Deep in the Piney Woods

Southeastern Alabama from Statehood to the Civil War, 1800–1865

Tommy Craig Brown

THE UNIVERSITY OF ALABAMA PRESS
Tuscaloosa

The University of Alabama Press
Tuscaloosa, Alabama 35487-0380
uapress.ua.edu

Typeface: Minion

Cover image: Illustration of the Alabama piney woods region by nineteenth-century artist Basil Hall; courtesy of Thomas Fisher Canadiana Collection, University of Toronto
Cover design: David Nees

Library of Congress Cataloging-in-Publication Data

Names: Brown, Tommy Craig, 1969- author.
Title: Deep in the piney woods : southeastern Alabama from statehood to the Civil War, 1800–1865 / Tommy Craig Brown.
Other titles: Southeastern Alabama from statehood to the Civil War, 1800–1865
Description: Tuscaloosa, Alabama : The University of Alabama Press, [2018] | Includes bibliographical references and index.
Identifiers: LCCN 2018009871| ISBN 9780817319977 (cloth) | ISBN 9780817392017 (ebook)
Subjects: LCSH: Wiregrass Country (Ala.)—History—19th century. | Wiregrass Country (Ala.)—Politics and government—19th century. | Wiregrass Country (Ala.)—Race relations—History—19th century.
Classification: LCC F326 .B856 2018 | DDC 976.1/3—dc23
LC record available at https://lccn.loc.gov/2018009871

Contents

Illustrations

FIGURES

TABLES

Acknowledgments

Thanks first to Kenneth Noe for his encouragement, timely advice, and important feedback that strengthened the work. Bill Trimble, Kelly Kennington, and Kim Key read the entire manuscript and provided valuable comments. I owe a debt of gratitude to the Department of History at Auburn and the excellent historians who supported me along the way.

I am particularly grateful to Auburn University Libraries, my academic home, and the many colleagues and coworkers who have been incredibly gracious and supportive. The libraries also provided funding for indexing this book. To my colleagues in the Special Collections and Archives Department, I owe special thanks for their help and encouragement. Dwayne Cox, former head of the department, read the entire manuscript, provided important suggestions, and routinely encouraged me to stay the course.

This book would not have been possible without librarians and archivists who tirelessly work to preserve and make available the primary and secondary sources that drive historical research. Much appreciation goes to the staff members at the Alabama Department of Archives and History in Montgomery, the National Archives and Records Administration in Washington, DC, the Louis Round Wilson Library Special Collections at the University of North Carolina in Chapel Hill, the Chattahoochee Valley Libraries in Columbus, Georgia, and the Stuart A. Rose Manuscript, Archives, and Rare Book Library at Emory University in Atlanta, Georgia.

I am most grateful for my wonderful family and my faith in God. To my wife, Amy, your tireless devotion, boundless optimism, and unwavering support have been a constant source of strength. To my children, Sarah, Rebekah, and Jackson, your giant hugs and encouraging words have inspired me to "keep moving forward!" My mother, Martha Longwith, prayed for and encouraged our family every step of the way. And, finally, when the challenges of life seem too great to overcome, I am reminded of the Lord's exhortation to Joshua: "Be strong and courageous. Do not be afraid; do not be discouraged, for the Lord your God will be with you wherever you go" (Joshua 1:9).

Introduction

The Battle of Gettysburg was a bloody affair for the Army of Northern Virginia's 15th Alabama Infantry. On July 2, 1863, the second day of a three-day fight, the regiment's multiple assaults against the extreme Federal left anchored atop Little Round Top failed to take the ground. The intensity of the struggle was especially keen at the points where Confederates temporarily breached the Union line. There, hand-to-hand combat signified the engagement's ferocity as the Federals beat back their Rebel attackers. By dark, dozens of Alabamians from the 15th Alabama and hundreds of other men from both sides were dead, wounded, or missing. Union colonel Joshua Lawrence Chamberlain of the 20th Maine Infantry remembered that men were everywhere "torn and broken, staggering, creeping, quivering on the earth."[1]

Twenty-nine-year-old private Crawford Dillard and eighteen-year-old private Warren Jones both made the charge up Little Round Top that day as members of the Dale County Beauregards, officially recognized as Company E, 15th Alabama Infantry. Back home, the men were neighbors and had joined the Beauregards along with dozens of relatives and friends as "later enlisters" in March 1862.[2] Dillard was the oldest of four brothers, all of whom eventually enlisted to fight with the company. Along with his wife, Mary, and two young children, he farmed a small plot of land just outside Newton, Alabama. Their total net worth was about $1,000. While they owned no slaves themselves, Dillard's father, who lived nearby, did own two young slave children. Warren Jones, on the other hand, was one of five teenage boys still living at home when the war began. His father, Moses, a widower who had migrated from Georgia in the mid-1850s, owned a large farm, five slaves, and enjoyed a net worth of nearly $20,000. Crawford Dillard survived the Battle of Gettysburg, fought in no fewer than thirty engagements as a Confederate soldier, and remained committed to the war effort for the duration of the conflict. Warren Jones died on July 16, 1863, from wounds he received during the assault at Little Round Top.[3]

These two men, their families, and the community they represented are just a small sampling of whites from southeastern Alabama who supported the Confederate war effort during the American Civil War. When the war broke out in 1861, Alabama's southeastern piney woods—known during the antebellum period as the pine barrens or pine lands—included the southernmost counties of Conecuh, Covington, Coffee, Dale, and Henry, as well as the northernmost counties of Butler, Pike, and Barbour. Four decades earlier, the territorial legislature organized the entire region as one county, Conecuh. From 1819 to the early 1840s, the state assembly divided the region into seven additional counties, an organization it retained until after the Civil War.

The eight-county geographical region represented in this study is based upon the physical boundaries, sociopolitical associations, and economic ties that defined southeastern Alabama from statehood through the Civil War. The region incorporates both the traditional Wiregrass counties (present-day Coffee, Dale, Geneva, Henry, and Houston) as well as counties in south-central Alabama (present-day Escambia, Covington, and Conecuh) just north of the Florida line. Butler, Pike, and Barbour counties, along with the towns of Greenville, Troy, Clayton, and Eufaula—all of which fall traditionally within the Black Belt—are included here because of their role as important trading hubs and because of the political influence they often exerted over the southernmost counties. Eufaula was also home of the Eufaula Regency, an influential political machine that, in many ways, dominated politics in neighboring counties during the volatile decade of the 1850s.[4]

Historians who have written about Alabama's southeastern piney woods have usually done so briefly and within the framework of broader topics. Walter Lynwood Fleming's antiquated *Civil War and Reconstruction in Alabama*, for instance, devotes fewer than five pages to the piney woods during the war years. Other early histories of the state, including Albert Burton Moore's *History of Alabama* and Lewy Dorman's *Party Politics in Alabama*, contain few references to the region outside of Barbour and Butler Counties. Two exceptions are Willis Brewer's classic history of the state, originally published in 1872, and Thomas McAdory Owen's multivolume *History of Alabama and Dictionary of Alabama Biography*. Both include numerous and useful references to piney woods counties, politicians, and soldiers, but the region as a whole is not the sole focus of either work.[5]

More recent studies of the state's history have likewise provided little in the way of a comprehensive narrative of the piney woods story. Malcolm McMillan's *Disintegration of a Confederate State* and Mills Thornton's *Politics and Power in a Slave State* make only passing references to the region. Bessie Martin's study of Alabama desertions during the Civil War and Margaret Storey's book on Alabama Unionists include useful information on certain piney woods counties, but neither viewed the region as central to their research. The same holds true for David Williams's examination of the lower Chattahoochee Valley, which concentrates on the Wiregrass counties closest to the Chattahoochee River, and Christopher McIlwain's recently published *Civil War Alabama*, a revisionist political history of the war years that includes useful but understandably limited information on southeastern Alabama. On the whole, then, while scholars have provided brief glimpses into the piney woods story, an in-depth, comprehensive examination of the region's history has yet to be published.[6]

This study seeks to fill this long-standing gap in Alabama's historiographical record by focusing solely on the southeastern piney woods from 1819 until the end of the Civil War. The region, especially the southernmost counties, has all too often been portrayed as nothing more than isolated backwoods where poverty reigned, slavery was often inconsequential, Unionism was disproportionately strong during the Civil War, raiders and bushwhackers created havoc on the home front, and deserters outnumbered the faithful in Confederate armies. While all of these factors to various degrees have become part of the piney woods narrative, a more detailed analysis of the region's history reveals a much more complicated story. By exploring the complexities of the region's social, political, cultural, and economic institutions, this study presents a fascinating portrait of a region persistently overlooked and frequently underappreciated.

From the beginning, white Alabamians in the piney woods supported both the fledgling market economy of the antebellum years and the institution of slavery that symbolized the market's growth in the South. The booming cotton economy paved the way for many yeoman farmers to become slave owners, allowing some to expand their work force. Even smallholders who owned no slave property often had a vested stake in the system. Solomon Easters and Francis Peacock, for instance, owned small farms in the Gainer's Store community in Pike County, just a few miles north of the county line. Solomon and Francis were siblings, and their father, William, with fourteen slaves (a large slaveholder by piney woods standards), lived within a few miles of both farms. It is not difficult to imagine the ways that small landowners such as Solomon and his wife and Francis and her husband benefitted from William's slaveholding status. Landless tenant farmers, overseers, teachers, and slaveless skilled tradesmen such as blacksmiths, carpenters, masons, saddlers, and furniture makers likewise benefitted from the system as they hired out to their slaveholding neighbors. In this way, the tentacles of slavery not only influenced slaveholding families, but also reached many nonslaveholding households.

For the overwhelming majority of black families in the piney woods, the institution of slavery governed every aspect of their daily lives. Yet slavery in the region varied—from the wealthy plantation districts located in the fertile river valleys, to the small-scale yeoman farms scattered across the sandy-loam plains of the southernmost counties. And while nearly half of the region's slaves lived and worked as field hands on large, commercial-style plantations, a sizeable percentage labored on small farms with just a few slaves. Sociocultural interactions between blacks and whites also reveal the varied and complex nature of antebellum slavery in a majority-white region such as the piney woods. Legal cases involving slaves and whites further demonstrate the convoluted circumstances surrounding racial relations in a system that counted slaves both as property with no rights and as human beings who deserved at least some protections under the law.

By the outbreak of the Civil War, the Democratic Party was the party of choice for a majority of white Alabamians in the piney woods; yet this had not always been the case. From the 1840s to the late 1850s, most of the counties in the region identified with the Whig Party. This alliance was especially true in Conecuh, Covington, Butler, Pike, and Barbour, the counties most likely to identify with the Black Belt. The Eufaula Regency, a politically powerful faction of states' rights Whigs, advocated secession as early as 1849. Over time, the group convinced more and more people that Alabama's destiny as a slave state could only be realized outside the Union. Residents of Henry, Dale, and Coffee counties remained staunchly Democratic throughout most of the antebellum period. The resilience of the region's Whig Party, and its later surrogate, the American or Know Nothing Party, demonstrates the effectiveness of party leaders such as Thomas Hill Watts and Henry Hilliard. Whig dominance declined in the late 1850s as sectional animosity drove at least some Whigs to the Democratic Party. Former Whigs-turned-secessionist-Democrats such as John Gill Shorter, for instance, helped convert Eufaula into a Democratic stronghold by the outbreak of the war.[7] Every piney woods county except Conecuh voted to send immediate secessionists to the secession convention in 1860, even though the vote itself may not have been representative of the majority of the region's population.

Inasmuch as the piney woods contained some of the least populated counties in the state, that so many men assembled, organized, drilled, and headed off to war is remarkable. Yet thousands of men volunteered to serve in companies with colorful names such as the Coffee Rangers, Covington Grays, Henry Pioneers, and Dale Beauregards. Piney woods soldiers experienced their first taste of battle at Shiloh. The region's soldiers also fought well in battles such as Gettysburg, the Wilderness, Cold Harbor, and Franklin. As the war dragged on into its third and fourth years, however, growing problems and disaffection at home—combined with demoralizing battlefield losses—challenged even the most diehard Confederates. Conscription, food and salt shortages, rising casualty rates, and Union incursions into Alabama turned some piney woods families against the war. Governors John Gill Shorter and Thomas Hill Watts, meanwhile, went to great lengths to support the families of indigent soldiers, and south Alabama appears to have received its share of this aid. Despite conflict between Confederate enrolling officers and Alabama authorities, conscription and recruitment efforts continued to bear fruit; though some of these new recruits proved to be wholly unreliable, going so far as to stage a mutiny in one regiment. The final year of the war was the most challenging for both soldiers and civilians alike. The southernmost counties contended with increasing numbers of bushwhackers, deserters, and Unionists, as piney woods families often found themselves under siege from friend and foe alike.

Historians must always ask themselves, so what? Why does this study really matter? Piney woods Alabamians played a central role in the Indian wars of the 1830s, raised record numbers of hogs and cattle during the antebellum period, produced some of the state's most prominent politicians, bolstered the Whig Party's base of support, and raised several of the Confederacy's most distinguished regiments. Because much of the state's history has concentrated on the Tennessee Valley, the hill counties, and the Black Belt, southeastern Alabama deserves a more prominent place within the social, political, cultural, and economic fabric of the state's storied past.

Deep in the Piney Woods

1

"The Wilderness Is All before You"

Settlement

In present-day Conecuh County, Alabama, just southeast of Evergreen, County Road 25 winds through the rural countryside. The paved but narrow road is only about five miles long and connects two equally inconspicuous highways. While the trees, wildlife, and farmland provide relaxing views, there is nothing to indicate the presence of a once-thriving community: no signs, no historical markers, no buildings, no ruins. Yet, nearly two centuries ago, the area along modern County Road 25 was the site of a comparatively small but flourishing community centered on the county seat town of Sparta. In 1860, with a population of at least one thousand inhabitants, there were four merchants, two blacksmiths, three grocers, a wheelwright, a judge, and numerous farmers, laborers, overseers, and slaves. Sarah Kennedy made a good living as a hotel keeper. M. J. Murphy served as the town's constable. E. W. Martin was the community's only lawyer. Brothers William and Samuel McCormick were chair makers. And Ellen Williams served as the town's school teacher.[1]

For much of the antebellum period, Sparta was also home to one of a handful of land offices in Alabama. During its three decades of operation, the Sparta Land Office issued more than five thousand land patents to settlers in the present-day counties of Escambia, Covington, Conecuh, Geneva, Henry, Dale, Coffee, Pike, and Barbour. From 1820 until the town's demise at the end of the Civil War, residents of Sparta and land-hungry settlers who passed through its streets actively participated in the historical development of a region known as the piney woods.[2]

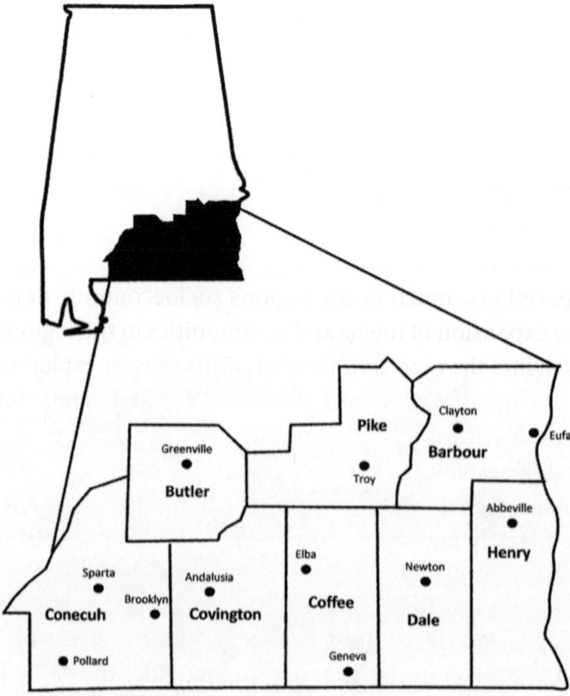

1.1. Piney Woods Region in 1860

The piney woods of southeastern Alabama encompassed an area from the Chattahoochee River west to the Old Federal Road, and north from the Florida/Alabama line (Ellicott's Line) to the thirty-second parallel (see Figure 1.1). The Creek Indian land cession of 1814 opened up the region for migration and settlement. In 1817, the Alabama territorial assembly created Conecuh County, a massive geopolitical division that originally encompassed the entire region, including "all that tract of country lying east of the Federal Road and not included in any other county now established."[3] It stretched from the Federal Road east to the Chattahoochee River, and from the Montgomery County line south to the border of Spanish West Florida. The 1818 territorial census recorded a total population of 1,395 inhabitants, including 1,092 whites and 303 slaves.[4] As the population increased, the legislature carved up Conecuh County into smaller units. In 1819, following Alabama's entry into the Union, the state legislature divided the piney woods into Conecuh, Henry, and Butler counties. The legislature created Covington County and Pike County in 1821; Dale in 1824; Barbour in 1832; and Coffee in 1841.

The region differed in its development from the neighboring counties in southwestern Alabama and the Black Belt counties just to the north. While much of southwest Alabama relied upon the Alabama and Tombeckbee rivers, the southeastern piney woods depended upon river systems that emptied into the Gulf of Mexico east of Mobile Bay. The land itself differed in many ways from other regions of the state with relatively poor, sandy loam soils dominating vast stretches of the region, particularly in the piney woods' southernmost counties. And with the exception of a handful of communities on the periphery, much of the region's socioeconomic development—especially the expansion of towns and communities in the region's interior—took place well into the nineteenth century. This chapter explores the region's settlement and maturation: its geographical features; confrontations between Native Americans and whites; migration and settlement; the spread of revival and the establishment of churches; and the evolution of communities and towns. It challenges the perception of the piney woods as nothing more than a sparsely populated, economically backward wilderness by exploring the rich complexities of the region's early settlement and development. Settlers from every socioeconomic background began migrating into the region, leaving their homes in the Eastern Seaboard states to start afresh in the piney woods. Large farms and cotton plantations developed in the most fertile areas to the north and along the rivers, while smallholders grew crops and raised livestock in the sandier soils. Larger towns such as Eufaula, Troy, and Greenville became centers of banking and commerce, while small towns and communities formed the social, cultural, and economic nucleus of much of the region.

Throughout most of the nineteenth century, the most conspicuous features of the region's landscape were its immense forests of longleaf and slash pine trees. The longleaf pine, so named because its needles averaged from eight-to-twelve inches in length, was by far the most prevalent species, with specimens growing often to one hundred feet or more in height. Basil Hall's vivid descriptions of the pine forests he encountered in southeastern Georgia in 1828 would have been equally applicable to the forests in southern Alabama. "It was a long time before I got tired of the scenery of these pine barrens," he noted. "There was something . . . very graceful in the millions of tall and slender columns, growing up in solitude, not crowded upon one another, but gradually appearing to come closer and closer, till they formed a compact mass, beyond which nothing was to be seen."[5] Ten years later, while surveying the ridges just west of the Conecuh River for the Alabama, Florida, and Georgia Railroad, William Campbell remarked that "the growth of pine along these vallies, and on the bordering ridges, is not surpassed by the most luxuriant forests of Georgia or the Carolinas."[6] Stands of timber discouraged undergrowth and promoted a distinctly open environment on the forest floor. One historian has observed that, not unlike longleaf forests throughout the coastal plain, "the general flatness of the land and absence of thick undergrowth enabled the traveler to pass through the pine forests with as much ease as over a prairie." Only the oak, hickory, elm, and other hardwood species populating the creek and river bottomlands interrupted an otherwise continuous expanse of virgin pine timberland.[7]

Perhaps as conspicuous as the longleaf pine was the abundant wiregrass, *aristida stricta*, growing beneath the evergreen canopy. Wiregrass flourished throughout the piney woods but was especially pervasive in the farthest southeastern corner of the region. It grew in large clumps, four-to-eight inches wide at the base, with hundreds of round, wire-like blades rising from each clump, often reaching heights of eighteen inches or more. Seeding was rare and took place only when the main clump was exposed to fire. Indeed, frequent fires, both man-made and natural, benefitted the forest's ecosystem by suppressing invasive undergrowth, regenerating new wiregrass growth, and promoting the development of new seed pods. The tender new grass shoots served as an excellent source of nutritious forage for grazing livestock, a fact readily apparent to the region's Indian inhabitants as well as to early nineteenth-century pioneering whites who migrated to the area. "In this section stock rearing is profitable," observed Lewis Troost, an engineer with the Mobile and Alabama Railroad, "and is attended with little trouble; the piney woods bordering on the streams affording natural perennial pastures."[8]

The creeks and rivers that drained the piney woods provided the most fertile bottomland in the entire region (see Figure 1.2). The Chattahoochee River, for example, not only formed the eastern boundary of the region and the state but its bottomland also eventually became home to some of the wealthiest plantations in the region. From its source in the Appalachian Mountains of northern Georgia, the river flows south 418 miles, where it converges with the Flint River to form the Apalachicola. In the nineteenth century, steamboats could navigate the Chattahoochee from Columbus, Georgia, southward an average of only five months out of the year. At other times, extended droughts limited steamboat activity, while log jams, overhanging tree branches, and rocky shoals often obstructed the channel, rendering daylight navigation difficult and nighttime travel almost impossible. On the other hand, keelboats and flatboats drawing no more than twenty-two inches of water could usually navigate the river year round.[9]

To the west, the Choctawhatchee River rises in Barbour County just below the town of Clayton and flows in a southwesterly direction through the present-day counties of Henry, Dale, and Geneva. The Pea River, the

1.2. Major Rivers in Southeastern Alabama

Choctawhatchee's main tributary, originates in present-day Bullock County, where it flows south and empties into the main channel in Geneva County. The Choctawhatchee then crosses the Florida line and continues for another fifty miles or so until it reaches Choctawhatchee Bay. As to navigation, at least three steamboats and dozens of flatboats and keelboats operated routinely on the river. One contemporary observed that "previous to the year 1861, a large tract of country, embracing the counties of Dale, Geneva, Coffee, Barbour, and Henry . . . depended on the river as the only outlet by which their produce could reach the market."[10]

The Conecuh River and its main tributaries—the Sepulga, Pigeon, and the Patsaliga—traversed the present-day counties of Pike, Butler, Covington, and Conecuh, effectively draining the westernmost portion of the piney woods. Navigating the river was most promising below the falls of the Conecuh, an area of rocky shoals located just west of the once-thriving town of Montezuma. Shallow-draft vessels transported everything from cotton to lumber down the river to the port town of Pensacola. "Large quantities of pine lumber are procured from the forests," one writer remarked, "and conveyed down the Conecuh River in small boats or rafts."[11] Once they reached Pensacola Bay, flatboat captains found it more profitable and practical to sell their boats for scrap lumber rather than attempt the impossible task of hauling the vessels back upstream. Efforts to establish steamboat travel failed as the river's treacherous sandbars, submerged logs, and unpredictable currents made this kind of navigation impossible.

During the eighteenth and early nineteenth centuries, rivers served as important travel, transportation, and trade routes for the region's first inhabitants, the Creek Indians. Major Creek towns could be found primarily along the banks of the Chattahoochee, while smaller settlements were located in present-day Butler and Conecuh counties on the Conecuh. The vast interior was sparsely settled with little more than scattered villages and hunting camps dotting the landscape. Paul Starrett notes that, "in lower Alabama in the vast section west of the Chattahoochee River there were no permanent villages of enough significance to appear on maps although there were some individual settlements of prominent mixed bloods to the east of the extreme lower Alabama River."[12]

Like Native Americans in other regions of the United States, the Creeks who lived within the piney woods or along the periphery adapted to their environment by successfully utilizing the region's national resources. The Creeks routinely hunted white-tailed deer, wild turkey, and black bear, all of which feasted on abundant stands of wild persimmons, crabapples, strawberries, blackberries, and native grasses. Native peoples understood the link between healthy game animals and the beneficial role that fire played in maintaining a vibrant ecosystem. Burning the forest kept undesirable vines, brush, and briars in check, prevented unnecessary debris build-up (a major cause of catastrophic fires), and encouraged the regeneration of nutritious wiregrass and other plants favored by large and small game.[13]

In addition to hunting, the Creeks (after European contact) actively participated in the deerskin trade, raised cattle and other livestock, and perhaps most importantly, farmed. While most families planted small garden plots next to their homes, the communal crops growing along the outskirts of towns were the primary sources of Indian agriculture. The Creeks grew squash, turnips, beans, potatoes, and a number of other crops, but their mainstay was corn. Anthropologist Robbie Ethridge maintains that "although the Creeks had a diversity of wild and domesticated foods by the turn of the nineteenth century, corn, supplemented with beans and squash, was still the staple food crop."[14] Corn was nutritious, simple to cultivate, flourished in many different types of soil, and was versatile as a foodstuff. Adam Hodgson, a wealthy English businessman who traveled through Creek country in 1820, documented that "the Indians often set out on long journies through the forests, without any other provision than a preparation of the flour of Indian corn, gathered while green, with honey. This mixture," he observed, "dried and reduced to powder, they carry in a small bag, taking a little of it with water, once or twice in 24 hours; and it is said, that if they have the ill luck to kill no deer . . . they will subsist on it for many weeks, without losing their strength."[15]

An important theme illustrating the socioeconomic complexities of early piney woods history revolved around the precarious relationship between Indians and whites. The Creeks' entanglement with white settlers was most pronounced in the Euro-Indian deerskin trade that developed during the eighteenth century. Over time, Native Americans became dependent upon the marketplace and gradually adopted Anglo economic and cultural practices. Andrew Frank argues that, by 1810, "many Creeks herded cattle, owned slaves, spoke and wrote English, grew cotton, wore European clothing, fenced their lands, and intermarried with white Americans."[16] Kathryn Braund further demonstrates that Creek participation in the commercial marketplace ultimately altered traditional Indian socioeconomic patterns and facilitated the ultimate decline of both the deerskin trade and the Creek way of life.[17] The influx of white settlers and unscrupulous traders following the American Revolution exacerbated growing tensions among whites, Anglo-friendly Creeks, and Indian factions hostile to the new geopolitical and economic dynamic.

The US government's purchase of the Louisiana Territory from France in 1803 set the stage for new conflicts between Native Americans and white settlers. Government officials hoped to establish a postal road connecting the Georgia frontier, the Mississippi Territory (which included the present-day state of Alabama), Mobile, and the newly acquired port of New Orleans. They hoped that the route would expedite trade and communication, and facilitate military movements should the Spanish or British in West Florida threaten the American frontier. Two years later, a handful of Creek Indian leaders led by William McIntosh signed the First Treaty of Washington, allowing the government to construct the route through the heart of the Creek nation. The Federal Road, as the route became known, crossed the Chattahoochee River just north of present-day Columbus, Georgia, stretched westward to the headwaters of the Alabama River, then followed the ridges in a southwestwardly direction to Mobile. The road officially opened in November 1811.[18]

The influx of white traders, herdsmen, and settlers that followed the road alarmed Creek Indians hostile to American encroachment to such a degree that, by 1813, armed conflict in south Alabama appeared to be inevitable. While most of the subsequent fighting took place outside the southeastern piney woods, the battles and skirmishes that occurred along the region's periphery had profound consequences for the area's eventual development. In July 1813, local militia attacked a band of militant Red Stick Creeks in present-day Escambia County in what became known as the Battle of Burnt Corn Creek. Four weeks later, seven hundred Red Sticks attacked Fort Mims in neighboring Baldwin County, killing more than two hundred white settlers, militiamen, allied Creeks, and slaves. The ensuing Creek War involved numerous battles and skirmishes throughout the Mississippi Territory, Georgia, and Tennessee, culminating in Gen. Andrew Jackson's defeat of a large contingent of Red Stick Creeks at the Battle of Horseshoe Bend. Following the battle, Jackson's treaty negotiations forced all the Creeks to forfeit millions of acres of land in the Mississippi Territory and in Georgia.[19]

The defeat of the Red Sticks at the hands of Andrew Jackson and the subsequent removal of thousands of Native Americans farther west spurred white migration and settlement. The 1814 Treaty of Fort Jackson ceded more than 23 million acres of Creek land in Alabama, Mississippi, and portions of Georgia to the US government. Twenty years later, the Third Treaty of Washington transferred all remaining Creek lands east of the Mississippi River into government hands. Both treaties resulted in massive numbers of white settlers and slaves pouring into Alabama in hopes of acquiring cheap and abundant federal land. In fact, the exodus from Eastern Seaboard states was so large that contemporaries hyperbolically called it "Alabama fever," a condition that infected large numbers of Americans and spread rapidly throughout the east with overwhelming effect. "Scarce any of those who were attacked by it ever recover," wrote Georgian Samuel McDonald, "it sooner or later carries them off to the westward."[20] James Graham made similar humorous observations from his Lincoln County, North Carolina, home: "as soon as one neighbor visits another who has just returned from Alabama he immediately discovers the same symptoms which are exhibited by the one who has seen alluring Alabama."[21]

Historians have speculated upon the push-and-pull causes that precipitated migration, but most suggest that a combination of factors including economic downturns, soil exhaustion, lower crop yields, and pressing debt obligations in the east, combined with the abundant and fertile lands available in the west, drove tens of thousands of Americans to leave their native eastern soils for greener pastures. One recently published history of Alabama finds that "those who flocked to Alabama were disillusioned with worn-out fields and poor economic conditions in the East and were attracted by cheap land from the Indian cession, high cotton prices, and dreams of wealth."[22] Lacy Ford notes that in South Carolina, "a steady stream of upper Piedmont whites flowed into the Southwest between 1830 and 1850, while during those same years whites abandoned the lower Piedmont for the cotton frontier in unprecedented numbers." Ford estimates that by 1850 more than forty-five thousand former South Carolinians lived in all of Alabama and another twenty-six thousand had relocated to Mississippi.[23] In his study of poor white people in North Carolina, Charles Bolton similarly argues that "poor whites, yeoman farmers, and rich planters . . . all joined the westward trek to the Old Southwest." Alabama fever drained 280,000 of that state's residents west; fifty thousand settled throughout Alabama and Mississippi. "The attraction for poor whites," Bolton observes, "as for other classes of southerners, was a seemingly inexhaustible supply of land that seemed suitable for growing cotton and making men wealthy."[24]

Migration and settlement in the piney woods never became as robust as in the Black Belt or the Tennessee Valley. Settlement in the region's interior—particularly the area lying between the Choctawhatchee and Conecuh rivers—was especially problematic due to the area's unreliable waterways and sandy soils. This area "is but thinly settled," wrote William Campbell in 1838, "its remoteness from navigable water courses, and the absence of artificial communications, (except the miserable county roads, which scarcely answer for neighbourhood purposes) have tended not only to prevent emigration to the country, but to induce many . . . to abandon their improvements and seek other lands, less generous in productions, but more accessible to market."[25] Nevertheless, the population of the piney woods on the whole rose steadily from 9,756 in 1820 to 27,775 in 1830—a 184 percent increase over ten years—with most of that growth occurring along the region's periphery. Over the next thirty years, the population grew threefold, from 27,775 residents in 1830 to 127,887 in 1860 (see Table 1.1).

Much of the region's growth was a result of natural increase, but the 1860 census reveals that 40 percent of the population was born outside the state of Alabama. When counting only white adults over the age of twenty, that percentage rises to more than 50 percent. In Pike County's Gainer's Store community, for example, a sampling of 520 residents demonstrates that 214, or 41 percent, were not native Alabamians. A similar sampling of 367 whites in Henry County's Green Mill Beat shows that 44 percent migrated to the area sometime before 1860. In the town of Geneva, in Coffee County, 209 of the 520 whites sampled hailed from other states. Eufaula was the one place in the region that qualified as an urban commercial center. It also contained a notably large percentage of nonnative Alabamians. Fifty-seven per-

TABLE 1.1. Population changes in the Piney Woods, 1820–1860

County	1820	1830	1840	1850	1860
Barbour			12,024	23,632	30,812
Butler	1,405	5,650	8,685	10,836	18,122
Pike		7,108	10,108	15,920	24,435
Henry	2,638	4,020	5,787	9,019	14,918
Coffee				5,940	9,623
Dale		2,031	7,397	6,382	12,197
Covington		1,522	2,435	3,645	6,469
Conecuh	5,713	7,444	8,197	9,322	11,311
Totals	9,756	27,775	54,633	84,696	127,887

Source: Historical Census Browser, University of Virginia Geospatial and Statistical Data Center, http://mapserver.lib.virginia.edu/collections/ (accessed April 16, 2012).

cent of the 480 whites sampled, for example, were born outside of the state. A large portion of these were native Northerners or Europeans; individuals from Connecticut, New York, Ireland, England, and France were among the nonnative population of Eufaula. On the whole, the overwhelming majority of migrants coming into the piney woods were native Georgians followed by South Carolinians, North Carolinians, and a variety of individuals from other states and countries.

White settlers who made the trek into southern Alabama came from a variety of socioeconomic backgrounds. For the planter class and those who aspired to join their ranks, land and slaves were the keys to fortune. "Before they reached their adulthood," historian James Oakes contends, "most slaveholders had been conditioned to accept migration as the prerequisite to success. It is no surprise, therefore, that the antebellum master class was one of the most mobile in history."[26] Success never came easily and settlers migrating into the piney woods hoping to prosper had to adjust quickly to frontier conditions.

In 1837, for instance, twenty-two-year-old planter John Horry Dent moved his wife and infant son from the Lowcountry district of Colleton, South Carolina, to Barbour County. Dent arrived during the waning days of a Creek Indian uprising perpetrated by a small band of Native Americans desperately trying to stave off white settlement. About the same time that Dent settled his slaves in the area—largely by renting them out to other planters—dozens of citizens from Pike, Barbour, and Macon counties petitioned Alabama Governor Clement Comer Clay, demanding that he remove all the re-

TABLE 1.2. Nonnative Alabamians in four Piney Woods communities

	Gainer's Store, Pike County	Green Mill Beat, Henry County	Geneva, Coffee County	Eufaula, Barbour County
Representative sample	520	367	520	480
Georgia	116	110	126	123
South Carolina	66	25	38	45
North Carolina	23	19	25	31
Other	9	10	20	74
Total non-natives	214	164	209	273

Source: United States Census, Pike County, Henry County, Coffee County, Barbour County, Alabama, 1860, Schedule 1.

maining Creeks from the area.[27] With the possibility of violence still in the air, Dent chose to temporarily forego building a house in the country and moved his family to Clayton. At one point, he compared frontier Alabama to the older, more settled parts of the state: "Old Alabama, then (contrasted with the Indian Nation just incorporated as a part of the State), presented an appearance of wealth, refinement and elegance in comparison with the new territory, yet to be cleared up, built up, and settled by civilized people, its present population being Adventurers, Speculators, and pioneer farmers who were moving in to settle fresh plantations to make cotton."[28]

Less than a year later, using slaves as collateral, Dent purchased a plantation ten miles north of Clayton, along the banks of South Cowikee Creek. He promptly put his slaves to work clearing land, building temporary slave quarters, and erecting a makeshift home for his family. "At this pine land abode," he later recollected, "we had hurriedly knocked up a double pen log cabin, rough as rough could be, but made it sufficiently comfortable to keep out rain and shelter us from the Sun."[29] Within a few years, "Good Hope," as Dent called his plantation, boasted a framed plantation home, four hundred acres of cleared, arable land, five hundred acres of timber land, a profitable cotton gin, and numerous barns and outbuildings. In 1840, his slaves harvested sixty-seven wagon-loads of corn and seventy-three bales of cotton, with the average bale weighing more than four hundred pounds. For the next twenty years, Dent bought and sold at least five plantations, continued to invest in slaves, harvested record amounts of cotton, and became one of the wealthiest men in the region. By the outbreak of the Civil War, he owned ninety-six slaves and enjoyed financial assets of nearly $200,000.[30]

While Dent and wealthy planters like him migrated and settled their families, yeoman and poorer farmers of lesser means took risks of their own by moving into the region. In 1822, sixteen-year-old James W. Clark migrated with his family from Georgia to Brundidage, Pike County. For nearly a decade, he worked odd jobs and clerked in his older brother's general store in Montgomery. He eventually settled down, married Harriet Kelly of Linwood, Pike County, and bought two forty-acre plots of land just a few miles north of his father-in-law's farm. The plots were located just three miles from the sloughs of the Conecuh River, and Clark later recalled the dangers he and other settlers faced, especially when wild animals from the river's swampy bottomlands ventured too close. "Bear tracks in the swamps were as thick as chicken tracks in the yard," he recollected some years later. Bears, coyotes, bobcats, and the occasional wolf posed serious threats to chickens, pigs, cattle, and other domesticated livestock. Despite the dangers, Clark worked his small farm and slowly accumulated enough resources that by 1850 he owned two hundred acres of land and was worth about $1,000. The evidence suggests that at some point during the 1850s he relocated to Coffee County, bought a small farm, and rented three slaves who worked his farm and picked hundreds of pounds of cotton each year.[31]

James Clark's experience was not unlike those of thousands of slaveless yeoman and poor farmers who migrated west with aspirations for a better life. David M. Braswell was another settler who moved his family from Crawford County, Georgia, to Pike County in the late 1840s. A few years later, he relocated his family farther south to Coffee County. By 1860, Braswell, his wife, Penelope, and their three teenaged boys worked a small twenty-acre farm just outside the small town of Elba. In a similar fashion, Reuben Kemp migrated with his wife and five children from Marion County, Georgia, to the Open Pond community in southeastern Henry County in the 1850s. His three hundred-acre farm, including sixty improved acres, produced nine hundred pounds of cotton in 1860. It is not clear whether Kemp rented slaves to pick his cotton, but the evidence suggests that he, his wife, and his sons worked the farm with little outside help. Like Kemp, James Parker left his native Georgia for Covington County sometime around 1842. A decade later, his family's two-hundred-acre farm was worth about $400. Parker owned no slaves but did employ eighteen-year-old James Drake as a farm laborer. As the 1850s drew to a close, Parker added two hundred acres of land to his holdings, bought a female slave, and by the outbreak of the Civil War, enjoyed a net worth of nearly $3,000.[32]

In many ways, the women who settled the Old Southwest experienced events differently than the men. They left families and tightknit familial relationships behind to face uncertain futures without the immediate support of established kinship networks. These networks fostered a unique female culture among white women in the Eastern Seaboard states, a culture of time-honored interdependency. Through courtship, marriage, childbirth, child rearing, and the death of loved ones, women cherished and relied upon their relationships with other women. Joan Cashin argues that women "relished interdependent relations with their female relatives. These kinship bonds provided women with valuable practical, social, and emotional resources." In many, if not most, cases migration severed these relationships either permanently or temporarily. "Women accepted the partial separations from relatives that happened when they married," Cashin suggests, "but migration portended losses that were radical and permanent because it could remove women so far from their kinfolk that those relationships might deteriorate, and eventually collapse."[33]

Fear and anxiety, perhaps more than anything else, occupied the minds of women migrating into the piney woods, especially at the beginning of the settlement. Trekking into areas often still inhabited by Native Americans was unnerving to women whose primary responsibility was to protect, care, and comfort their children. News related to the massacre of white settlers at Fort Mims and other such incidents, whether factual or not, spread like wildfire among potential migrants living in the Eastern Seaboard states. Moreover, the birthing process for women of childbearing age was stressful enough even in the best of circumstances. Mortality rates for women and newborns in the early nineteenth-century were high by modern standards, and the thought of giving birth with little or no support from close female relatives or friends must have been terrifying. Depending upon one's socioeconomic circumstances, setting up house under frontier conditions with young children or babies in tow was challenging, even for women who relied upon slave labor for help. Finally, the untimely death of husbands added additional burdens to many women, especially those whose economic circumstances were uncertain.

Caroline Alley, for example, migrated from Randolph County, Georgia, to Dale County with her husband, Alford, in 1852. Their three children, John, Mary, and Martha, were all under the age of six; young Martha was barely two years old. Alford's service in the Creek War earned him a government land grant of forty acres just a few miles southeast of Newton. The Alleys were poor by the standards of the day and Caroline's circumstances worsened with the birth of two more children and the untimely death of her husband in the mid-1850s. Yet Caroline's determination and willingness to take risks eventually improved her family's economic prospects. Following her husband's death, she sold her small farm and bought eighty acres of government land not far from her original homestead. Two years later, Alley's eleven improved acres produced two hundred pounds of corn, twenty pounds of sweet potatoes, and 56 dollars' worth of slaughtered livestock. On the whole, her family's net worth increased from a census-reported zero dollars in 1850 to a modest $400 ten years later. This was no small feat for a single mother of five farming the southernmost reaches of the piney woods.[34]

Women of the slaveholding class faced many of the same challenges as their lower-class neighbors, but enjoyed a level of assistance that others such as Caroline Alley did not. Several years prior to their migration to Alabama, for instance, Mary Elizabeth Morrison brought a human dowry of forty-five slaves to her marriage to John Horry Dent. At least half of the slaves Dent brought to Alabama belonged to his wife, and the evidence suggests that she supervised the labor of at least some of her slaves.[35] Twenty-four-year-old Rebecca Gunn's move from Georgia to Henry County in 1860 must have been somewhat easier considering that a portion of her husband's nineteen slaves was almost certainly at her disposal.[36] Joan Cashin argues that "slave men and slave women did the hardest work on the frontier, and they spared plantation mistresses many of the strenuous, exhausting, and dangerous chores that other white women had to perform."[37] Nevertheless, the high percentage of male slaves on the southwestern frontier demonstrates that clearing forests, breaking new land, and planting crops took precedence over nearly all other human endeavors. Many plantation mistresses found themselves butchering chickens and hogs, chopping wood, caring for sick slaves, washing clothing, tending gardens, and completing tasks previously carried out in whole or in part by slaves.

As more and more families migrated and settled the piney woods, religion and the establishment of frontier churches helped alleviate some of the emotional and spiritual isolation many people experienced. Indeed, the increasing popularity of frontier revival meetings intensified social interaction by introducing new levels of sociocultural complexity to rural communities throughout the region. Settlers and itinerate ministers spoke often of the abundant lawlessness and wickedness that permeated the region early on. In 1826, Methodist missionary Josiah Evans frankly described his estimation of the communities in the southernmost piney woods: "I know of but one class of persons that the present state of the lands seems to suit, and that class is no advantage or honor to any country."[38] A year later, the minutes of the Alabama Baptist State Convention noted that "the wilderness is all before you, behind you, around you; the inhabitants of the waste places are in the midst of you and before your eyes, a living spectacle of ignorance, superstition, and crime."[39] Frontier missionaries certainly had their work cut out for them.

Baptists and Methodists ultimately made the greatest headway in the piney woods. Characteristic of both denominations were the frequent camp meetings held in towns and communities throughout the region beginning in the 1820s. Meeting dates, places, and times spread primarily by word of mouth. Dozens of families gathered at the appointed time; most came prepared to camp for days or possibly even weeks at a time. Singing, praying, and fiery sermons often led to dramatic religious conversions. In the spring of 1823, for instance, Methodist preacher John Triggs delivered a sermon in Henry County that was so moving, one of the congregants abruptly stood up, interrupted the service, "and begged the congregation to pray for him. This produced considerable excitement among the people, and many came forward weeping and desiring our prayers."

In a nearby community a few weeks later, another of Triggs's sermons persuaded a Mrs. B to join the church. Her husband, infuriated by her Christian conversion, demanded that she move out of the home and threatened to beat her if she talked to anyone about their altercation. Witnesses recalled that for several days he cursed and raged against the itinerate minister, blaming the congregants and the whole of Christendom for his wife's newfound religion. Finally, a confrontation with his brother about the matter "reached his heart, so that he went home, begged his wife's pardon, and sent for some of the Society to pray for him. They gathered and prayed for him nearly all night. He has since very much reformed, and his wife found peace to her soul."[40] Josiah Evans remembered yet another episode involving a seventy-three-year-old blind man during an 1826 camp meeting in Henry County. On the third day of the meeting, the man in question experienced a spiritual conversion so powerful that he "exhorted all around him to draw near the Lord. I have been in the dark fifteen years," he implored, "I have not been able to see my way, nor have I seen the sun; but now, glory to God, I can see my way to heaven as well as any of you!"[41]

While Methodist missionaries made inroads into the piney woods, the Baptists were far and away the most successful. Like many of their Methodist counterparts, itinerant Baptist ministers traveled for weeks on end preaching at small churches and conducting camp meetings throughout their circuits. For at least two decades, Alexander Travis crisscrossed southeastern Alabama, preaching revivals and planting churches. Each year, after the midsummer crop lay-by and again following the fall harvest, he toured his circuit. His traveling schedule became so demanding and his preaching so popular, he eventually hired an overseer to help manage his farming pursuits. "So great was his reputation as a preacher," one historian notes, "that one poor woman without a horse or mule reputedly once walked twenty miles to hear him preach."[42] Like Travis, David Wood was among the first Baptist ministers to operate in the southern part of the state. He migrated from Twiggs County, Georgia, to Conecuh County two years before Alabama's statehood. Wood was perhaps the most unique itinerant preacher in Alabama, for he was totally blind. His physical handicap was by no means an impediment to his impressive skills as a minister. He was "an indefatigable preacher" whose influence and talents aided in the establishment of Baptist churches throughout the piney woods.[43]

Like their white counterparts, African Americans participated in religious revivals and joined religious denominations. Wayne Flynt notes that before 1840 it was not unusual for blacks and whites to attend services together, "perhaps with slaves in the back rows, but at least in the same building."[44] Methodist and Baptist itinerant preachers reported annually the total number of black and white parishioners in their respective districts. In 1823, for example, John Triggs reported to the Methodist Annual Conference that the Chattahoochee Circuit, for which he was responsible, included 182 whites and fifty-nine blacks. Ten years later the three Methodist circuits that served the piney woods reported a total of 1,340 white and 207 black members.[45]

By the late 1830s, the growth of slavery and the rise of Northern abolitionism prompted serious concerns on the part of white Southerners. While state governments enacted stricter laws regulating the social and economic aspects of slavery, Southern churches became increasingly proslavery as well, aggressively attacked their abolitionist brethren, and shifted their approach to African American congregants. Attendees at the 1840 meeting of the Bethlehem Baptist Association, which included representatives from no fewer than six churches in Conecuh and Butler counties, unanimously adopted a resolution condemning the American Baptist Antislavery Convention held earlier that year in New York City.[46] "We think ourselves compelled to declare against men who misrepresent and slander us," they responded, and "recommend our brethren at the South to speak out their sentiments fully and fearlessly."[47] Within five years the Methodist and Baptist denominations split into Northern and Southern factions, with slavery being the root cause.

Baptist and Methodist efforts to evangelize piney woods slaves increased dramatically during the 1840s and 1850s. Wilson Fallin argues that by evangelizing slaves, white Southerners hoped to deflect abolitionist criticism that slave owners cared little for their slaves' spiritual well-being. Denominational associations adopted resolutions urging churches to provide services for black congregants if they did not already do so. They also encouraged individual slave owners to arrange for religious activities and promote their slaves' spiritual welfare. The Bethlehem Baptist Association instructed its churches that "where there is a sufficient colored population to justify it, make arrangements for a separate service for them at least one Lord's day in each month, and oftener, if practicable." Slave owners, too, were encouraged to "so arrange the order of their family devotions as to have their servants present, and especially where they cannot attend upon the more public means of grace."[48]

These efforts produced mixed results. In Conecuh County's Bellville Baptist Church, African Americans accounted for half of the membership—104 white members to 103 "colored." About ten miles away, the black membership of Beulah Baptist Church outnumbered the white members 105 to 53. On the other hand, smaller churches such as Catawba Springs and Sepulga reported only a handful of black members.[49] Overall, churches located in more remote areas of the piney woods (where slave populations were sparse) naturally counted few slaves among their membership, while those in closer proximity to the region's towns enjoyed larger populations of both black and white members.

Like the influx of religion, the establishment of communities and towns became an essential part of piney woods historical development, adding to the region's social and economic complexity. The towns that dotted the region ranged in size and scope from the cotton-rich enclaves in and around Eufaula and Troy to more traditional, frontier-like conditions that existed in the townships just north of the Florida line. As such, they resembled other predominantly white belt regions of the South. Historian John Inscoe refers to such areas, irrespective of their size or perceived unimportance by outsiders, as "concentrated communities," that is, communities that "generated much of the area's progress, diversity, and entrepreneurial spirit."[50] Eufaula (known before 1843 as Irwinton) in Barbour County, Troy in Pike County, and Greenville in Butler County were centers of economic and social activity for more than half of the piney woods.

For nearly a century, Eufaula's central location on the banks of the Chattahoochee River served as an important cotton market and trade magnet for farmers in bordering counties. During the antebellum period, cotton-laden wagons from Henry, Dale, Coffee, and Pike counties frequently clogged the roads leading to Eufaula. Mary Love Edwards, a Dale County resident whose family lived in the Clay Bank Creek community, remembered that "Eufaula and Greenville were the cotton markets for the Dale County farmers before and for some time after the [Civil War]. It usually took the cotton wagons five or six days to make the trip to market and return. They would carry cotton and return loaded with dry goods and groceries for the Westville merchants."[51] One-time postmaster and newspaperman Thomas Jackson observed that while "steamboats were plying the Chattahoochee, supplying the merchants with goods . . . the town was boasting of a lucrative wagon trade" from every county in the southeastern corner of the region.[52] By 1860, Eufaula was home to thirty-five merchants, ten carriage makers, eight druggists, a dozen physicians, and numerous cabinet makers, carpenters, teachers, and clerks.

Edward Young, one of the town's wealthiest merchants, moved to Eufaula from New York in the mid-1830s. He established a small mercantile business and amassed a personal fortune that by the outbreak of the Civil War amounted to more than $50,000.[53] L. J. Leaird not only sold clothing, dry goods, tools, books, and groceries from his general store on Broad Street but he also provided "a convenient warehouse for the accommodation of his customers . . . where he is prepared to store cotton on terms to suit them [and] advance them money on cotton, stored or shipped, at such rates as cannot fail to give satisfaction."[54] Alfred Bernstein's mercantile was substantially smaller than Young's and Leaird's, but with two clerks, a store full of merchandise, and a net worth of $6,500, his family lived comfortably.[55] These merchants and others like them played an important role in the economic development that characterized both the community and the region during the antebellum period.

Greenville was established in the early 1820s and Troy about a decade later. Both towns grew rapidly and served as essential markets for communities farther south. When the Conecuh River fell to levels too dangerous for river transport, farmers in Covington County hauled their crops to Greenville, Evergreen (in Conecuh County), or Pensacola. Even when creeks and rivers were full, driftwood, fallen trees, and other debris clogged the channels to such an extent that farmers often chose to move their products overland rather than risk losing the fruits of weeks or even months of labor. Greenville further benefitted when federal officials relocated the land office from Cahaba to Greenville in 1854. More than forty thousand acres of federal land sold in Butler and Covington counties between 1854 and 1860. During the decade of the 1840s, Butler County's total population grew by just 20 percent—from 8,685 in 1840 to 10,836 in 1850. By contrast, the population nearly doubled between 1850 and 1860 to 18,122, due in large part to the relocation of the land office. Thus, by the late 1850s, the town of Greenville had become a bustling community with more than 1,400 residents including twenty-one merchants, more than forty mechanics, at least six hotel owners, and numerous doctors, druggists, and lawyers.

Opportunities for economic growth expanded as town populations increased. Benjamin West sold his small farm in Pike County in the early 1850s, moved his family to Greenville, and opened a livery stable that served the ever-growing populace. By 1860, he owned ten slaves; employed a hostler, a carriage driver, and a harness maker; worked a five-hundred-acre farm; and enjoyed a net worth of $38,000. Not everyone fared as well, however, as local markets sometimes remained constrained. In 1856, brothers Richard and John Branscomb moved from Macon County to Greenville, where they opened a saddler's shop just on the outskirts of town. Writing to his father less than a year later, Richard complained, "I fear we will do bad business here this year. . . . Our opponent has got the ascendency over us and takes very unfair means to put us down in the community."[56] By 1860, the brothers had moved back to Macon County.[57]

In the 1840s, Troy became an important destination due in part to its proximity to Montgomery, one of the largest commercial centers in the entire South. Troy merchants relied upon Montgomery markets to buy their cotton and supply them with affordable manufactured goods. Merchant and cotton buyer Joel D. Murphree was one of many businessmen who bought cotton from local farmers, shipped it and sold it in Montgomery, and sold merchandise on credit to families throughout the region. Murphree began his career some ten years earlier when, as a struggling newcomer to the area, he bought groceries from Montgomery, hauled them back to Troy, and sold them out of the back of a makeshift wagon.[58]

As in Eufaula and Greenville, economic opportunities in Troy increased as the antebellum era progressed. In 1857, Archibald Lockard acquired a mercantile store from a Mr. Weiss. He immediately restocked the shelves and storage room, hired a younger kinsman to help run the store, and built a thriving new business.[59] A year after Lockard opened his establishment, one of the town's most respected and well-known business owners died. Nearly twenty years before Lockard's new venture, Ann Love, a widow and mother of at least six children, built the first hotel in Troy after the county seat relocated there from Monticello. In 1838, using money from her late husband's estate as well as funds from her existing tavern in Monticello, Love bought the old courthouse lot and building at public auction. She tore down the old structure, hauled the lumber to Troy, and built a new hotel and tavern from the remnants. She died in 1858 a respected entrepreneur, slave owner, and something of a local legend, no small feat for a widow in the nineteenth-century South.[60]

Other towns in the five southernmost counties, while not nearly as prosperous as those closer to the Black Belt, offered local residents important goods and services, not to mention legal and social activities. From Evergreen, Sparta, and Andalusia to Elba, Newton, and Abbeville, the daily commercial activities that took place in these towns were for many residents a gateway to the larger market economy. Fifty-year-old Elizabeth Eason, for instance, worked out of her home in Newton as a seamstress. Her personal estate of just $100 was supplemented by her two sons, Green, a mechanic worth $1,900, and William, a wagoner worth $475. The Eason family's combined 1860 income of $2,475 was five times the per capita income of the average Dale Countian. John W. Dowling spent his boyhood and teenage years as a farmhand on his father's small farm. In 1858, Dowling, Frances M. Martin, and James H. Carroll formed a grocery partnership in Ozark. Although the Civil War interrupted the firm's business and it eventually dissolved, Dowling continued to invest his time and resources as a grocer. By 1870, he owned one of the most prosperous enterprises in town.[61]

Small town merchants elsewhere in the southernmost piney woods operated limited but necessary establishments. Merchants such as Andalusia's Isa Smith, Abbeville's Moses Green, and Geneva's William Lee stocked nails, hand tools, plows, clocks, shoes, boots, guns, clothing, and other goods especially coveted by farmers in their respective communities. The majority of businesses such as these were small, but a handful of merchants built large enterprises rivaling those in bigger towns. In 1850, Henry W. Laird was a young, single, up-and-coming merchant renting a room at Elizabeth Chisolm's boardinghouse and tavern in Montgomery. He soon relocated to Geneva, speculated in land, and opened a general store that became one of the largest and most profitable in the county.[62] Alexander Gordon moved with his uncle from Georgia to Henry County around 1817. He worked in his uncle's store near the town of Franklin and eventually bought his own mercantile business in Abbeville. By the late 1850s, Gordon was one of the wealthiest merchant/planters in the region with twenty thousand acres of land, sixty-four slaves, and a personal net worth of more than $130,000.[63]

From the 1820s to the 1850s, the settlement and maturation of the piney woods mirrored the complexity and development of other majority white areas of the Old Southwest. The region's residents were witnesses to, or active participants in, the Creek Indian War, Indian removal, migration and settlement, the spread of revival and religion, and the establishment of communities and towns. As the country became increasingly settled, economic issues stood at the forefront of continuing regional development. For most piney woods residents, farming dominated all other economic endeavors. From poor and middle-class farmers to the wealthiest slaveholding nabobs, nearly every family was touched to some degree by the cotton economy and the peculiar institution upon which it rested.

2

"Of All the Hardy Sons of Toil"

Class and Race in the Piney Woods

In 1860, William Dick was one of the most prosperous farmers in Dale County, Alabama. He and his wife, Mary, along with their eight children, lived in the Saw Mill community just a few miles northeast of Newton. With eleven hundred acres of land, thirteen slaves, and a net worth of nearly $22,000, his family enjoyed a higher standard of living than most Dale Countians. Dick's two next-door neighbors, William Andrews and Joseph Foxworth, were close in proximity but far-removed economically. Andrews's four hundred and sixty–acre farm and personal estate were worth a modest $2,500. As an aging widower, he relied increasingly on his twenty-year-old son, Elisha, and three teenage daughters to work the farm. Foxworth, on the other hand, owned no land and reported to the census taker just $25.00 of personal wealth. He and wife, Eleanor, had five boys, aged two through eleven. They more than likely worked the land of their wealthy next-door neighbors as tenant farmers. While none of these households shared the same socioeconomic status, all three benefitted from growing one of the South's most profitable cash crops, cotton.[1]

Families such as the Dicks, their slaves, the Andrews, and the Foxworths represent a microcosm of a larger socioeconomic whole that included wealthy planter elites, yeoman farmers, poor whites, and slaves. This chapter explores the socioeconomic conditions that existed in the piney woods during the late antebellum period. It considers both class and race as crucial elements in the region's development. With the exception of northern Barbour County—which contained more than one-third of the region's slave population—much of the piney woods, and especially the southernmost counties, has often been portrayed as an area where poverty reigned, the slave population was inconsequential compared with the Black Belt, and most whites showed only slight interest in supporting an institution in which they purportedly had little economic stake. This oversimplification tends to trivialize the region's unique place in history and suggests that the overwhelming majority of whites in southeastern Alabama had little interest in the cotton economy or the institution of slavery. While it is certainly true that the majority of white families owned no slaves, it is equally important to note that many embraced the market economy and supported the expansion of both cotton production and slavery. Indeed, the evidence suggests that, in some communities, the tentacles of slavery often reached much deeper into the socioeconomic fabric than heretofore understood, touching everything from domestic disputes and the legal system to labor practices and kinship networks.

Historians often use census and economic data to identify and categorize socioeconomic classes, usually based upon a set of shared characteristics common to each group. By examining the class structures that existed in the antebellum South, scholars provide a more accurate understanding of nineteenth-century Southerners, thus helping to clarify the times in which they lived. However, identifying and classifying wealthy white slaveholders and their slaves has been, in some respects, less challenging than categorizing the vast sea of yeoman, middling, and poor whites at the center and bottom of the economic ladder. Frank Owsley's "plain folk," for example, included a large and diverse class of "landowning farmers who belonged neither to the plantation economy nor to the destitute and frequently degraded poor-white class."[2] Bill Cecil-Fronsman, J. William Harris, and Wayne Flynt all blur the lines that separated poor whites from plain folk. Common whites—as Cecil-Fronsman prefers to call them—occupied a "middle strata [that] was so broad and diverse that any attempt to provide a rigid definition of it is doomed to failure."[3] Flynt likewise argues that "it is impossible to separate poor whites from middle class yeoman," while Harris similarly notes that "the line between farmer and planter, laborer and tenant, even artisan and farmer were not always clear, since people on either side of the line were often more alike than different."[4]

On the other hand, historians such as Lacy Ford, Samuel Hyde Jr., Steven Hahn, and Stephanie McCurry all provide more precise frameworks for categorizing the various classes, including slaveholders, in the antebellum South.[5] Despite using a wide range of sources and formulas, and arriving at varied conclusions, these authors generally divide white Southerners into lower, middle, and wealthy strata, although the term "middle class" as used for the

Southern yeomanry remains controversial. Most recently, Joseph Glatthaar's heavily statistical study of the Confederate Army of Northern Virginia includes an in-depth class structure analysis of the soldiers who fought in Robert E. Lee's army—an army that included approximately eighteen hundred soldiers from Alabama's southeastern piney woods. Using 1860 census data, Glatthaar combines soldiers' (and their immediate family if they resided at home) real and personal property and creates three categories of economic wealth: the lower or poorer class constituted individuals or families worth $0–$799; middle-class wealth ranged from $800–$3,999; the upper class enjoyed wealth of $4,000 and higher.[6] Given its precise nature, this chapter applies Glatthaar's useful analytical framework to Alabama's piney woods.

In the 1850s, Frederick Law Olmsted wrote about the poor white families he encountered during his travels into the piney woods region just south of Raleigh, North Carolina. "A family of these people will commonly hire or 'squat' and build a little log cabin," he noted. "They will cultivate a little corn, and possibly a few roods of potatoes, cow peas, and coleworts. They own a few swine, that find their living in the forest."[7] Although Olmsted also spent time in northern and central Alabama, had he journeyed deeper into the state's southeastern piney woods, he would have noticed many similarities between the poor Alabamians who lived there and the poor Southerners he observed elsewhere. Unfortunately, his New England upbringing and preconceived notions of wealth often distorted his conclusions about the poor whites he encountered; his writings often denigrated Southern farmers who failed—in his mind, at least—to measure up to his New England standards.[8] Yet, a growing number of historians have eschewed this interpretation of the poor, namely that common whites embraced isolation and shunned the market economy, arguing instead that, by the middle of the nineteenth century, common whites participated freely, if not fully or enthusiastically, in the market.[9] In his study of Ashe County, North Carolina, Martin Crawford aptly notes that while "self-sufficiency remained the prime objective of the community's farm households . . . few could afford to stand aloof from market production, for its benefits potentially outweighed the risks involved."[10] Land ownership and cotton production was the norm for many of the South's poorer families, though this was certainly not the case in every household. While few lower-class households in the piney woods of Alabama could afford to participate in the market economy to the same degree as the upper classes, their inclusion nevertheless signified a willingness on their part to take at least nominal risks in order to expand their economic prospects.

Glatthaar estimates that nearly 51 percent of American households in

1860 qualified as lower class.[11] Compared to the rest of the nation, then, approximately 43 percent of households in Alabama's piney woods qualified as lower-class, by his definition, eight percentage points lower than the national average. In the five southernmost counties, the numbers increase to 54 percent, while the three northernmost counties stood at 42 percent. Compared to Barbour, Pike, and Butler counties, in other words, the southernmost counties had a higher number of poor households, but still only slightly higher than the national average. The numbers are skewed, however, because Eufaula, an important cotton transportation hub, and the cotton-producing communities concentrated in northern Barbour County contained large numbers of wealthy planters, bankers, doctors, cotton factors, and merchants. By removing these beats from the equation, the percentage of lower-class households for the entire region rises slightly to 46 percent while the figures for the southernmost and northernmost counties stands at 51 percent and 41 percent, respectively. Simply put, these numbers suggest that on the whole the region was better off than the national average economically and, when considering only the southernmost counties, equal to the rest of the nation by percentage of lower-class households (see Table 2.1).

For many lower-class families in the piney woods, land ownership and cotton production were an important means to increase wealth. To this end, poor farmers used every available method within their power to acquire land and plant cotton. The 1860 census taker, for instance, found forty-four-year-old Calvin Gilbert and his wife, Lucy, on a small Texasville farm about twenty miles southwest of Clayton in Barbour County. They had eight children. Milly was fifteen-years-old, Maranda fourteen, John twelve, Matilda ten, William nine, Daniel seven, Mary five, and Buford just a year old. Within a year, Lucy Gilbert gave birth to their ninth child, Henry. None of the children attended school that year. According to the agricultural schedule, Calvin Gilbert owned 80 acres of land, including 35 improved acres. He had a horse, one milk cow, a pair of working oxen, and three pigs. His harvest for the year included some peas and beans, one hundred twenty bushels of corn, and one hundred fifty bushels of sweet potatoes. His wife and the three older girls found the time to produce thirty-five dollars' worth of homemade manufactured goods. Importantly, the family's eight hundred pounds of cotton, worth more than $100 in 1860, and 152 gallons of molasses provided enough cash income and trading collateral to purchase goods and items necessary to support a large family. The Gilbert family's net worth of $750 suggests that their land and participation in the cotton economy likely improved their financial outlook.[12]

Like Calvin Gilbert, Marinda Watson took full advantage of her small

TABLE 2.1. Class divisions in the Piney Woods, 1860

County	Lower class	Middle class	Upper class	Total
Barbour[a]	1336 (47%)	600 (21%)	892 (32%)	2828
Barbour[b]	551 (43%)	350 (28%)	377 (29%)	1278
Butler	796 (40%)	583 (29%)	632 (31%)	2011
Coffee	757 (55%)	418 (31%)	195 (14%)	1370
Conecuh	517 (46%)	285 (26%)	308 (28%)	1110
Covington	515 (53%)	329 (34%)	132 (13%)	976
Dale	837 (48%)	671 (38%)	250 (14%)	1758
Henry	945 (53%)	470 (26%)	385 (21%)	1800
Pike	1091 (40%)	828 (30%)	810 (30%)	2729

Source: United States Census for Barbour County, Butler County, Coffee County, Conecuh County, Covington County, Dale County, Henry County, Pike County, Alabama, 1860, Schedule 1.

Note: County divisions include the number of families in each class category along with the percentage of total families in that county.

[a] Figures include all of Barbour County.

[b] Figures exclude Eufaula and the wealthy cotton-producing beats in northern Barbour County.

farm in Pike County's Indian Creek community. Probate court records reveal that, in September 1857, the same year of her death, Watson owned ten hogs, three cows, and two calves. She and her twenty-four-year-old son, Napoleon, worked a small potato patch, a cotton patch with an estimated two thousand pounds of unpicked cotton, and a field of corn estimated to produce seventy-five bushels of grain. Three bee stands would have provided enough honey and beeswax for family use with plenty left over to sell. Her home was unembellished but filled with items that suggest a humble yet comfortable living. Appraisers found a kitchen table with five chairs, earthen-ware plates, knives and forks, a coffee mill, some pots and pans, two beds with mattresses, bed clothing, a spinning wheel and loom, cotton yarn, and fifty pounds of ginned cotton. The total value of the family's personal possessions, crops, and livestock was less than $300. Watson's one hundred acres of land, valued at $500, and the cotton crop then growing on her land was her most prized possessions. Three years after his mother's death, Napoleon, now married with two young children, enjoyed a net worth of over $4,000, including one slave. That same year, he harvested eleven bales of cotton worth over $500. It is not entirely clear how Watson experienced such a dramatic shift in fortunes. It may well be that his inheritance, which included his mother's land, allowed him opportunities to improve his economic standing. The land alone would have at least given him valuable borrowing collateral. It is also possible that he or his wife relied upon kinship connections to help them expand their farming operations.[13]

While landowning families such as the Gilberts and the Watsons formed a significant portion of lower-class households, landless tenant farmers and common laborers also shared a place in the ranks of the lower class, though this group was far less likely to participate meaningfully in the cotton economy. Because of its poor, sandy soil, Covington County was one of the poorest counties in Alabama and home to the piney woods' largest percentage of landless poor. In 1860, the agricultural census reported that 331 out of 515 (64 percent) lower-class heads of households reported no improved acreage, no unimproved acreage, and zero farm value. The majority of these households were more than likely tenant farmers who raised livestock, grew modest amounts of corn and sweet potatoes, and harvested the occasional bale of cotton. The population schedule listed the majority as landless farmers whose wealth fell well below Glatthaar's $799 threshold for the lower class. Moreover, by adding up *all* of the lower-class households owning no land—including seamstresses, store clerks, watch repairers, shoemakers, cabinet makers, and other occupations unrelated to farming—the number of landless increases slightly to 336. Put another way, landless tenant farmers or common laborers made up almost two-thirds of the lower-class families in Covington. By way of comparison, approximately 45 percent of the region's lower-class households qualified as landless.[14]

The landless, regardless of whether they were tenant farmers or common laborers, struggled mightily at times just to survive. Illiteracy rates were high among this segment of the population, especially in Covington County and certain segments of the southernmost piney woods. The landless poor who grew cotton did so primarily for home use. Yet even landless tenant farmers used cotton and other crops as valuable sources of collateral. Twenty-five-year-old James Goodson and his wife, Missouri, for instance, lived in Coffee County, Alabama, where the census listed both as landless and illiterate. Goodson does not appear on the 1860 agricultural schedule, but the population schedule suggests that he farmed a small portion of his father's fifteen improved acres of land. Five years earlier, he borrowed thirty dollars from a planter in Dale County. His collateral was "the growing crop of corn and cotton now growing on the place of Edmon Goodson." It is unclear why he borrowed the money, but his crops provided the necessary security that allowed him to take a calculated risk. James Goodson's case also demonstrates that being landless was relative, especially if kinship networks provided opportunities to farm. Just a few miles away, William Lucas worked as a landless sharecropper. He purchased a horse on credit from Joseph Parrish, a local planter in Elba. "As I am imployed by James Morris of this county as a croper," the deed states, "and am to have one third of the corn peas and potatoes of said Morris crop to be made this year for my services as croper aforesaid that he hold my part . . . of said crop until the said notes are paid."[15] Importantly, the landless poor utilized both their value as workers and the crops that they produced to try and improve their immediate economic circumstances.

While poor households in the piney woods participated in the cotton economy on a limited basis, middle-class families contributed at a much higher rate. In 1860, Alabama-born proslavery apologist Daniel Hundley noted: "of all the hardy sons of toil, in all free lands the Yeoman are most deserving of our esteem. With hearts of oak and thews of steel, crouching to no man and fearing no danger, these are equally bold to handle a musket on the field of battle or to swing their reapers in times of peace among the waving stalks of yellow grain."[16] Despite the author's obvious celebratory tone, Hundley challenged what he believed to be an unfair portrait of Southern society in general and common folk in particular. The middle class, defined in this chapter as families whose total wealth equaled from $800 to $3,999, constituted the second largest class in the piney woods. And while it included teachers, tradesmen, merchants, ministers, and people of other nonagricultural pursuits, farmers comprised the overwhelming majority of middle-class households. Compared to the poor—especially the landless poor—these yeoman households were far more prosperous and more likely to meaningfully participate in the production of cotton and slaveholding.

While some middle-class farmers owned slaves, about 85 percent considered themselves freeholders who worked their farms alongside their own family members, the occasional hired hand, or slaves rented from neighboring slaveholders. In 1860, Stephen Satterwhite's 260-acre farm in Dale County included forty-five acres of improved land and 215 acres of unimproved land. He owned a horse and mule, three milk cows, three stock cattle, fifteen hogs, and forty sheep. His sheep produced around fifty pounds of wool and functioned as a ready source of meat, if the need arose. In addition, his two thousand pounds of ginned cotton was valued at approximately $260. At age seventy-two, Satterwhite may have been unable to take on some of the more grueling chores on the farm, but with three teenage children at home and one older son living next door, there were plenty of laborers to work the farm.[17]

Stephen Satterwhite's investment in livestock was a common means by which many piney woods farmers hoped to improve their personal economic standing. In fact, while cotton production was a high priority for most middle-class households, raising livestock provided an additional source of wealth. Historian Grady McWhiney observes that "in 1860 hogs and other Southern livestock were worth half a billion dollars—more than twice the value of that year's cotton crop; indeed, Southern animals probably were worth much more because there was every reason for owners to undercount the actual number of livestock they reported to tax collectors and census takers."[18] Cattle, sheep, and especially hogs were the livestock of choice in the Deep South, and piney woods families were no different (see Table 2.2). The northernmost counties led the way in livestock production. Barbour County farmers, for example, reported over seventy-four thousand head, while Pike County and Butler County farmers totaled 72,623 and 51,425, respectively. On a per capita basis, farmers in the southernmost counties maintained livestock herds equal in numbers to their neighbors to the North, and several counties surpassed state and regional averages (see Table 2.3). In swine production, Covington County's 3.1 per capita average, Dale County's 2.8, and Coffee County's 2.5 were the highest in the piney woods.[19]

Because livestock provided meat, milk, butter, lard, wool, and a host of other products for family consumption, as well as opportunities for trade and useful loan collateral, piney woods families kept as many hogs, sheep, and cattle as economic circumstances allowed. Moreover, by diversifying their holdings between livestock and cotton production, the region's farmers wisely increased their economic prospects. Coffee County's William Wilkins, for example, produced sixteen hundred pounds of cotton and raised forty hogs, ten sheep, twelve stock cattle, and eight milk cows on his four hundred and forty–acre farm near Geneva. The cotton was worth $200, the livestock $500, and the milk cows generated fifty pounds of churned butter. In neighboring Covington County, King Howard and his brother Elbert produced a combined sixteen hundred pounds of cotton, and raised six milk cows, eighteen stock cattle, twenty-four sheep, and forty-four hogs. Just a few miles down the road, Eliza Jackson's ten milk cows, eight stock cattle, and forty hogs—together with twelve hundred pounds of cotton and forty acres of improved land—a total value of $805, was just enough to place this single mother of eight children in the ranks of the middle class. It is worth noting, however, that for large families like Eliza Jackson's—straddling the fence between the middle and lower classes—poverty was just one swine disease away from wiping out a major source of the family's income. Importantly, middle-class farmers understood the potential profitability of combining cotton production with raising livestock.[20]

For freeholders such as William Wilkins, the Howard brothers, and Eliza Jackson, livestock, land, and especially cotton provided the keys to their economic wellbeing. The vast majority of nonslaveholding yeoman planted

TABLE 2.2. Livestock, 1860

County	Swine	Cattle	Sheep
Barbour	55,523	12,839	6,331
Butler	34,116	10,208	7,101
Coffee	23,859	9,294	3,685
Conecuh	21,996	10,135	5,612
Covington	20,527	5,872	4,369
Dale	34,011	6,721	7,872
Henry	33,938	7,367	4,310
Pike	55,156	11,785	5,682

Source: Joseph C. G. Kennedy, *Agriculture of the United States in 1860: Compiled from the Original Returns of the Eighth Census* (Washington, DC: Government Printing Office, 1864).

TABLE 2.3. Livestock per capita, 1860

County	Swine	Other	Population
Barbour	1.8	0.6	30,812
Butler	1.9	1.0	18,122
Coffee	2.5	1.3	9,623
Conecuh	1.9	1.4	11,311
Covington	3.1	1.6	6,469
Dale	2.8	1.2	12,197
Henry	2.3	0.9	14,918
Pike	2.3	0.7	24,435
Alabama	1.8	1.0	964,201

Sources: Joseph C. G. Kennedy, *Agriculture of the United States in 1860: Compiled from the Original Returns of the Eighth Census* (Washington, DC: Government Printing Office, 1864); Manuscript Census, Piney Woods Counties, 1860, Schedule 1.

cotton, even if it was only a bale or two. According to Robert Russell, an Englishman who visited Alabama in the 1850s, "it is worthy of remark, however, that a good deal of cotton is cultivated throughout the piney woods, and the larger portion of it seems to be raised by free labour."[21] For these families, cotton was an important resource for domestic manufacture, and cotton farming supplemented family incomes by providing extra cash or credit at the local mercantile. Stephanie McCurry demonstrates that middle-class yeoman farmers "marketed their cotton through local storekeepers and in that way secured the credit in goods without which they could not have survived the long year between harvests."[22] Lacy Ford likewise argues that South Carolina's "upcountry yeomen made a set of crop-mix decisions each year, balancing their need for a sure and steady food supply with their desire for cotton profits, a cash income, and a higher standard of living."[23] In this regard, piney woods yeoman were not unlike middle-class farmers of similar means in other cotton-growing, majority-white regions of the South. On average, over 70 percent of households with accumulated wealth of $800 to $4,000 harvested at least one bale of cotton. The averages increased in the northernmost counties and the counties bordering the Chattahoochee River and decreased in the southernmost counties, with Covington averaging only about 50 percent.

Given that large numbers of middle-class farmers supported the cotton economy, it was only logical for those who could afford it to purchase slaves, thereby increasing cotton production and extending slavery's influence into more and more of the region's households. Slaveholding among the yeomanry was not unusual and was, for many, the most obvious and direct route to achieving greater socioeconomic status. In his study of piney woods Georgia, Mark Wetherington notes that "a yeoman's status could rise head and shoulders above his neighbors when he combined slaveholding with cotton farming."[24] Historian Gavin Wright argues that the financial incentive for purchasing slaves was so great that it superseded all other investment endeavors, including land purchases. Slave owners, he insists, were not so much landlords as they were "labor lords."[25] Even with a modest amount of acreage, the average yeoman farmer could potentially reap immense financial benefits by purchasing slaves and planting cotton.

The great majority of yeoman or middle-class slaveholders, as defined by Glatthaar, owned between one and three slaves. Nearly 40 percent of slave owners in the piney woods came from the ranks of the yeomanry. By the 1850s, however, the value of slaves, especially prime field hands, increased to levels almost out of reach for many yeoman farmers. Some discovered a solution to the problem by investing in less costly adult female slaves or children. Slaveholders valued slaves according to their sex, age, and physical capabilities. Olmsted observes that young slaves began as quarter-hands, advanced to half-hands, and then three-quarter hands as they grew older and stronger, finally reaching the status of full hands "when mature, able bodied, healthy, and strong."[26] Because the market value for female slaves and children was lower than the price for men, yeoman farmers could purchase slave women at lower cost in hopes that the initial monetary outlay would pay off later; female slaves' future reproductive value promised significant returns on their investment.[27]

TABLE 2.4. Piney Woods crops, 1860

County	Corn	Cotton (bales)	Sweet potatoes	Orchard products
Barbour	909,973	44,518	273,851	$6,055
Butler	13,489	13,489	124,391	$875
Coffee	257,822	5,294	78,357	$0
Conecuh	302,610	6,850	72,370	$3,979
Covington	148,475	2,021	55,459	$97
Dale	341,239	7,832	109,129	$6,337
Henry	421,618	13,034	138,025	$100
Pike	823,752	24,527	243,079	$11,423

Source: Joseph C. G. Kennedy, *Agriculture of the United States in 1860: Compiled from the Original Returns of the Eighth Census* (Washington, DC: Government Printing Office, 1864).

James D. McRae from Dale County serves as an example of this approach. McRae owned a nineteen-year-old female slave, her three-year-old son, and twelve-month-old daughter. His forty acres of improved land produced three hundred fifty bushels of corn and four bales of cotton. The household also included an eighteen-year-old white laborer named William Rouse, who might have actually been McRae's kinsman. McRae's sole slave cabin was most likely a single room dwelling of log or plank-board construction with dirt or, if they were lucky, wood flooring. While his total net worth was a little over 3,000 dollars—at least half of which came from slave property—his investment promised to pay off as long as his female slaves remained healthy and produced additional offspring.[28]

Yet for James McRae and others like him, there was always the risk that a few bad crops or the untimely death of his most valuable slave might force him out of the slaveholding business. Scholars have demonstrated the tendency among Southern slaveholders to move in and out of the ranks of the master class, and piney woods farmers in Alabama were no different. Some yeoman climbed the slaveholding ladder while others, including large slaveholders, lost a portion or all of their slaves. James Oakes, for example, argues that movement between the various slaveholding classes was a common occurrence, especially during harvest time or anytime economic conditions warranted. Indeed, fluctuations in slave ownership often involved complicated kinship networks, unusual circumstances, or a combination of the two.[29] In 1850, Benjamin Stuart's family—Lucinda, Benjamin Jr, John, Mary, and Lucinda's aging mother, Elizabeth Shropshire—lived in Macon County,

Alabama, in the heart of the Black Belt. The slave schedule lists four slaves under Stuart's name, but some or all of them may have actually belonged to his mother-in-law. At some point over the next five years, the family moved to Coffee County, with the number of slaves increasing from four to seven. In 1855, eighty-seven-year-old Elizabeth Shropshire conveyed two slaves—an adult female slave named Amy and her five-year-old son, Simon—to her daughter Lucinda. By 1860, Benjamin and Lucinda Stuart lived in Dale County, Lucinda's mother was dead, all of the children had moved out of the household, and only two slaves remained. Presumably, the twenty-four-year-old female and the ten-year-old male listed on the slave schedule were Amy and Simon. With a little over $2,500 in net worth, nearly all of which came from the value of their personal estate and the two slaves, the Stuarts were solid middle-class slaveholders. Yet the family's changing fortunes demonstrate just how complex and potentially volatile slave owning could be. The Stuarts began the 1850s as middle-class slaveholders, briefly entered the ranks of the upper-class as the number of slaves grew to seven, and finished out the decade as yeoman slave owners once again. Despite the volatility, however, the Stuarts and other piney woods whites determined that the potential economic gain from owning slaves far outweighed the economic consequences of losing them.[30]

While middle-class whites increasingly embraced the cotton and slaveholding economy—and stood to gain economically if they could make the system work—it was the wealthiest families who controlled the vast majority of the region's slave population. Glatthaar defines the upper-class, slaveholder and nonslaveholder alike, as individuals with combined personal and real estate wealth of $4,000 or higher. In the piney woods, the vast majority of the well-to-do were in fact slaveholding farmers or planters. There were exceptions of course, but many wealthy doctors, ministers, attorneys, grocers, and merchants owned slaves and planted cotton. Osborn Johnson, for instance, a physician living in Pike County's Mount Ida community, owned an 880-acre plantation, fifteen slaves, and three slave cabins. He employed a full-time overseer, Joshua Calahan, and a school teacher, eighteen-year-old Isaac Parks. His farm produced fifty bales of cotton in 1860, three hundred pounds of rice, six hundred bushels of corn, seventy-five hogs, twenty sheep, ten stock cattle, and nine milk cows. For the Osborn Johnsons of the region, their diversification activities between slaveholding and professional pursuits strengthened their economic standing.[31]

Although Glatthaar's definition of the upper-class is useful, a more detailed examination of the region's wealthy slaveholders is necessary in the case of the piney woods. By further dividing the upper-class between middling slaveholders (not to be confused with middle-class) and large planters,

TABLE 2.5. Piney Woods slaveholders in 1860

County	Slaveholders owning 1–3 slaves	Slaveholders owning 4–19 slaves	Slaveholders owning 20+	Total
Barbour	367	541	235	1143
Butler	260	394	94	748
Coffee	124	103	12	239
Conecuh	132	196	70	398
Covington	82	56	6	144
Dale	159	144	11	314
Henry	201	226	62	489
Pike	400	478	121	999
Total	1725	2138	611	4474

Source: Joseph C. G Kennedy, *Agriculture of the United States in 1860: Compiled from the Original Returns of the Eighth Census* (Washington, DC: Government Printing Office, 1864) 223; Manuscript Census, Piney Woods counties, 1860, Schedule 2.

historians have drawn important distinctions between the two groups. Middling slaveholders, those who owned between four and nineteen slaves, accounted for nearly 50 percent of all slave owners in the region.[32] As a group, their wealth exceeded that of the slaveholding yeomanry, while some enjoyed a standard of living rivaled only by the planters (those who owned more than twenty slaves). Barbour County produced the largest number of middling slaveholders at 541—mostly due to the port town of Eufaula and the wealthy planting communities in the northern portion of the county—while Covington County's poor soil and relative isolation accounted for the region's fewest, 56 (see Table 2.5).[33]

Yet a closer examination of the statistics reveals that nearly two-thirds, or 64 percent, of middling slaveholders owned between four and nine slaves, clearly indicating that the distribution of slaves skewed substantially more toward the bottom end of the bracket than the top. Representative of this "lesser" group was A. J. Dunham, who lived in Butler County's Davison community. Dunham owned just four slaves: a twenty-year-old female, an eleven-year-old female, a three-year-old male, and a two-month-old baby girl. His 240-acre farm supported sixty-four head of livestock, including thirty hogs and twenty sheep. Dunham most likely relied upon his own labor, as well as that of his two teenage sons and the two older slaves, to tend the livestock, pick cotton, and harvest two hundred bushels of corn. His total net worth of over $6,500 placed him comfortably within the ranks of the middling farmers. Henry County farmer and physician John Little kept four slaves on his one hundred improved acres, where he harvested thirteen bales of cotton and two hundred bushels of corn. His estate was worth $6,150 in 1860. A few miles away, James John's slaves produced twenty-one bales of cotton. The value of John's nine slaves, only four of which would have been considered full hands, pushed his total net worth up to nearly $10,000. It is important to note, however, that the vast majority of middling slaveholders who owned fewer than ten slaves still worked or assisted with all of the various tasks on their farms, spending less time as slave managers and more time as self-working slave owners.[34]

Middling slaveholders who owned between ten and nineteen slaves—the top end of the bracket—made up less than 17 percent of the total number of slaveholders in the piney woods. Barbour County produced the highest number at 215, while Covington County again had the fewest, only eleven. A handful of slave owners in this group developed remarkably large entrepreneurial holdings that rivaled the planters. Covington's Hugh Blount, for example, owned an eight-hundred-acre plantation, sixteen slaves, three slave cabins, and enjoyed a net worth of almost $60,000. His slaves produced fifty-four bales of cotton, three thousand bushels of corn, and tended over one hundred head of livestock. Blount employed two overseers, Richard Webb and fourteen-year-old Daniel Knowles, although the latter was probably just an apprentice. To be clear, most middling slaveholders in this bracket never amassed Blount's level of wealth. William Harvey of Pike County was more representative of the norm. His estate records provide a useful glimpse into the middling slaveholder's world and the extent to which slavery directly impacted kinship networks in his and other slave-owning households. In the mid-1850s, he owned thirteen slaves worth about $9,000. Following his death in 1857, the estate record reveals that he divided his slaves into two families. One family included Richard and Betty, both in their forties, with their three children, thirteen-year-old Levi, five-year-old Shondra, and four-year-old Jerry. The second family included the mother, twenty-four-year-old Mondana (Montana?), and her seven children, Elizabeth, Jordan, Gracy Ann, Malsey, Elbert, Penny, and Rinda, all under the age of ten. According to the deed, Harvey left one family of slaves to his twelve-year-old daughter, Evelina, and the other to his ten-year-old son, David. The two children would eventually inherit their father's slaves along with the wealth tied to that inheritance.[35]

In the meantime, however, Evelina and David Harvey lived with their uncle, O. F. Knox, a physician, large planter, and one of the wealthiest men in Pike County. As the owner of forty slaves, his six hundred–acre plantation produced eighty bales of cotton, two thousand bushels of corn, and 120 hogs. He was one of just thirty men in the entire county who owned forty or more slaves. Indeed, piney woods planters who owned twenty or more slaves—the customary definition of the planter class—made up just 14 percent of all slaveholders in the region. Historians William Cooper and Thomas Terrill note that "in 1860, planters with more than 20 slaves accounted for only 12 percent of all slave owners, but they owned 48 percent of all the slaves. In contrast, 71 percent of the masters with fewer than 10 slaves held only 32 percent of the slaves."[36] In other words, half of the South's slaves belonged to a small percentage of the South's slaveholders. In Barbour County, 21 percent of the county's slaveholders owned 65 percent of the slaves. In Pike, Butler, and Henry counties, large planters controlled fewer than 50 percent of the slaves. In the southernmost counties of Dale and Coffee the distribution of slaves varied, with large planters controlling only around 25 percent. Covington County's nutrient-starved, sandy soil limited large slave owning operations to a small area, primarily along the Conecuh River just south of Andalusia. There, seven slaveholders owned 269 slaves, or 33 percent of the county's total. Among this small group, Nancy Feagin of the Fairfield community was the largest and most prosperous slaveholder in the county, with seventy-nine slaves.[37]

Many large planters hired overseers to organize day-to-day operations on their plantations and to manage their large slave populations. Planters expected overseers to be skilled agriculturalists, professional motivators, firm but fair disciplinarians, and expert organizers. Since few lived up to the planters' expectations, turnover rates were high; replacing overseers annually was commonplace. Barbour County planter John Horry Dent grew impatient with overseers whom he felt were more interested in high wages and lavish living than in carefully attending to cotton production and slaves. "Overseers this fall," he wrote in 1855, "are looking up for higher wages for next year. They are asking from 300 to 500, horse found, cook furnished, and provisioned in full. In short they are expecting easy times, and good pay." In Dent's estimation, the older, more experienced men proved to be highly unreliable: "I have generally found out that these experienced overseers rely more on hard driving than good management, they are close and pushing in the field, and negligent in the quarter and stock departments. Wasteful and extravagant with provision. Careless and regardless of stock, and cruel to negroes." Dent's solution was to hire young, inexperienced overseers who required much less pay, showed more enthusiasm and initiative for their job duties, and followed instructions without deviation. Dent's 1855 "unexperienced" overseer lasted about one year, which was actually the norm at the time, while his 1856 experienced man stayed on for only four months.[38]

Planters' constant difficulty dealing with overseers was only one of the many consequences of their quest to cultivate more and more cotton. Contemporaries (and a fair number of later historians) excoriated plantation owners for their relentless pursuit of land, cotton, and slaves at the expense of diversification and self-sufficiency. In 1849, the editor of *The Eufaula Democrat* encouraged planters to cut back their cotton production and invest more time raising livestock, cultivating food crops, and harvesting timber. "But our planters," the writer lamented, "instead of following these plain dictates of common sense, strain every nerve to add to the number of bales of cotton. Not only so, they invest every dollar of surplus capital they can scrape up, in purchasing negroes from Maryland, Virginia, and N. Carolina."[39] Furthermore, some planters exhausted the soil and abandoned their land in search of more fertile property farther west. "One of the most baneful consequences of *unsettledness* is seen in the *abuse* of the soil," the *Democrat* added. "All that can be made must be made immediately, without regard to an almost waste of the energies of the land. The most exhausting modes of culture are resorted to—the fixed intention of the planter being to emigrate as soon as the soil loses its fruitfulness."[40]

Although some planters moved farther west, most held on to their plantations and tried to improve the condition of the soil and increase their production of cotton. Farmers often turned to agricultural journals for ideas on slave and plantation management, established local agricultural societies, and experimented with crop diversification, soil enrichment, and other modern farming techniques.[41] *De Bow's Review*, for example, promoted the economic transformation of the South through urban development, industrialization, and innovative farming practices. For decades, the journal served as an intellectual resource for Southern planters, merchants, and wealthy entrepreneurs. Piney woods residents such as physician Jesse Hayley from Dale County, merchant William Laird from Coffee, middling slaveholder John B. Randolph from Butler County, and merchant-planter John McNab from Barbour all maintained regular subscriptions.[42] *De Bow's Review* and other popular journals such as the *American Agriculturalist* and the *American Cotton Planter* presented both full-length articles and news stories showcasing modern farming techniques. In 1844, the *Agriculturalist* reported that the Apalachicola Chamber of Commerce awarded Eufaula's Alexander McDonald "an elegant silver tea-set . . . as a premium for the best lot of 20 bales of cotton sold last season in the market."[43] McDonald credited the cotton's quality—for which he received 10 cents per pound or $800 total—to his knowledge of agricultural journals and the implementation of new farming techniques. In 1858, an Abbeville planter wrote to *The American Cotton Planter*, "I made upwards of ninety gallons of wine from the cultivated grape and wild muskadine [last year]. This year I have made upwards of seven hundred gallons of wine from the muskadine alone."[44] Agricultural journals routinely praised such diversification efforts.

Planters devoted to using new agricultural techniques frequently utilized manure as a way to fertilize their fields and increase production. Most found the practice beneficial and occasionally reported their findings to journals and farmers' organizations. At an 1846 meeting of the Barbour County Agricultural Society, Thomas Flournoy and Henry Folson described the process to their peers and suggested that planters who used manure as fertilizer achieved higher crop yields. "On those places the benefit of manuring was fully exemplified, particularly on Col. McDonald's plantation, which was in its natural state extremely sandy and poor, and apparently not susceptible of a high state of fertility."[45] John Horry Dent put dozens of slaves to work spreading manure on his fields in preparation for planting cotton and corn. Slaves raked pine straw, hauled it to the livestock pens, scattered the fresh straw in the pens, loaded the old, manured straw into the wagon, hauled it to a designated field, broadcast it, and returned to the woods to begin the process anew. Dent noted in his journal: "It is my wishes to turn my attention to stock on this plantation, in order that I can make a large supply of manure for resussitating my lands, as well as to have a supply of fresh meats for market, as well as for my table."[46] By adopting new agricultural techniques, large planters such as John Dent hoped to improve the soil, expand their profit margins, and increase their slave work force.

Planters' extensive holdings in both land and slaves placed them in the unique position of offering a number of goods and services to their neighbors. Common business transactions between planters and their neighbors tied increasing numbers of lower- and middle-class farmers closer to the cotton and slaveholding economy. Slave owners, especially large planters, frequently ginned and marketed their neighbor's cotton, rented out slaves, loaned money, and sold corn, meat, produce, and other surplus supplies. For the majority of smallholders, the costs of purchasing and maintaining a cotton gin was beyond their ability to pay. Planters ginned cotton for a fee, thus providing a much-needed service to the community in addition to strengthening ties between themselves and nonslaveholders.[47] In 1840, John Dent ginned a bale of cotton for Philip Johnson, six bales for G. B. Wheeler, five bales for William Brown, and one for Murdock McDuffie. Throughout the 1840s and 1850s, he ginned thousands of pounds of cotton for other farmers, made dozens of loans to neighbors, and conducted business with individuals from all sorts of economic backgrounds. In 1854, he loaned $500.00 to Buckner Williams; sold 945 bushels of corn to William Varner; and hired out a slave mechanic named Alfred to John McNeil "to fix his gin geer."[48]

Dent's plantation journals are littered with examples of business transactions such as these. Another planter, T. A. Lawrence from Dale County, loaned $100 to Nathan Stoddard, a landless tenant farmer who lived nearby. For collateral, Stoddard pledged a nine-year-old horse, two yearling steers, one yoke of oxen, one feather bed, and a wagon. If he failed to repay the loan, he risked losing a major source of personal wealth.[49] In addition, farmers who would have otherwise been unable to afford the purchase price of a slave could rent slaves from their slaveholding neighbors. Those with no familial workforce of their own—young farmers whose children were too young to work, for instance, or those with no apparent kinship connections with slaveholders—rented slaves for clearing land, plowing fields, planting crops, and harvesting cotton. These types of business transactions between slaveholders and nonslaveholders reinforced both the cotton economy and the extent to which the peculiar institution influenced white families who owned no slaves. Even among the lower and middle classes, smallholders had a stake in guaranteeing the permanence of slavery.

By examining planters such as John Dent, middle-class slaveholders and nonslaveholders, and lower-class farmers, this chapter demonstrates that many piney woods whites supported both the expansion of the cotton economy and the growth of slavery. It also suggests that slavery had far-reaching effects even in a majority white region such as the piney woods. At first glance, however, the statistics show that the total number of individual slave owners from all economic classes constituted only a small percentage of the total free population of each county. In Barbour County, only 8 percent of the population owned slaves. In Pike and Butler counties, the numbers averaged 6 percent and 7 percent, respectively. In the southernmost counties, Conecuh averaged 6 percent, Henry 5 percent, with Coffee, Covington, and Dale all at 3 percent. Yet, the perspective changes when one examines the numbers through the prism of *households*. Assuming that most slaveholders were also heads of their households, which was typically the norm in 1860, slaveholding households accounted for 42 percent of all households in Barbour County. Slave-owning households in Pike and Butler accounted for 37 percent, Henry at 27 percent, Dale 18 percent, Coffee 17 percent, and Covington at 14 percent (see Table 2.6). In addition, if one considers the number of households not recorded as slaveholding in the census, but indirectly connected to slaveholders through bonds of kinship, the figures rise a bit higher. Put another way, it is possible that up to half of the freeholders in Barbour, Butler, Pike, Henry, and Conecuh counties found themselves connected in one way or another with slavery. In Coffee, Dale, and Covington, the percentages may have averaged as high as 40 percent.[50] This is not to say that nonslaveholding families necessarily supported the

TABLE 2.6. Slaveholding households, 1860

County	Number of households (free population)	Number of slaveholders
Barbour	2,717	1,143(42%)
Butler	2,046	748 (37%)
Coffee	1,375	239 (17%)
Conecuh	1,117	308 (28%)
Covington	1,045	144 (14%)
Dale	1,767	314 (18%)
Henry	1,843	489 (27%)
Pike	2,734	999 (37%)
Total	14,644	4,384 (30%)

Sources: Muster Rolls of Alabama Civil War Units, 1861–1940, Alabama Department of Archives and History; *Brief Historical Sketches of Military Organizations Raised in Alabama During the Civil War—Reproduced From Willis Brewer's Alabama: Her History, Resources, War Record, and Public Men, From 1540 to 1872* (Alabama Civil War Centennial Commission, 1962); Thomas McAdory Owen, *History of Alabama and Dictionary of Alabama Biography in Four Volumes* (Spartanburg, SC: Reprint Company, 1978); United States Census, Barbour County, Butler County, Coffee County, Conecuh County, Covington County, Dale County, Henry County, Pike County, Alabama, 1860, Schedule 1.

institution just because their slaveholding kinsmen did, but it does lend credence to the idea that by 1860 more and more freeholders had a much greater stake in the system than they had just a decade before.

No socioeconomic study of the expansion of the cotton economy and growth of slavery in the piney woods would be complete without a closer look at the region's black population, nearly all of which was enslaved. By examining the region's slaves, one gains a better understanding of the institution's impact on the region. In the decade prior to the Civil War, the slave population in Alabama increased from 342,844 in 1850 to 435,080 in 1860, a 26.9 percent increase. During that same period, the number of slaves in the piney woods rose from 26,643 to 45,115, a 69 percent increase. The number of whites, meanwhile, grew from 70,905 to 82,772, only a 17 percent increase (see Table 2.7). Put another way, the piney woods as a whole saw a seven-fold regional increase in the number of enslaved persons, while statewide the numbers reflected only a three-fold increase. One possible explanation for the difference between state and regional numbers is that, by the 1850s, a large portion of southeastern Alabama was still being developed, while other regions of the state, principally the Black Belt and the Tennessee Valley, had reached a certain level of socioeconomic maturity. During the 1850s, for example, the white population in Black Belt counties increased on average about 10 percent, while the white population in Butler County grew by 57 percent, in Covington County by 78 percent, in Henry by 54 percent, and in Dale by 84 percent. The increase in white population, combined with a substantial increase in the percentage of slaves, suggests that by the outbreak of the Civil War the piney woods region remained in a state of expansion and development.[51]

A closer look at the numbers reveals that Barbour, Butler, Pike, and Henry counties contained over fifteen thousand of the 18,472 slaves added during the 1850s. In 1860, the three northernmost counties of Barbour, Pike, and Butler accounted for 50 percent of the region's free white population but over 70 percent of the region's slaves. Barbour County planters alone owned sixteen thousand slaves, accounting for over 50 percent of that county's total population and more than one third of the slave population in all of the southeastern piney woods (see Table 2.7). As has already been mentioned, the rich soil and large plantations in northern Barbour County accounted for most of the slaves in that corner of the region. In short, the vast majority of slave population expansion took place in the northernmost counties and along the Chattahoochee River. While the southernmost counties were not nearly as prolific in raw numbers—slavery's growth never matched the volume of growth of the communities in or near Eufaula, for instance—several of those counties witnessed sizeable increases in their slave populations nonetheless. Coffee County saw a 154 percent increase in slave population, followed by Dale County at 138 percent, and Covington County at a modest 71 percent. Covington's numbers are, of course, comparatively lower than the others due to its poor, sandy soils. Even so, the evidence suggests that slavery was a growing, vibrant institution throughout the Alabama piney woods, especially in the region's northernmost counties.[52]

For the majority of slaves, life in the piney woods was not unlike that of those who lived in other parts of the South. Approximately half of the region's slaves lived on plantations of more than twenty slaves, and many, if not most, worked as field hands in gangs in the cotton fields. On the other hand, a substantial number of slaves labored individually or in small groups alongside whites on smaller farms, a fact that increased slavery's influence in the region. Whether on small farms or large plantations, work was the all-encompassing reality in the life of a slave. With the exception of the youngest,

TABLE 2.7. Free and slave population in the Piney Woods, 1850 and 1860

	1850			1860		
	Population total[a]	Slave population	% of population[b]	Population total	Slave population	% of population
Barbour	23,632	10,780	46	30,812	16,150	52
Butler	10,836	3,639	34	18,122	6,818	38
Coffee	5,940	557	9	9,623	1,417	15
Conecuh	9,322	4,394	47	11,311	4,882	43
Covington	3,645	480	13	6,469	821	13
Dale	6,382	757	12	12,197	1,809	15
Henry	9,019	2,242	25	14,918	4,433	30
Pike	15,920	3,794	24	24,435	8,785	36
Total	84,696	26,643	31	127,887	45,115	35

Source: Joseph C. G. Kennedy, *Preliminary Report on the Eighth Census, 1860* (Washington, DC: Government Printing Office, 1862).

[a] The population totals are aggregate totals that include "whites," "free colored," and "slaves" according to Kennedy's *Preliminary Report*.

[b] Represents the percentage of the slave population relative to the total population in each county.

the elderly, or the physically disabled, slaves were expected to work. John Dent took annual or semiannual assessments of his slaves. On one occasion in 1855, for example, he evaluated his ninety-two-slave workforce. He assessed sixteen men—including Maywood, Sam, Frank, Grandison, and Israel—as full hands. He also rated strong, healthy women like Hannah, Charlotte, Mary, Violet, Flora, and twelve others as full hands. He listed two of the five boys and three of the six girls as full hands while the rest graded out as three-quarter or one-half hands. Dent expected every prime hand to work seventeen to twenty-three acres of land for a total of seven hundred acres.[53]

On most large plantations, hierarchies of slavery existed as a kind of planter-imposed class structure. In general, field hands occupied the lowest rungs on the hierarchical ladder while house servants and skilled laborers held positions closer to the top. The slave driver, however, ranked higher than all other slaves and possessed a level of authority and responsibility that most slaves did not. Slave owners chose drivers whom they considered loyal, disciplined, knowledgeable, and able to lead. According to one historian, "slave drivers were both [agricultural] generalists and specialists in the performance of their management duties, but more than anything else perhaps they had to be 'people managers' who knew how to set goals and to motivate the field laborers."[54] Most drivers supervised their own gang of slaves who, depending upon the season and structure of the gang, cleared land, dug field trenches, repaired fences, plowed fields, planted seed, weeded crops, and harvested the yield.

In the mid-1850s, Dent temporarily resolved his growing dissatisfaction with overseers by replacing them with reliable slave drivers. "Our best policy," he insisted, "is to take a trusty sensible negro and make a driver of him. His services are worth his labor, and by proper training, a mutual confidence and interest will be established, causing him to be invaluable."[55] During the spring of 1856, Dent fired his overseer and placed several drivers in charge. He put Venture in charge of the slave quarters and the "hoe department"; Bob took charge of the mule and lot department as well as the plow department; and Brown assumed full responsibility for the plantation house and premises. Dent considered Venture, who shows up frequently in his diary, as one of the most important and trusted drivers on the plantation. Venture often supervised mixed gangs of slaves including boys and girls, girls and women, and women and men. Though his methods as a slave driver are not disclosed in Dent's writings, Venture apparently achieved the desired results.[56]

Perhaps the most telling and intimate examples of slavery's impact on the piney woods involved sexual encounters between the races. Since the late 1960s, historians have generally agreed that sexual liaisons between slaves and whites—whether coerced or consensual—occurred much more frequently than previously understood. In Alabama, black men who engaged in interracial sex with white women risked almost certain death. Bondswomen raped at the hands of their masters had no legal recourse. Yet, even a cursory examination of the census records from piney woods counties reveals that miscegenous relationships produced large numbers of mulattos throughout the region. William H. Houghton of Dale County owned a twenty-two-year-old black female, a four-year-old black female, and a twelve-month-old mulatto female. That same year, Pike County's Charles Ingram owned a twenty-three-year-old black female, a ten-year-old black female, and a young mulatto baby girl. Down the road, miscegenous relationships produced six of Marcus Burson's eleven-slave workforce. Slave schedules document hundreds of similar instances involving slaveholders from a variety of socioeconomic backgrounds. The evidence is only circumstantial of course, but one cannot help wondering about the conditions and circumstances surrounding each case. Again, whether consensual or not, the slaveholders themselves, their sons, other kin, overseers, or perhaps even neighbors may have been complicit in these cases.[57]

The sexual exploitation of slave women was all too real in the antebellum South, but to cast them as nothing more than victims would be to deny their agency in the matter. In the mid-1850s, Belinda Mosser filed suit in the Chancery Court of Pike County against her husband, Samuel. She successfully argued that he had committed adultery with one of her house servants, an eighteen-year-old mulatto slave named Holland. Samuel Mosser, a middling slave owner, farmer, and merchant, appealed the ruling to the Alabama Supreme Court. Testimony revealed that while Belinda was away on a trip to Florida, Samuel engaged in numerous sexual encounters with Holland. Faitha Wood, the Mossers' white housekeeper, testified that Samuel Mosser frequented the kitchen when Holland cooked, routinely summoned her to his store (especially when there were no customers around), and reportedly spent more time alone with Holland than he did his own wife. "I have seen her go into his bed-room," Wood testified, "and the door was shut-to; and I heard a voice, which I took to be Mosser's, say, 'lie down.' . . . It was about 8 o'clock at night when she went into the room, and she had not come out at 2 o'clock in the morning." Wood further testified that the couple spent the night together numerous times during Mrs. Mosser's absence.[58] Samuel Mosser insisted that Holland was nothing more than a nurse who assisted him with his various ailments. And even if sex were involved, he argued, the case should be dismissed "on the ground that adultery cannot be committed with a slave" (a charge summarily dismissed by both courts). One witness suggested that the housekeeper fabricated the whole story. "There was no good feeling between Mrs. Wood and Holland," the witness recounted. Wood's whiteness did not deter Holland from frequently mouthing off and then "flirting out of the room with a great air."[59] The evidence suggests that Samuel Mosser committed adultery; Holland routinely defied white authority and engaged in an affair with her owner's husband; Faitha Wood and Belinda Mosser challenged patriarchal power; and the Alabama Supreme Court crushed that challenge by upholding Samuel Mosser's appeal. Importantly, Holland's legal status as both person and property placed her at the center of a domestic dispute that, under normal circumstances, would have remained within the confines of the local judiciary.

Legal disputes involving whites and slaves function as a microcosm for understanding the significance of slavery in the piney woods. Like most slave states, Alabama viewed slaves as both chattel property and persons. In 1859, the Alabama Supreme Court reaffirmed decades of legal and judicial precedent:

> In the administration of the criminal law, a slave is not regarded merely as property. On the contrary, the courts recognize his existence as a person, his capacity for crime, and his subjection to criminal responsibility. Where a crime has been committed, either by or against a slave, the law, upon high ground of public policy, takes him out of the hands of his master, whose claims of ownership, and the rules of civil rights dependent thereon, are for the time forgotten, and the slave becomes a person with well defined rights and liabilities, and is protected and punished as such.[60]

Criminal law applied to slaves who assaulted other slaves, but white involvement complicated the issue. In 1854 and 1855, two Barbour County farmers pooled their resources to rent Dinah and Bob from a local slaveholder. While not legally recognized as a married couple, the two slaves lived together "as man and wife" in the home of one of the farmers, a Mr. Vining.

A pattern of domestic abuse quickly ensued between the couple. At one point, Bob beat Dinah so severely that Vining whipped him and then sent him to live at the other farmer's house. On another occasion, Dinah was clearing a field about three hundred yards from the main house. At her side stood seven-year-old Martha "Lou" Vining, the farmer's daughter who "was much attached to [Dinah] and frequently followed her out into the field." Sometime around midmorning, Bob, who had been splitting rails off in the distance, approached the two and demanded that Dinah hand over her axe. During the ensuing struggle, he wrested the axe from Dinah's hands and struck Martha in the head, killing her almost instantly. Dinah later testified that Bob intentionally killed the child and intended to kill her as well: "I came here to kill you and Lou," he allegedly said, "I have killed her and now I mean to kill you." Upon cross-examination, however, Dinah changed her story and admitted that Bob might have accidentally struck Martha during the struggle.[61]

Court cases such as those involving Holland, Dinah, and Bob are interesting beyond their immediate legal importance. It is curious, for example, that the entire episode involving the death of Martha Vining apparently took place out of the purview and hearing range of her father and other whites. Further, an axe-wielding, knife-toting male slave with a propensity for violence evidently warranted no apprehension on the part of the white farmer in charge of his whereabouts. Perhaps, on the other hand, these seeming curiosities were not at all unusual. Historian Anthony Carey suggests that slavery in the Chattahoochee Valley "combined ultimate rigidity—the iron fact of servitude—with surprising flexibility, particularly in the areas of slave hiring and slaves' engagement with the market."[62] Indeed, slaves routinely worked independently, especially on smaller farms where masters may have been engaged elsewhere. Even slaves on large plantations, especially carpenters, mechanics, and other craftsmen, enjoyed a fair degree of free movement. John Dent routinely sent slaves to work on neighboring plantations, farms, and even businesses in Eufaula. Joseph Park's slaves frequently traveled several miles to Jeremiah Henderson's general store to purchase goods. On one occasion, Park requested of Henderson: "sir, please let Andy have goods to the amount of five dollars & his wife Missouri seven dollars worth and I will see that you get your pay."[63] These examples demonstrate a fluid environment wherein slaves and whites interacted on a routine basis, and often under the least restrictive circumstances.

By 1860, many—if not most—piney woods whites embraced both the expansion of the cotton economy and the institution of slavery that made it possible. The evidence suggests that slavery's impact on the region was significant, particularly in the northernmost counties but also extending into the poorer counties to the south. From lower-class farmers to the region's wealthiest planters, many white families had a stake in the system. Even farm families with no apparent connection to slavery had every financial incentive to plant and harvest as much cotton as possible. Others rented slaves from their more prosperous neighbors, an affordable way to expand their cotton production. Middle-class farmers who could afford to purchase slaves did so, even if it meant investing in less costly bondswomen or young children. Wealthy slave owners increased their workforces; some even adopted progressive farming techniques to enrich nutrient-depleted soil and increase their holdings. Put simply, cotton farming and the institution of slavery touched nearly every community in the piney woods to one degree or another. In the minds of many whites, it was a system worth preserving, no matter what.

3

“Let the Union Stand”

Piney Woods Politics, 1819–1845

The Cooper Institute in New York City was filled to capacity that night. “At a quarter past seven the house was full,” the *New York Herald* reported the next day, “at half past it was crowded to repletion; at a quarter to eight the side windows were thrown open to the public, and at eight o’clock . . . the people were packed together as grains in a keg of gunpowder.”[1] The main speaker was tall and slender, a well-known politician in his home state but largely unfamiliar to most Americans in other sections of the country. While considered a political moderate within his party, his views on slavery in the territories drew sharp criticism from sectional radicals. During the speech, his fervent appeals to patriotism and historical tradition thrilled the audience, eliciting thunderous applause from everyone within earshot of his voice. “The Union,” he exclaimed, “must be preserved! Glorious objects lie before us; our destiny as a nation is not yet fulfilled. Let us accomplish the grand and beneficent objects of our destiny.”[2]

It was not Abraham Lincoln that stirred the crowd that chilly September night in 1860, but rather Alabama’s Henry W. Hilliard, a proslavery politician whose strong support for the Union prompted him to canvass the North in support of Constitutional Union Party candidate John Bell. In Alabama, Hilliard was a well-respected teacher, minister, and three-time US congressman. During his time in Congress, he represented the Montgomery district, an area that included most of the counties in the piney woods. He canvassed the region extensively and understood the people and their politics. He was as radical in his approval of slavery, and the right of Southerners to take their slaves into any territory in the Union, as the most fervent fire-eater.[3] Yet even Lincoln's election did not convince him that secession was the only viable option to protect slavery and "southern rights."

Not unlike other regions in the South, antebellum politics in the piney woods revolved around personalities and parties linked both indirectly and directly to local, state, and national issues and events. In some counties, voting patterns and party loyalties remained relatively stable. In others, party identity shifted over time. As the Democratic and Whig parties took shape in the 1840s, the most consistently Democratic section of the region included Dale, Henry, and Coffee counties, tucked into the region's extreme southeastern corner. Party loyalty was especially strong in these counties, where Jacksonian Democracy persisted and where fiercely loyal Democratic leaders strengthened the entire party structure. With the exception of one presidential election, only a handful of trusted local Whigs was able to win there. Barbour County, just to the north, was pro-Whig for much of the antebellum period, becoming solidly Democratic only in the late 1850s. And while the remainder of the region strongly supported the Whigs, Democrats made small but important political inroads even there as sectional tensions heightened.

This chapter explores the political history of the piney woods from 1819 to 1845, the personalities and parties involved, and the ways in which sectionalism and national events affected regional politics and party identity. It contends that, like Henry Hilliard, the region was overwhelmingly pro-Union and, with the exception of the counties located in the extreme southeastern corner of the piney woods, decidedly pro-Whig. It further argues that the personalities and politics of local and regional political leaders—like Hilliard for the Whigs and Coffee County's Gappa T. Yelverton for the Democrats—drove much of the region's political development. Finally, this chapter challenges the perception that majority white regions were politically simplistic, predominately Democratic enclaves, arguing instead that party politics in Alabama's piney woods were vibrant, diverse, and often complex.

Alabama's first constitutional convention took place in 1819 in preparation for the state's entry into the Union. Forty-four delegates met in Huntsville that summer to iron out the provisions that would guide the state for nearly fifty years. The majority of the delegates were from northern Alabama, with Madison, Limestone, Shelby, Franklin, Lawrence, and Blount counties sending a combined nineteen representatives. The region with the second largest delegation included the counties along the Tombigbee and Alabama rivers. Montgomery, Clarke, Dallas, Monroe, and Washington counties sent twelve men to the convention. "Of this number," Malcolm McMillan suggests, "there were at least eighteen lawyers, four physicians, two ministers, one surveyor, one merchant, and four planters or farmers. Since no information is available on the profession or occupation of the other fourteen, it may be surmised that they were the 'lesser' men and that most of them were farmers or laboring men, rather than professional men."[4] One of these so-called lesser men was sixty-two-year-old Samuel Cook from Conecuh County, the piney woods sole representative at the constitutional convention. Cook was a Revolutionary War veteran, a former member of the Mississippi territorial legislature, and chief justice of the Conecuh County court. An unpretentious man of modest means, he owned only one slave. His economic status was well below the planters who made up a majority of the convention's delegates.[5]

Alabama's constitution was one of the more liberal of its time. Along with Kentucky, the state was one of only two in the South to approve universal white male suffrage. The constitution minimized qualifications for holding state legislative office and excluded property holding, religious, and tax-paying requirements. While planters pushed for a representation model that favored slave owners in the state legislature, delegates from majority-white counties spearheaded efforts to guarantee broader apportionment. Slavery was protected but provisions were added to guarantee that slaves would be treated humanely and receive some legal protections. Delegates from majority-white counties, such as Samuel Cook, were responsible for amending the original draft of the Constitution, creating a more democratic document. Malcolm McMillan notes that these "'plain men' abolished the militia qualification for suffrage, defeated the efforts of the planters to count three-fifths of the slaves as a basis of representation in the state legislature, reduced the minimum age for senator and representative, curtailed the power of the governor, reduced residence requirements for voting and for election to the senate," and guaranteed that county clerks and other local officials were elected by the people rather than appointed by the legislature.[6]

For residents of the piney woods and Alabamians in general, the presidential election of 1824 was the first truly contentious presidential race in which they voted.[7] Kentucky's Henry Clay, Georgia's William H. Crawford, Massachusetts's John Quincy Adams, and Tennessee's Andrew Jackson all competed for the presidency as Republicans. Albert Burton Moore argues that in Alabama, "Crawford had the support of the Georgia planter faction; Adams was strong among the Carolina and Virginia planters, though they did not relish his New England background; and Clay had influential followers among the small protection element. But the great mass of plain people . . . were devotedly attached to Andrew Jackson."[8] His exploits against the Creek Indians at the Battle of Horseshoe Bend in 1814 and his overwhelming victory against the British at New Orleans ten months later was more than enough to secure a loyal following in Alabama on election day. Alabamians delivered Jackson nearly 70 percent of the 13,619 statewide votes. Piney woods voters likewise supported Jackson by wide margins. Conecuh County, for example, returned two hundred votes for Jackson, eighty-three for Adams, fourteen for Crawford, and only two for Clay. More than 70 percent of the voters in Covington, Henry, and Pike counties cast their votes for Jackson. For the five piney woods counties in existence at the time, 66 percent of the voters supported Jackson. Only Butler County gave a slight edge to John Quincy Adams, with ninety-six votes going to Jackson, forty-two for Crawford, and 102 recorded for Adams.[9] Unfortunately for Jackson's supporters, none of the candidates won a clear majority of electoral votes nationally, even though Jackson was the popular favorite. The House of Representatives decided the election when Henry Clay, one of Jackson's long-time political enemies, used his influence to convince legislators from Kentucky, Missouri, Louisiana, and Maryland to support John Quincy Adams.

From 1824 to 1828, the Adams administration became increasingly unpopular in Alabama. Adams supported the Cherokees in their court battle against Georgia's ultimately successful attempts to survey and sell Indian lands to white settlers. This policy gave cause for concern to those settlers living in close proximity to Creek Indians in the piney woods.[10] Adams also favored increased tariffs aimed at protecting American-manufactured products from cheaper European competition. Southerners not only feared that higher tariffs would force them to buy costly Northern goods, but resented duties that appeared to benefit one section of the country to the detriment of the other. Beyond that was the fear that the loose construction of the Constitution that allowed tariffs might also be used to restrict or abolish slavery.[11] In January 1827, the Alabama General Assembly passed a resolution condemning such tariffs proclaiming "that the imposition of taxes and duties by the Congress of the United States for the purpose of protecting and encouraging domestic manufactures is an unconstitutional exercise of power, and is highly oppressive and partial in its operation."[12] Nevertheless, with the passage of the Tariff of 1828, Adams signed into law the highest tariff in the history of the young republic.

Given Adams's unpopularity in the state, it is not surprising that Jackson won 90 percent, or 16,737, of the 18,614 votes cast in Alabama during the 1828 presidential contest.[13] In the piney woods, Butler, Covington, and Henry counties likewise returned large majorities for Jackson. Out of 270 voters in Henry County, only four supported Adams. Election returns for Pike, Conecuh, and Dale counties were apparently never submitted to the General Assembly for verification, but given the overwhelming victory for Jackson in the rest of the state, there is little reason to believe that these counties would have delivered significant votes for Adams.[14]

While national events proved exciting and important, most piney woods residents were more directly affected by policies implemented by the state legislature. William Freehling has noted that instate political rivalries "led to endless localistic skirmishes over state promotion of market enterprise and of moral behavior, concerns productive of huge voter turnouts in nonpresidential years, matters having nothing to do with slavery or loyalty or anything national at all."[15] In Alabama, the General Assembly wielded a formidable degree of power over the daily lives of the citizenry. It chose all of the state's governmental officials (except for the governor), appointed state and county judges, selected the board of directors for the state bank, and installed the board of trustees for the state's flagship university, the University of Alabama. It also created counties, regulated state and local tax policies, chartered schools and corporations, approved militia organizations, legitimized common marriages, sanctioned divorces, approved name changes, and controlled numerous other state and local activities. Yet state legislators remained keenly aware of their constituents' wishes and were highly responsive to the popular will. Those who failed to live up to expectations risked losing their seats in the next election. Members of the House of Representatives faced the voters annually, while state senators ran for reelection every three years. "Voters used their power with great freedom," J. Mills Thornton notes, "and rates of reelection to the Alabama legislature, from the very beginning, appear to have been quiet low."[16]

Throughout the 1820s and 1830s, representatives from piney woods counties came mostly from the ranks of the slaveholders. Conecuh County's Samuel W. Oliver, for instance, owned eighty-six slaves and worked a substantial plantation just west of Sparta. He became one of the most powerful members of the state House of Representatives, rising to the level of speaker during the 1826 and 1827 sessions. James Ward from Henry County owned seventeen slaves, while Butler County's Nathan Cook held seven. Pike County's Jacinth Jackson, Charles A. Dennis, and Philip Fitzpatrick owned ten, five, and five slaves, respectively. Although each of these men commanded a measure of respect in their home communities, none of them—with the exception of Oliver—would have been considered elites within the legislature. In an effort to improve his meager reading and writing skills, the functionally illiterate Jacinth Jackson, for instance, enrolled in the same grammar school as his children. "Even though Jackson was a man of some substance in Pike County," Mills Thornton observes, "when he entered the legislature he encountered men of far greater economic and intellectual stature than he."[17]

Nevertheless, each man—regardless of his socioeconomic status or level of education—represented the voters back home in the best possible manner, particularly if he wanted to retain his seat in the legislature. Each year, legislators received dozens of petitions and appeals from constituents related to everything from divorce and taxes to the construction of local roads and county courthouses, to the emancipation of slaves, county annexations, and even name changes. Legislators had to be responsive to such requests. In 1825, for instance, Nathan Cook presented a petition "of sundry inhabitants of Montgomery County" requesting that their lands be annexed into Butler County. A year later, militia officers from Pike County called upon their representative, Charles Dennis, to petition the legislature for the creation of an additional militia regiment. Similarly, Conecuh County resident Anthony Presler petitioned the legislature to legitimize his daughter, Matilda Shuffel, and change her name to Matilda Presler.[18]

During the first two decades of statehood, the General Assembly also enacted numerous statutes regulating both the institution of slavery and the conduct of free blacks. The law banned blacks and mulattos from selling whiskey or any type of "spirituous liquors." First-time offenders paid a $10 fine, with subsequent offenses assessed at a fine plus up to twenty-five lashes on the bare back. Nearly every member of both houses of the legislature supported the bill, including Conecuh County's Sam Oliver and Henry County's Ben Harvey, the only two representatives from the piney woods at that time. Another statute guaranteed that slave owners receive up to half of the value of any slave tried and convicted for committing a capital crime. The state financed the program by taxing slaveholders, to be paid at a rate of one cent for every slave under the age of ten and two cents on slaves between the ages of ten and sixty. The bill barely passed the House, with three of the four piney woods representatives joining other south Alabama legislators in voting against the measure.[19] Taxing slave owners to pay for the program was apparently just as unpopular in the piney woods as it was in the Black Belt.

On the national front, meanwhile, Andrew Jackson's presidency became entangled in numerous controversies, including the tariff and nullification debacle, the president's fight with the Bank of the United States, and his Indian removal policies. Jackson remained immensely popular in the South, particularly in states such as Alabama. William Freehling points out that "Old Hickory was the Southwest's man, the perfection of the region's mentality and persona."[20] To the satisfaction of many Alabamians, he rejected numerous internal improvement projects, vetoed the rechartering of the national bank, and cleared a path for the eventual opening of thousands of acres of Indian lands to white settlement.[21] Early twentieth-century historian Theodore Jack notes that "probably no state was more loyal . . . to the president, or more earnest in its support in general than was Alabama."[22]

Alabama joined South Carolina and most of the other Southern states in condemning the Tariff of 1828.[23] Signed into law by President John Quincy Adams, the tariff was designed to protect the growing industrial sector in the Northern states. Textile manufacturers found it difficult to compete with cheap European goods and hoped the new taxes would revive their struggling industries. Southern cotton producers argued that the "tariff of abominations," as they called it, not only raised the price of cheap fabric (the material they bought to clothe their slaves) but also triggered inflation on many other manufactured items. According to Daniel Howe, "the protective tariff raised the price of textiles and thus diminished the demand for southern cotton at the same time as it increased the cost of maintaining slaves. The cotton planters were morally wrong about slavery, but they were economically right to complain that the tariff did not serve their interest."[24]

Some Southern politicians insisted that the law's protectionist designs violated the constitution. The power to tax was specifically designed to raise revenue and never intended to be used as a support mechanism for struggling textile manufacturers. The Alabama General Assembly protested the tariff, arguing that while raising revenue and regulating commerce were legitimate powers exercised by the central government:

> It is not of these powers that we complain, but it is the assertion of another, and a very different one. It is the assertion of the power to impose a duty on any article of foreign commerce, not because we want revenue, or the regulations of commerce, as such require improvement; but because we want to exclude the foreign in favor of the domestic fabric. This power is not granted in the Constitution, and must be sustained, if at all, by the pliable doctrine of implication, and as it is not necessary to the power to raise revenue or regulate commerce, it cannot be sustained as an incidental or implied power. On the contrary it is a substantial, distinct power, resting on assumption, and fraught with frightful danger. . . . The unlimited nature of this power and the dangerous purposes to which it may be applied, renders it odious and unfit to mingle in human affairs.[25]

In an 1832 speech before the General Assembly, Governor John Gayle warned that "this partial and unjust legislation in the National Government is hastening a crisis in our affairs which involves in its consequences the dissolution of the Union."[26] The legislature similarly denounced the tariff as "unequal, unjust, oppressive and against the spirit, true intent and meaning of the constitution; that if persevered in, its inevitable tendency will be to alienate the affections of the people of the Southern States from the general government."[27]

In July 1832, Jackson signed a compromise tariff into law that lowered rates and repealed some of the more onerous elements of the previous law. The bill reduced duties on nearly everything manufactured outside the United States and cut the taxes on woolen cloth from 45 percent to just 5 percent, an obvious concession to plantation owners. The legislation passed the House of Representatives with healthy majorities from both Northern and Southern members. It then passed the Senate, with most of the yea votes coming from the North and about half from the South. Alabama's delegation was split. Representatives Clement Comer Clay and Samuel Wright Mardis voted yes, along with Senator Gabriel Moore, who cast a vote in favor of the law in spite of his support for South Carolina and partiality toward John C. Calhoun. Dixon Hall Lewis and Senator William Rufus King, both solid nullifiers, opposed.[28]

Alabama's General Assembly joined other Southern state legislatures approving resolutions supporting the new lower tariff rates. The measure passed the House overwhelmingly, with only nineteen dissenters, the majority of which came from South Alabama, including all six piney woods representatives. In an open letter to the public, some of the men who voted against the resolutions, including Julian Devereux from Covington County and Pike County's Jesse Reaves and Lawson Keener, argued "that South Carolina has cause to be dissatisfied with the oppression of her citizens, and although [she] may have mistaken her remedy, every attempt at this time to take the part of congress in its unauthorized oppressions, will only serve to strengthen the arm of the general government."[29] While careful not to support nullification, these men argued that the Tariff of 1832 still included far too many elements of protectionism and failed to adequately address the South's grievances. Mills Thornton notes that during this time there emerged in the Black Belt a growing states' rights faction willing to defy the Jackson administration. Because piney woods counties were economically connected to the Black Belt, especially to Montgomery, it makes sense that the region's representatives refused to support the 1832 tariff.[30]

Not satisfied with the new, lower tariff, South Carolina nullified both the Tariff of 1828 and 1832. At this point, most Southerners refused to support the Palmetto State's promotion of nullification as a remedy for protective tariffs. Indeed, the Ordinance of Nullification generated a backlash of opposition from every corner of the South, including Alabama. "As sure as [nullification] shall succeed," Governor Gayle warned, "its triumphs will be stained with fraternal blood, and the proudest of its trophies will be the destruction of constitutional liberty."[31] The General Assembly condemned the concept as "unsound in theory and dangerous in practice, that as a remedy it is unconstitutional and essentially revolutionary, leading in its consequences to anarchy and civil discord, and finally to the dissolution of the Union."[32]

Yet not all of Alabama's political leaders joined the chorus condemning nullification. A small but vocal number of states' rights advocates warned of the danger that encroaching federal power posed to individual liberty. US Representative Dixon Hall Lewis, who had opposed the compromise tariff of 1832, openly and forcefully supported both nullification and secession. US Senator Gabriel Moore, a fierce onetime supporter of Andrew Jackson, likewise embraced John C. Calhoun and moved closer to the radical states' rights position. In 1834, the General Assembly passed a joint resolution demanding Moore's resignation, in part because he supported nullification. "Senator Moore has evinced a strong partiality," the resolution stated, "if not positively committed himself in favor of the heretical doctrine of nullification, which the people of this state hold to be . . . fatal to the harmony and perpetuity of our inestimable Union." Moore refused to resign.[33]

With the exception of an outspoken minority, most Alabama politicians, including those from the piney woods, supported the 1832 compromise tariff and condemned nullification. The region's politicians were simply not ready to support such a radical move as displayed by South Carolina. Within months, Henry Clay, hoping to placate the belligerent Carolinians, submitted yet another compromise tariff that temporarily calmed the storm. The Tariff of 1833 gradually reduced all tariff rates across the board so that no rate exceeded 20 percent. "Objectively," Daniel Howe notes, "the nullifiers had lost. The other Southern states had not rallied to their side. Both the legislative and executive branches of the federal government had demonstrated their resolve to suppress nullification."[34]

Meanwhile, a new and growing challenge to sectional harmony simmered just beneath the surface. In the early 1830s, New England abolitionists such as William Lloyd Garrison and Theodore Dwight Weld initiated a radicalized version of antislavery that, unlike its more moderate predecessor, demanded an immediate and uncompensated end to the institution. Through letters, pamphlets, and newspapers such as Garrison's *Liberator*, abolitionists argued forcefully that the old ploys for soft-peddling slavery and pushing gradual emancipation schemes simply were not enough. They began distributing propaganda through the mail, first in the North and then in the slave states. Spearheaded by the American Anti-Slavery Society, supporters flooded the Southern states with an estimated 175,000 letters and pamphlets.[35] Butler County representative John W. Womack angrily insisted in 1835 that "the Anti-Slavery Societies in the Northern and Middle States are doing all they can to destroy our domestic harmony, by sending among us, pamphlets, tracts, and newspapers—for the purpose of exciting dissatisfaction and insurrection among our slaves."[36]

Proslavery advocates such as Womack moved quickly at both the state and federal levels to suppress the distribution of antislavery publications. The Jackson administration instructed postmasters in the South to withhold any mail connected with abolitionist organizations and "direct that those inflammatory papers be delivered to none but who will demand them as subscribers."[37] The US House of Representatives adopted a "gag rule," forbidding members of Congress from reading antislavery petitions on the floor of the house. On the state level, Alabama's General Assembly passed a resolution calling upon Northern governors to take action against those organizations responsible for the publication of antislavery materials: "If rash, wicked and bigoted fanatics are suffered, under the shield and protection of the laws of the States in which they live, to poison the minds of our slaves, to render them more dissatisfied with their condition, and excite them to acts of violence and blood-shed against their masters, the harmony of the Union will be greatly disturbed."[38] Governor John Gayle went so far as to demand the extradition of New York abolitionist Ransom G. Williams, a black minister and publishing agent indicted in absentia by a grand jury in Tuscaloosa, for aiding in the publication and distribution of the *The Emancipator*, an antislavery newspaper published by Elihu Embree in Jonesborough, Tennessee. Ironically, while the majority of Northerners opposed abolitionism, Southern attacks against abolitionist newsprint raised the ire of the Northern public and strengthened the resolve of those committed to slavery's demise.[39] "It is my solemn opinion," John Womack wrote in the aftermath of the immediate controversy, "that this question (to wit slavery) will ultimately bring about a dissolution of the Union of the States."[40]

Womack, a lawyer, state representative, and editor of the *Greenville Whig*, was one of several politicians who helped organize what soon became Alabama's Whig Party. A contemporary of Womack described him as an energetic, tall, muscular young man who stood "straight as an Indian, and with a person and manner at once dignified and commanding—a voice deep, sonorous, and well modulated."[41] Like other nascent Whigs, he opposed Andrew Jackson as an overly powerful and increasingly intrusive threat to individual liberty and states' rights. Jackson, he complained, was not above using his office to directly persuade individual state legislators to use their influence to pressure US senators to fall in line with the administration's legislative wishes.[42] "I do most solemnly object and protest against this practice of the president of the United States," Womack wrote in a letter published by several of the state's Whig newspapers, "of addressing any communication whatever to the members of a state legislature for the purpose of influencing their actions and opinion. It is without precedent, and fraught with fearful and dangerous consequences."[43] By the late 1830s, the Whigs "identified *themselves* as the true bearers of the states-rights, strict-construction torch that in their minds Jackson had so ignominiously let fall."[44]

For nearly a century after the Civil War, historians viewed Alabama's Whig Party as the "broadcloth" party of privilege, while simultaneously portraying the Democratic Party as the common man's political haven. Historian Clement Eaton once pointed to an aphorism that "wherever you found rich soil, there you would find a cotton bale, and sitting on the bale a Negro, and nearby would be a Whig in a silk hat. . . . The Democrats, on the other hand, were strong in the pine barrens and areas of high illiteracy of the white population, of low land values, and of small proportion of slaves."[45] More recent scholars have debunked much of the traditional approach. Over the past half-century, these authors and others have argued that the Whig Party in Alabama, and in the South generally, garnered support from a broad base of citizens from all socioeconomic backgrounds and classes.[46] While it is true that Alabama Whiggery drew sizeable numbers of supporters from Black Belt counties, the same can be said for the Democrats. Similarly, majority-white counties, such as Conecuh and Covington in the piney woods became Whig Party strongholds. As J. Mills Thornton notes, "a closer examination of the parties will reveal them not as elitist institutions, but as subtle agents of the social faith. Reaching deep into the citizenry, the parties were perhaps the most comprehensive and assiduous reflectors of Alabamians' desires."[47]

In the piney woods, what historians refer to as the second two-party system initiated a twenty-year struggle between Democrats and Whigs. Although neither party claimed preeminence over the entire region, there were a number of sections that each party could rely upon for support in any given election (see Table 3.1). In Henry, Dale, and Coffee counties, the Democratic Party sustained a distinct advantage in local, state, and national politics from the late 1830s to the Civil War. Jacksonian Democracy had taken root there and remained a powerful element throughout the antebellum period. Anthony Carey argues that the "Democracy's greater hostility to banks and corporations proved lastingly attractive in regions where both were few, and themes of states' rights and limited government matched the mood of countless yeoman who desired mostly to be left alone."[48] Such was the case in the region's extreme southeastern corner where opposition to state-funded internal improvements, especially railroads, remained high for two decades prior to the war.[49] In addition, local party leaders such as Coffee County's Gappa T. Yelverton, Angus McAllister from Henry County, and Dale County's James C. Ward zealously promoted the Democratic Party

TABLE 3.1. Presidential elections and party politics, 1836–1856

County	1836	1840	1844	1848	1852	1856
Barbour	W	W	W	W	**	D
Butler	W	W	W	W	W	A
Coffee	*	*	D	W	D	D
Conecuh	W	W	W	W	D	D
Covington	W	W	W	W	D	D
Dale	D	D	D	D	D	D
Henry	D	D	D	W[1]	D	D
Pike	W	W	W	W	D	D

W = Whig majority vote
D = Democratic majority vote
A = American majority vote
NR = No returns available.
* = County did not exist.
** = Barbour countians cast a majority vote for third party states' rights candidates George Troup of Georgia and Mississippi's John A. Quitman.

[1] Whig Party candidate Zachary Taylor, a slaveholder, won Henry County by a margin of eight votes.

Sources: Clanton W. Williams, "Notes and Documents: Presidential Election Returns and Related Data for Antebellum Alabama," *Alabama Review* 1 (October 1948); Clanton W. Williams, "Notes and Documents: Presidential Election Returns and Related Data for Antebellum Alabama," *Alabama Review* 2 (January 1949); David Young, *Whig Almanac* (1849); "Presidential Election in Alabama," *Weekly Alabama Journal*, February 5, 1856.

while endorsing its candidates at every level. Although rare, Whigs were occasionally victorious there. In 1841, Dale countians sent Archibald Justice to the state house, one of only a few local Whigs ever elected from that county. Conecuh County's William A. Ashley defeated Coffee County Democrat Josiah Jones for the state senate in 1855. Yet Ashley's victory is best explained by the fact that at the time Coffee was in a heavily Whig district that included both Covington and Conecuh counties. The same circumstance applied two years later when Whig candidate Daniel H. Horne won the district. On the national stage, Zachary Taylor carried Coffee and Henry counties by slim margins in the presidential election of 1844, but both counties came back into the Democratic camp four years later. With rare exception, then, Democrats were heavy favorites in the southeastern corner of the piney woods.

During that same time, the Whigs maintained a formidable presence in

Butler, Conecuh, and Covington counties. Like their neighbors to the east, Conecuh and Covington were comparatively poor counties with few slaves. Yet their destiny aligned more with the personalities and policies of the Whigs. Butler County's Thomas Hill Watts, Conecuh's William Ashley, Covington's Alfred Holley, and Henry Hilliard from Montgomery County were profoundly influential. The Whigs also performed well in state and national elections in Pike County before 1852, and in Barbour up until 1856. On the whole, then, the Whig Party enjoyed substantial support throughout most of the piney woods region during the antebellum era. Counties such as Pike and Barbour trended toward the Democratic Party in the 1850s, but did so slowly, and still retained sizeable numbers of Whig voters until late in the decade.

In the presidential elections of 1836 and 1840, the Whig Party made substantial inroads into Alabama politics. In 1836, the party delivered nearly half of Alabama's forty-nine counties to Whig Party favorite Hugh Lawson White of Tennessee. Four years later, the party secured victories in twenty-three counties. Statewide, the Democrats carried both elections, but the ranks of the opposition grew nonetheless. In both elections, the Whigs relentlessly attacked Democratic candidate Martin Van Buren. A native New Yorker, they insisted, could not be trusted to protect slavery; rumors flourished that Van Buren maintained numerous friendships with prominent Northern abolitionists.

The economic downturn that hit the country in 1837 also provided a wealth of political fodder for the Whigs—just in time for the 1840 election.[50] The Whigs were organized and motivated in 1840 behind the candidacy of William Henry Harrison, an old Indian fighter and war hero in the Andrew Jackson mold. Political meetings took place throughout the state, but the party's main convention in Tuscaloosa "was a large assemblage, with all the emblazonry of coon skins, log cabins, and hard cider, which excited considerable enthusiasm."[51] Popular Whig politician Henry Hilliard observed that "delegations came from the remote counties, some of them bringing with them log-cabins on wheels drawn by fine horses, and displaying the symbols of pioneer structures; the gourd, the string of red pepper, a barrel of cider, the latch-string of the door conspicuously hung on the outside, and the raccoon."[52] Harrison's nationwide victory in the presidential election still did not translate into a win in Alabama, but the growing popularity of the Whig Party in the state gave Democrats reason enough to worry.

In the piney woods, the presidential elections of 1836 and 1840, together with the gubernatorial election of 1837, created much political fanfare throughout the region. In the 1836 presidential race, Whig Party candidate White carried Barbour, Butler, Conecuh, Covington, and Pike while Van Buren was victorious in Dale and Henry. The votes in Barbour, Henry, and Pike were close, with Pike countians giving the nod to White by fewer than ten votes. In 1840, Whig candidates Harrison and John Tyler won overwhelming victories in Barbour, Butler, Conecuh, and Covington, and carried Pike by 51 percent of the vote. Van Buren again won by respectable margins in Dale and Henry counties, the heart of Jacksonian Democracy in the region.[53]

The governor's race of 1837, meanwhile, pitted Democratic candidate Arthur P. Bagby, a recent Democratic convert, against piney woods favorite Samuel W. Oliver, the Whig candidate originally from Conecuh County who had relocated to Dallas County in 1837. Oliver was well known as one of the largest slaveholders in south Alabama. He served eleven terms in the Alabama House of Representatives, was elected speaker of the house at least twice, and served one term as a state senator. Although he ultimately lost the election to Bagby, he won every county in the piney woods except Henry. Even in Dale County, local and regional devotion to Oliver appears to have trumped party loyalty, at least in this instance.[54]

By 1840, the generation of piney woods politicians led by men such as Samuel Oliver began to yield to a new stable of leaders. These energetic young politicians profoundly influenced their home communities as well as the region as a whole. Many of these men would later provide both political and military leadership during the Civil War. Walter Crenshaw of Butler County, for example, served six nonsequential terms as a member of the state House of Representatives and multiple terms as a state senator. The son of prominent circuit court judge Anderson Crenshaw, Walter was only twenty-one years old when he became one of the youngest members of the General Assembly. He was a lawyer, planter, a local militia captain, a prominent member of the Whig Party, and was to become one of the largest slaveholders in Butler County.[55]

Another young Butler countian, Thomas Hill Watts, represented the county in the 1840s. Watts, too, was a lawyer, planter, and large slaveholder who, by the outbreak of the Civil War, owned over two hundred slaves. He campaigned enthusiastically for Harrison during the 1840 presidential election and served as one of the electors for Zachary Taylor's 1848 presidential campaign. He rose quickly through the Whig ranks, becoming one of the party's most popular leaders statewide, a position that eventually led to the governorship.[56]

Eufaula's John Gill Shorter was yet another of the region's rising young politicians. Shorter was born in 1818 near Jasper County, Georgia. In the mid-1830s, he and his family relocated to Eufaula, known at the time as Irwinton. John Gill and his father, Reuben, were loyal Jacksonian Democrats who never wavered in their support for the Democratic Party. John graduated from the University of Alabama, practiced law in Eufaula, and served

3.1. Henry Washington Hilliard (courtesy of the Alabama Department of Archives and History)

as a Democratic state legislator, senator, and circuit court judge—no small feat for a young Democrat living in a strongly Whiggish county.

On the national stage, no piney woods county produced a US senator or member of the US House of Representatives until 1855 when Eli Shorter was elected to the House. Before that, Montgomery County's Henry Washington Hilliard was the closest thing to a native son that the region had in Washington. Hilliard, a Whig, represented the Montgomery congressional district, a district that for much of the antebellum period included every county in the piney woods except for Butler.[57] Although he was born in Cumberland County, North Carolina, in 1808, he spent his boyhood, teenage, and college years in Columbia, South Carolina. He entered South Carolina College at age fifteen and graduated three years later. Within the next five years, Hilliard studied law in Columbia and in Athens, Georgia; engaged in Methodist mission work and preaching in and around Columbus, Georgia; edited the *Columbus Enquirer* after the paper's original editor moved to Texas; and began a brief stint as an English professor at the University of Alabama.

Hilliard's biographer, David Durham, notes that his "growing reputation as a lawyer, scholar, preacher, editor, and orator was remarkable for a young man who had just reached the age of twenty-three."[58]

But it was a eulogy delivered before the Alabama General Assembly in honor of the deceased Charles Carroll of Carrollton that launched his political career. Hilliard's speech, delivered on December 7, 1832, was a masterpiece of oratory. His words also provided a window into his political beliefs and principles. Hilliard "was a Whig of the State Rights school," a contemporary once observed, "ardently devoted to the interests of the South, yet in his patriotism embracing the whole country."[59] He revered founding fathers such as Carroll, the last surviving signer of the Declaration of Independence. He was also a strong and forceful advocate for the Union and was, according to J. Mills Thornton, "a careful conservative who was Alabama's closest analogue to Daniel Webster."[60] Hilliard's speech in part reflected these values, values shared by the majority of piney woods voters. "If the cause of freedom goes down here," he proclaimed, "it is in the dust throughout the world—it is driven back forever: lost are the hopes of mankind; vain the sufferings and toils of patriots; vain the blood of martyrs. Let these things inspire us; let us tell the patriots who, amid the dark systems of other lands, bend their gaze upon us, that we will be faithful."[61] Nineteenth-century public speeches were replete with such poetical phraseology and soaring rhetorical analysis, important elements that played to Hilliard's strengths and advanced his political career. According to William Garrett, "few men could charm an audience by the gracefulness of manner, ease and beauty of delivery, and rich imagery of conception, more than Mr. Hilliard."[62]

From the beginning, Hilliard's influence upon the piney woods, the Whig Party, and Alabama politics in general, was impressive. He represented Montgomery County in the General Assembly in 1838 and 1839; served as one of twelve Alabama delegates to the national Whig convention; was chosen as an Alabama elector on the Harrison-Tyler presidential ticket of 1840; and campaigned energetically for Harrison's election that same year. Not only was he instrumental in helping the Whigs gain seats in Alabama's General Assembly but he also played an important role in his party capturing two of the state's five seats in the US House of Representatives. In 1842, Hilliard mounted an unsuccessful challenge to Montgomery's powerful Democratic incumbent congressman, Dixon Hall Lewis. Hilliard's loss wiped out any chance for the Whigs to secure majority status for their party in Alabama's congressional delegation that year.[63] For the time being at least, his political ambitions were stifled by a Democratic Party bent on protecting Lewis's seat and determined to arrest the growth of Whiggery throughout the state.

In an effort to stem the rising Whig tide, Democrats in the General Assembly unleashed two legislative weapons against their opponents, the General Ticket System and White Basis voting. The General Ticket System allowed the whole of the electorate to select all of the states' representatives without regard to legislative district, thus utilizing Democratic majorities in North Alabama to unseat a handful of Whigs in the South. Proponents claimed that the General Ticket System would guarantee a more accurate representation of Alabama's Democratic voting majority as well as ensure a unified, one-party congressional delegation in Washington. "The General Ticket System," Governor Bagby contended in 1840, "gives to a majority of the whole people of the State, at all times, whatever may be their political opinions, the entire, undivided weight of the whole representation in congress."[64] In fact, Democrats introduced the bill specifically to protect Dixon Hall Lewis's seat from an almost-certain Whig takeover by Hilliard.

The debate in the General Assembly over the General Ticket System was long, animated, and, at times, theatrical. In the House, Whigs used every parliamentary procedure at their disposal—including motions to postpone votes, adjourn the chamber, and table the bill—to debate, lobby opposition, and defeat the legislation. In a final act of desperation, they launched a futile attempt to prevent a quorum by walking out of the session on the day the bill was adopted. Whig members later protested that "we remained until our appeals were unheeded; the voice of our constituents strangled; freedom of speech denied. . . . And we left when that hall . . . had been seized by an organized party, and converted into a slaughter house of every principle of protection and security in legislation, which government affords to the weak; the inestimable right to dissent."[65] The bill passed with fifty votes in the affirmative and twenty-three against; more than half of the absentee members returned to the floor to cast their votes against the bill. In the final days leading up to bill's passage, "the scene of noise and disorder in the House at times, and especially when the Whig members retired, and after they came back in squads" was chaotic. "Some of them even mounted the desks in defiance of the Speaker's call to order."[66]

Although there is no detailed voting record of individual members in the General Assembly, the evidence suggests that piney woods representatives rejected the General Ticket System. Whigs understood that the legislation was nothing less than a bold-faced attempt on the part of the Democrats to destroy Whig political power in South Alabama. William Garrett notes, for instance, that support for the bill took place almost entirely along party lines. If so, seven of the ten legislators from the piney woods opposed the legislation, with representatives from Barbour, Conecuh, and Covington counties solidly against the bill, Henry County in favor, and Pike County split.[67] In addition, several weeks after the bill's passage, thirty-seven legislators issued an official minority protest to the proceedings. Five of the region's ten representatives—including Barbour's John W. Mann and William T. Shanks, Butler's Walter H. Crenshaw, Conecuh's William A. Bell, and Covington's Laird B. Flemming—signed the document. The signers accused the speaker of the house and the majority party of disregarding established House rules, violating parliamentary procedure, suppressing debate, and generally trampling upon the rights of the minority. "Several gentlemen had prepared themselves . . . who had not spoken upon the question, when one of the majority rose and called the previous question; which was carried affirmatively by the majority; the minority silenced; the debate suppressed; the law passed over every barrier, which the constitution had interposed, to the reckless spirit of an infuriated party."[68]

The General Ticket System succeeded in stacking the deck in favor of the Democrats in the 27th Congress but its unpopularity, even in strongly Democratic north Alabama, led to its quick demise in 1842. That same year, Democrats in the General Assembly gerrymandered the state's congressional districts—now increased from five to seven by the 1840 census—and changed the state's apportionment ratio to a whites-only basis.[69] In this way, congressional representation would be based upon the white population only, thus diminishing the Whig Party's power in the Black Belt. The measure passed the House on a largely partisan basis by a vote of forty-six to thirty-eight, with seven Democratic defectors joining the minority. Support in the piney woods was mixed, with representatives from Covington, Dale, and Coffee counties favoring the bill, while Barbour, Butler, Conecuh, and Pike were opposed. Curiously, four of the region's ten representatives, including Henry's James Pynes and William Gamble, did not cast a vote at all. The bill's opponents, meanwhile, accused the majority of violating the Constitution's three-fifths provision. They claimed that the provision weakened the slave states' voting power, encouraged Northern abolitionists, and gave "to the northern part of the State an undue advantage over the south in electing members of Congress."[70] Historian Carlton Jackson has argued that "the White Basis bill helped eliminate much Whig power at a time when the party contained as much as 45 percent of the voting population."[71]

Alabama Whiggery experienced yet another setback in the presidential election of 1844. In the national contest, the relatively unknown Democrat, James K. Polk, defeated an experienced, well-known, and generally popular Whig candidate in Henry Clay. While Polk won comfortably in the Electoral College, the popular vote was much closer, with Clay coming to within forty thousand (out of 2.7 million votes cast) of a majority. Margins for victory were close on both sides. Clay carried Tennessee by the razor-thin margin of 113 votes while Polk won New York and Michigan by 5,106 and 3,442 votes, respectively. Clay's waffling on Texas annexation cost him votes in both the North and the South. "Personally I could have no objection to the annexation of Texas," he wrote, "but I certainly would be unwilling to see the existing Union dissolved . . . for the sake of acquiring Texas."[72] To some Southerners at least, Clay's apparent willingness to sacrifice slavery's expansion on the altar of Unionism was unacceptable. Polk's position on Manifest Destiny, on the other hand, played well in the deep South and in Western states, where westward expansion engendered hopes of free land and increased opportunity.[73] Writing to a group of antiannexationists in April, 1844, Polk made his intentions clear: "I have no hesitation in declaring that I am in favor of the immediate re-annexation of Texas to the territory and government of the United States."[74]

In truth, Alabama Whigs were overly confident about their candidate's chances, so much so that supporters "did not think it possible that a leader who shone so conspicuously before the people . . . was to be defeated by a man so far his inferior."[75] Yet, Polk's unequivocal stance in favor of Texas prompted 60 percent of the state's electorate (36,846 out of 62,431 votes) to support the Democratic candidate. The evidence suggests that, like other areas of the state, Clay's candidacy underwhelmed voters in the piney woods, a region where Whiggery usually enjoyed stronger support. While Clay carried the usual Whig strongholds of Barbour, Butler, Conecuh, Covington, and Pike, he did so by narrower margins than previous Whig candidates, especially when compared with Harrison's 1840 polling results (see Table 3.2). Clay carried Covington County by a paltry nine votes, for example, while Harrison's victory four years earlier garnered more than 74 percent of the vote in that county.[76] Polk, in contrast, made gains in every piney woods county and scored particularly well in traditional Democratic strongholds such as Henry and Dale.

One man who admired Henry Clay and worked especially hard for his campaign was Henry Hilliard. Indeed, if there was a ray of hope for despondent Whigs in the months following Clay's defeat, it was Hilliard's successful 1845 bid for Congress. At this juncture, the Montgomery District included the counties of Pike, Barbour, Coffee, Henry, Dale, Covington, Montgomery, Macon, and Russell. Hilliard and his Democratic opponent, John Cochran of Eufaula, canvassed the district with great enthusiasm and even met on one occasion in Glennville, Barbour County, for a three-hour debate. Hilliard worked especially hard, "never losing an opportunity to visit doubtful parts of the district." In Covington County, for instance, where Clay had won by less than a dozen votes, Hilliard took the time, "drove through it once more, and was rewarded for my attention by a majority of a hundred and ten votes at the Congressional election."[77]

While on the stump, Cochran attempted to ride Polk's coattails by stressing his support for Texas annexation, but Hilliard countered that he and a

Table 3.2. Piney Woods vote in presidential elections of 1840 and 1844

County	1840 (Harrison)	1840 (Van Buren)	1844 (Clay)	1844 (Polk)
Barbour	1,028	642	1,113	860
Butler	710	274	666	405
Conecuh	533	209	441	277
Covington	188	65	148	139
Dale	367	672	209	616
Henry	325	391	367	546
Pike	653	627	862	768

Source: Clanton W. Williams, "Notes and Documents: Presidential Election Returns and Related Data for Antebellum Alabama," *Alabama Review* 1 (October 1948); "Alabama: Official Returns of Election Counties," *Mobile Advertiser*, December 5, 1844.

number of other Southern Whigs also supported annexation, while arguing that prominent Democrats such as Martin Van Buren opposed the measure. He also "appealed to the people to restore the Whigs to power that they might arrest the tendency of the Democratic Party to encourage sectional strife, which must bring ruin upon the country."[78] Hilliard won the election to become the lone Whig in Alabama's delegation to the Twenty-Ninth Congress. While national politicians such as Clay may have stumbled, Hilliard's political principles, charismatic personality, and energetic canvassing demonstrated once again his popularity among voters in the piney woods. For the time being at least, the Whigs remained the party of choice for the majority of voters in the region.

Hilliard's influence on piney woods voters as well as his effect on the staying power of the Whig Party in the region cannot be overemphasized. His staunch support for states' rights and slavery, combined with an outspoken defense of the Union, appealed to a majority of the citizenry. By traveling throughout the region meeting face-to-face with the people he wished to represent, he connected with poor and middle-class white voters in a way that others could not or perhaps would not. At a time when the Democratic Party utilized every means within its power to destroy Whiggery in South Alabama, Hilliard was one of the party's most outspoken and influential advocates. His ability to connect with the people of the piney woods helped to keep the spirit of the Whig Party alive.

4

"Disruption of the Ties Which Bind Us Together"

The Politics of Secession, 1845–1861

On January 11, 1861, Judge Gappa T. Yelverton of Coffee County stood before the secession convention on the floor of the House Chamber in Montgomery and submitted a request to his fellow delegates "that the secrecy be removed from the proceedings of this day." Just moments before, the convention had voted, by a count of sixty-one to thirty-nine, to take Alabama out of the Union. They quickly adopted Yelverton's motion and opened the chamber doors to the public. "The wild shouts and rounds of rapturous applause broke in upon the ear of the convention, and startled the grave solemnity that presided over its deliberations." A group of women from Montgomery presented a "secession flag" to the convention large enough "to reach nearly across the ample chamber." Outside, cheering crowds swelled, prominent delegates offered speech after speech, citizens fired their weapons in the air in celebration, and the city's cannons fired periodically throughout the remainder of the day and into the night. For delegates such as fire-eater William Lowndes Yancey, the celebration of secession was a decades-long dream come true.[1]

Sixteen years earlier, on March 4, 1845, just days before the new Congress was to be seated in Washington, the US House and Senate approved resolutions admitting Texas to the Union as a slave state. Three months prior, the Alabama General Assembly passed, by large majorities, its own set of resolutions supporting annexation, instructing Alabama's US Senators to do everything within their power to push the Texas issue forward. Every piney woods legislator voted with the majority.[2] Other slave states passed similar measures in support of swift and decisive federal action. “The Texas issue,” historian William Cooper contends, “proved again that in the South nothing could withstand the force of a political issue closely connected with slavery.”[3] A year later, the United States went to war with Mexico over Texas; slavery’s expansion remained at the forefront of sectional politics.

This chapter explores the politics of slavery and secession in the piney woods from 1845 to Alabama’s secession convention in 1861. It argues that a majority of the region’s voters continued to support the Whig Party and its surrogate, the Know Nothing Party—thanks, in no small part, to the influence of Henry Hilliard—despite pronouncements from the state’s Democratic leadership that Northern Whigs could not be trusted when it came to the issue of slavery. Even with the national collapse of the Whig party structure in the late 1840s, the party’s base support remained largely intact. Nevertheless, as national events and sectional politics became increasingly contentious, many piney woods voters migrated slowly, almost reluctantly, into the ranks of the radical secessionists. Organizations such as the Eufaula Regency and leaders like John Buford nudged the region closer to accepting the secessionist point of view as mainstream rather than radical. John Brown’s raid in 1859, followed by Abraham Lincoln’s election to the presidency a year later, prompted strong reaction throughout the piney woods. Many of the region’s communities ultimately supported both secession and civil war.

Although Henry Hilliard initially opposed the Mexican War, as did most Whigs, he supported the effort once war was declared, and broke ranks with powerful elements in his own party who sought to defund the war. “If the question were now presented to me between peace and war,” he rejoined in a speech on the House floor, “I should undoubtedly be in favor of peace. But no such election is presented to us. The spectacle before us is a war in progress, our own country on one side, a foreign country on the other.”[4] Hilliard defended the Polk administration’s prosecution of the war and supported America’s bid to acquire California in any treaty negotiations with Mexico.

Yet Hilliard and most other Southern politicians from both parties strongly condemned what came to be known as the Wilmot Proviso. In August 1846, Pennsylvania Democrat David Wilmot dropped a political bombshell by proposing an amendment that would ban slavery from any territory gained from Mexico as a result of the war. Borrowing language from the Northwest Ordinance of 1787, the provision declared “that, as an express and fundamental condition to the acquisition of any territory from the Republic of Mexico by the United States . . . neither slavery nor involuntary servitude shall ever exist in any part of said territory, except for crime, whereof the party shall first be duly convicted.”[5]

The Proviso seemed an affront to Southerners who wished to take their slaves into United States territories. Whether it was crossing the Appalachians from the Eastern Seaboard into Kentucky and Tennessee in the late eighteenth century, or migrating from Georgia and the Carolinas into Alabama and Mississippi, territorial expansion had always been one of the keys to economic opportunity. Political power, too, appeared to be in jeopardy. New territories closed to slavery would necessarily be divided up into free states, thus empowering the antislavery states at the expense of the South. Few believed that slavery would flourish in California, but the importance of excluding the institution was not lost on Southern politicians.[6] Michael Holt argues that the "significance of the Proviso was symbolic. They regarded it as a humiliating insult by the northern majority, a denial of the equal rights of white southerners, even when they had no intention of exercising those rights, and an attempt to subjugate southerners to northern dictation."[7]

Response to the Proviso was almost entirely sectional, with Northerners in support and Southerners vehemently opposed. Henry Hilliard's speech before the House sounded more like that of a fire-eating radical than a moderate Whig:

> If this be done, this government will become unequal, and its days will be numbered. The spirit still lingers in the South which produced our Revolution—a spirit which will contend for political rights to the very last. The people of those states love this Union; they glory in the past, and hope for the future. They will cling to the pillars of the Constitution as long as they can; they will listen to the parting words of Washington, still vibrating in their ears, as long as endurance is possible; but, when they find that they were to be down-trodden, they will be constrained, though it be with deep grief, to give up an alliance which is to be marked only by wrongs and oppressions, and gather about their homes and their property.[8]

Resolutions from the Alabama General Assembly condemned the Proviso, denied the right of the federal government to prevent slavery in the territories, denounced Northern politicians who injected their antislavery views into federal policymaking, and pledged to support presidential candidates who condemned the "spirit of fanaticism."[9] Like many other Southerners, many piney woods inhabitants set aside party divisions to oppose a common foe in Northern "provisoism." One letter-writer suggested that Wilmot had unleashed "a demon spirit which hears no argument and under the pretext . . . of doing god's service, is prepared to perpetuate any outrage, however great upon the constitution of our country, and the rights of the South."[10] William Lowndes Yancey and other proslavery radicals also attempted to use the Wilmot controversy to create a permanent slave-state voting bloc. Yancey even attempted to persuade Hilliard, who had earned a reputation for routinely defying his party's positions on important issues, to join the effort. Nevertheless, neither Hilliard nor his piney woods constituency (nor most Southerners, for that matter) were ready to abandon the existing two-party system to create something that many acknowledged would destroy the existing Union.[11]

The Wilmot Proviso and the presidential contest of 1848 gave both political parties an opportunity to redefine themselves—or at least readjust their positions on slavery—so as to satisfy their sectional constituencies, keep the parties intact, and attack their opponents. Democrats nominated Michigan Senator and well-known political moderate Lewis Cass as their candidate. Cass opposed the Proviso and became an advocate for popular sovereignty, a position adopted by party leaders from both sections.[12] The Whigs chose Mexican War–hero Zachary Taylor, a slaveholder from Louisiana who owned multiple plantations and more than one hundred slaves. Taylor was not a politician and never took a stand publicly for or against the Proviso. Southerners nonetheless were certain that his status as a planter placed him on their side of the issue. In the North, antislavery elements refused to support Taylor, choosing instead to endorse the fledgling Free Soil Party. Conversely, most Northern Whigs eagerly supported the Jackson-like war hero.[13]

Taylor won the election nationally, but lost the state of Alabama to Cass by fewer than nine hundred votes. In the piney woods, the Whigs recaptured many of the votes they lost as a result of Clay's disastrous 1844 campaign and made noticeable headway in the heavily Democratic counties of Dale, Henry, and Coffee. Taylor carried Barbour, Butler, Conecuh, and Covington by at least two-to-one margins, scraped together wins in Henry and Coffee counties, and secured a comfortable victory in Pike County. Only Dale County remained the piney woods Democratic Gibraltar. Dale County aside, there was simply no way that Lewis Cass could compete with the slaveholding war hero.

In 1849, radical Democrats led by Yancey and a small group of equally radical states' rights Whigs known as the Eufaula Regency saw an opportunity to unseat Henry Hilliard who, despite his strong condemnation of the Wilmot Proviso, remained far too moderate for their liking. Stirred up by the Proviso, the debate over slavery in the territories, and the newly organized Free Soil Party in the North, the Regency, an informal faction of lawyer-planters from Barbour County, contended that secession had now become a viable option to protect slavery. The Regency wielded powerful political influence throughout the southeastern corner of the piney woods, especially in

Pike, Henry, Dale, and Coffee counties. Among the group's leaders were John and Eli Shorter, two brothers who were partners in a law firm in Eufaula. In 1850, Eli was a young, twenty-six-year-old lawyer and planter who owned forty-four slaves and an estate valued at more than $35,000. He was an unapologetic radical who argued for the right "of a sovereign State to secede from the Union whenever she determines that the Federal Constitution has been violated by Congress, and that the Government has no Constitutional power to coerce such seceding State."[14] His older brother, John Gill Shorter, owned only eleven slaves at the time of the 1850 census, but his estate was valued at around $40,000. During his career, he was a state senator, member of the state house, long-time judge, and eventually became governor.

Other influential members of the Regency included John Cochran, Edward C. Bullock, Jefferson Buford, and James Pugh. Cochran was a lawyer, judge, and Southern rights' proponent who had once been defeated by Hilliard in a run for Congress. "I pray God that the South may tear herself from the power of the monster which does not conceal its purpose," he wrote in 1851. "I do not think the Union will be dissolved immediately, but I believe, and rejoice in the belief, that at this moment there is amongst us here a leaven of disunion, which by a more or less rapid, but perceptively certain, process will leaven the whole lump."[15] Bullock, Buford, and Pugh, meanwhile, were partners in one of Eufaula's most influential law offices. Bullock earned a reputation as one of the finest lawyers in eastern Alabama. He served as a state senator, edited a local newspaper, and mentored up-and-coming law student and future Civil War general William C. Oates. Buford was perhaps the most dominant member of the Regency. He was a former Indian fighter and state legislator.[16] His style of radicalism called for a gradual move toward secession rather than the immediate separation sought by Yancey. He believed, rightly, that the masses were not yet ready for secession. "No great, valuable and lasting achievement was ever consummated without long and much toil," he wrote. "With us it requires a long, very long time for new ideas to enter and imbue the public mind, and they must sink . . . into our very bones and marrow and become part of our being before they develop the fruit of action."[17] In other words, Southern independence hinged upon the white population's willingness to accept secession as mainstream and separation from the Union as absolutely necessary. As a result, many of the radicals understood the need to be patient, resourceful, persuasive, and—most of all—persistent.

One of the first steps to achieving the revolution that Buford and others desired was to replace Hilliard with one of their own. Buford's law partner and fellow states' rights Whig, James L. Pugh, challenged Hilliard in a campaign that came to be known as the "War of the Roses," a reference to fifteenth-century wars between English royal families. The Democratic Party decided not to run a candidate of its own, choosing instead to throw its full support behind Pugh. As a fellow Whig, Pugh had supported Hilliard's rise to political prominence, but like other radicals, he put his states' rights philosophy well ahead of party loyalty. Hilliard, on the other hand, attempted to walk a tightrope between his love for the Union, his support for slavery, and his opposition to secession.[18]

The campaign was bitter. The radicals accused Hilliard of selling out the South by failing to support the extreme states' rights position. Yancey traveled all over the district stumping for Pugh. A scheduled debate between Hilliard, Yancey, and Pugh at Mt. Meigs was canceled when the participants failed to reach a compromise over the order of the speakers.[19] Pro-Whig newspapers charged Pugh with being nothing more than a pawn in the hands of the Democrats to destroy the Whig alliance and empower the most radical elements in Alabama politics. In a fiery speech before a large crowd in Montgomery, Hilliard attacked the radicals, "these self-constituted leaders of the Democratic Party, who professed to be the truest friends of the South, say that at the last election they allowed me to return to Congress without opposition; I say to these gentlemen today, I intend to return to Congress, and I defy you to prevent it. The heart of the people in this great district beats in full sympathy with me, and they will stand by me while I uphold the standard of the Constitution and the Union."[20]

When the dust settled, Hilliard won reelection by fewer than eight hundred votes (see Table 4.1). Coffee, Dale, and Henry counties voted solidly for Pugh, while Barbour and Pike went for Hilliard. That Hilliard won Barbour County by a margin of just eight votes is still surprising given that Pugh was the hometown favorite. Without the counties of Macon, Montgomery, and Russell, Hilliard would have lost the election. Yet with the exception of the region's southeastern corner, the piney woods—including Conecuh and Butler, which supported moderate Whig candidate William J. Alston by comfortable margins that year—remained a predominantly Whig region. With some exceptions, most residents of piney woods counties were not willing to risk dividing the Union over the Wilmot Proviso, which they believed had no real chance of becoming law anyway. Nor were they all that incensed over a seemingly irrelevant faction of abolitionist radicals whom people believed would never amount to much. Hilliard won the election but the Regency established an important beachhead of radicalism in Barbour and surrounding counties that eventually moved many Whigs into the camp of an increasingly radical Democratic Party.[21]

Proslavery radicals became even more emboldened with the passage of the Compromise of 1850, a law they once again insisted would put the South

TABLE 4.1. 1859 congressional election, District 2

Counties	Hilliard (Whig)	Pugh (Whig)
Barbour	992	984
Coffee	302	441
Covington	231	202
Dale	400	647
Henry	407	637
Macon	1,393	672
Montgomery	1,068	867
Pike	1,014	870
Russell	963	658
Total	6,770	5,975

Source: David Young, *The Whig Almanac, 1849. Calculations for the Year 1849* (New York: Greeley and McElrath, 1849), 59.

at a political disadvantage and threaten slavery. Two years earlier, the United States acquired 500,000 square miles of territory from Mexico in the aftermath of the Mexican War. "This outcome translated the Wilmot Proviso from theoretical possibility into hard reality," William Cooper has noted, a reality that further polarized extremists in both sections of the country.[22] While the organization of the Mexican Cession and legislation regarding California's entry into the Union were important, it was the status of slavery that led to heated exchanges in both chambers of the US Congress. Even moderates such as Hilliard argued that to exclude slavery from the whole of the territories, as many antislavery legislators had called for, was just one short step away from eliminating the institution from the states where it already existed. "It must be acknowledged," Hilliard contended, "that there is a mere difference of degree between having a right questioned and assaulted and having it wrested away, but your demand now to appropriate the entire territory acquired from Mexico at the close of a national war in which the whole country participated . . . has aroused a spirit which you will find it no easy task to subdue."[23] Whigs meeting in Conecuh County argued that Southern politicians should insist upon "a constitutional guarantee or an undoubted equivalent, that the subject of slavery will not be again interfered with south of that line by the Federal Government in any manner whatever."[24]

Southerners, therefore, were surprised when President Zachary Taylor pushed for immediate statehood for California, Utah, and New Mexico, a move that would have resulted in each new state entering into the Union as a free state.[25] Like most Southerners, Alabamians were outraged that their slaveholding president would betray their trust by taking such a stance. Whigs especially found themselves in a politically untenable position and pleaded in vain with Taylor to rethink and redefine his position. Henry Hilliard, who was hoping to secure a foreign ambassadorship from the administration, openly broke ranks with the president. "I have bestowed upon this great question the most earnest reflection," he explained in a speech on the floor of the House. "I have studied it thoroughly and with the most sincere respect for the motives of the President [and] I find it impossible to give my support to the policy which he recommends."[26] Taylor never yielded his position and would surely have vetoed the Compromise of 1850 had he lived long enough to do so.

Meanwhile, in June 1850, an assembly of delegates from nine slaveholding states met in Nashville, Tennessee, to plot a unified course of action related to territorial expansion in the southwestern territories. The Alabama General Assembly appointed thirty-six delegates but only fourteen Democrats and seven Whigs attended. Historian Lewy Dorman once suggested that, while most of the delegates were Democrats, few were of the radical persuasion.[27] William Yancey, for instance, refused to attend the convention, as did most of the extreme states' rights politicians. Conspicuously absent was Henry Hilliard who, along with other prominent Alabama Whigs, discouraged their friends from attending. To the Whigs, any convention at this juncture was premature, and even if it were necessary, the legislature should have allowed the people to choose their own delegates. "As to the Nashville Convention," Hilliard maintained, "my opinion as things now stand, is against it. I adhere to the position taken by me last summer—that no convention ought to be held in advance of some act of aggression on the part of the government. The most the legislation should have done was to . . . empower the government, in the event of an aggression, to call a convention of the people to consider the question in all its bearings."[28]

As it turned out, the convention unanimously adopted a series of resolutions that a majority of Whigs, including Hilliard, largely supported. Avery Craven has observed that, given all of the controversy, the document was noticeably subdued in tone. While the delegates insisted upon Southern rights in the territories and demanded that the federal government meet its obligations to protect slave property, there was no mention of secession—an important point consistent with the Unionist affections of a majority of Southerners. Both Democrats and Whigs rallied in Montgomery, condemned the "blind and bigoted fanaticism" of Northern abolitionism, and supported the resolutions. Yancey and the radicals denounced the resolutions, held rallies throughout the state, and attempted to win people's support for secession.

A meeting of Yancyites in Abbeville, Henry County, for instance, passed its own resolutions "proclaiming that a secession by the Southern States from the [nation] is the rightful and efficient remedy," and must necessitate a "withdrawal of their delegated authority and rights from the Union which has ceased to answer the ends for which it was established, and become an engine of robbery and oppression."[29] While secession may have gained some converts in the extreme southeastern corner of the region, the piney woods as a whole remained overwhelmingly opposed to the idea.

In this atmosphere, Henry Clay proposed, and Congress eventually passed, a series of compromise resolutions whereby California would be admitted as a free state, New Mexico and Utah would theoretically be open to slavery, the slave trade would be abolished in the District of Columbia, and attempts to recover fugitive slaves would have the full support of the federal government. Texas agreed to give up its claims to New Mexico, relinquish a large chunk of territory north of the Missouri Compromise line, and hand over its massive debts, to be paid by the United States. Despite cries from the fire-eaters that the bill undermined slavery, the majority of Alabamians (and Southerners as a whole) supported the Compromise. Henry Hilliard voted in favor of the resolutions as did both of Alabama's senators and the majority of the House delegation. State senator James Johnson insisted that the law was "intended as a final adjustment of all the difficulties which had heretofore existed or could be . . . anticipated in connection with the subject of slavery."[30]

In the aftermath, members from both houses of the Alabama General Assembly offered numerous resolutions, some more supportive of the Compromise than others. Piney woods legislators were more or less divided in their support. Barbour County's John Gill Shorter and John W. Jackson, Butler's John McMullen, Dale's Edwin R. Boon, and Henry's Alexander J. McAllister all opposed resolutions supporting the Compromise. In their minds, weakness was provocative. They were convinced that any compromise on the issue of slavery in the territories would invite further aggressions against the institution. Conversely, Coffee County's William Holley, Conecuh's William Ashley, Covington's George Snowden, and Pike County's Levi Freeman and Richard Benbow voted in the affirmative. They were willing "to take the measures as a final settlement of the Territorial questions, so far as slavery was concerned, in the hope that . . . slavery agitation would cease."[31] Three of the region's four state senators also voted to uphold similar measures favoring the Compromise in the Senate. Yet, while Shorter and a handful of other disunionists statewide called for immediate secession, there is no evidence to suggest that other members who opposed the Compromise were similarly ready to adopt such drastic action. Indeed, given the choice between moderate Unionist James Abercrombie, chosen by the Whigs to replace the retiring Henry Hilliard, and radical Yanceyite John Cochran, piney woods residents chose the former. One historian argues that "the [congressional] elections of 1851 battered the secessionists" statewide and affirmed the widespread sentiment that Alabamians were once again not willing to abolish the ties that bound them to the Union.[32] Despite the radical element in their midst, piney woods whites were simply not convinced that secession was the best remedy.

In the wake of the Compromise of 1850, the national Whig Party struggled to regain its former prominence. Issues such as immigration and temperance divided Whigs. Many Northern Whigs refused to support the Compromise and slowly drifted into the ranks of the Free Soil Party. In the South, James Abercrombie was one of only twenty Whigs elected to the US House of Representatives (out of a total of seventy-eight seats) from all of the slave states. Democrats controlled the legislatures in every Southern state except North Carolina and Tennessee. Party leaders hoped to reenergize the ranks by nominating Winfield Scott for the presidency in 1852, but Southerners bristled at the thought of electing another Taylor-like war hero. On the other hand, Democrats united behind the Compromise of 1850 by nominating Franklin Pierce, a New Hampshire native who promised to uphold the law in its entirety and unapologetically pledged his support for Southern institutions.[33]

Pierce defeated Scott in a landslide. Alabamians supported Pierce by nearly two-to-one, but voter turnout, especially among disenchanted Whigs, was much lower than in previous presidential contests. Every county in the piney woods except Barbour voted for the Democratic ticket. Yet, the evidence suggests that if Whig voters had turned out in the same numbers as they had in 1848 the results might have been different. In Pike County, for instance, only 379 voters cast a ballot for Scott in 1852 as opposed to the 935 votes Taylor received in 1848, a 59 percent decline. Democrats, on the other hand, increased their turnout margins by 11 percent overall. The fire-eaters, meanwhile, ran their own slate of candidates, featuring George Troup of Georgia and Mississippi's John A. Quitman, but made little headway in the region outside the Eufaula Regency's Barbour County, where the ticket picked up a voting majority, and Henry County, where they ran a close second behind Pierce.[34]

In 1854, the divisive issue of slavery raised its head once again, this time in a portion of the Louisiana Purchase known as the Nebraska Territory. Senator Stephen A. Douglas's Kansas-Nebraska Act divided the territory, nullified the old Missouri Compromise prohibitions on slavery, and established popular sovereignty as a means by which slavery could be introduced into the region. The act created a firestorm in the North, shattered what was left of Whig Party unity, and provided a launching pad from which the newly formed Republican Party would unleash a barrage of condemnatory declarations aimed at the "slave power" menace in the South. Gamaliel Bailey, radical abolitionist and editor of the *National Era*, encouraged all antislavery men in the North to "rally as one man for the reestablishment of liberty and the overthrow of the Slave Power."[35]

Down South, orphaned Southern Whigs with states' rights leanings migrated into the Democratic Party, while Unionist Whigs—the majority of the Party—and a sizeable number of disaffected Democrats drifted temporarily into the ranks of the American, or Know-Nothing, Party. Like their Whig predecessors, southern Know-Nothings swore that they were the true guardians of slavery and defenders of the Union. Henry Hilliard proposed "to aid that party to the full extent of my ability. . . . Let us appeal once more to the masses of the North to be faithful to the Constitution; and if we fail to awaken their patriotism, we know how to die in defence of our institutions."[36]

In the wake of the Kansas-Nebraska Act, thousands of settlers flooded into the territory. While most went in search of affordable farm land and greater opportunity, others went specifically to fight either for or against the extension of slavery into the region. Both proslavery and antislavery partisans moved into the region equipped with guns, ammunition, and an unwavering devotion to their respective causes. Eufaula's Jefferson Buford notably organized a group of four hundred emigrants, mostly men from Alabama and Georgia, with the grand scheme of establishing a permanent proslavery settlement in the territory. He and a small band of hand-picked recruiters traveled throughout the piney woods region, making stops in Greenville, Troy, Elba, Daleville, Newton, Abbeville, Franklin, and other communities. Buford's fiery temperament, his appeals to white supremacy, and his warnings against racial amalgamation, must have been enticing. Abolitionism, he suggested,

> cannot stop short of universal freedom, equality and fraternity; and when it emancipates, it must protect its beneficiaries by giving them right to her arms—to vote—to testify—to make laws—nay! by sending the federal army to defend them, and to fight their battles. It is therefore . . . a question of races, equally affecting every white skin in the land—it is a question of whether the inferior race, ceasing to be producers and tax payers, shall become drones and eat up the hive—whether the stenchy Ethiopian shall sleep with the white man—sit with him in church—jostle him in the street—thrust him from the assembly, the witness stand, the jury and the ballot box—marry his

> daughters, make and administer his laws—steal his pigs and put him in prison for complaining—a question in which every white skin [is] equally interested.[37]

In April 1856, "Buford's Battalion," about 350 strong at this point, received a grand send off in Montgomery, complete with political speeches, a sermon by popular minister Isaac Taylor Tichenor, and a cheering crowd of more than five thousand supporters from all over the state. In a stroke of irony, an African American band entertained the crowd at the same time that banners proclaiming "The Supremacy of the White Race" and "Kansas, the Outpost" flew overhead. Addressing the crowd from atop a bale of cotton, Hilliard championed white supremacy and fervently defended Southern rights, but only within the context of the Union.[38]

The expedition went by train from Montgomery to Mobile, then by ship to New Orleans, steamed up the Mississippi River to St. Louis, and overland to the Kansas Territory. Proslavery Missourians welcomed "with open arms those gallant sons of Alabama and other Southern States, now on their way to their new homes in the Kansas Territory. . . . We hereby pledge ourselves to them . . . that we will aid and assist them in every proper way, and should emergencies require, we will march shoulder to shoulder with them to the last struggle for Southern rights."[39] As it turned out, Buford's ruffians arrived just in time for some of the bloodiest fighting in the Kansas civil war. They notably participated in the attack on the free-state settlement in Lawrence, although Buford reportedly tried to stop some of the more blatant destruction of private property.

The attack on Lawrence sparked John Brown's murderous raid on a slave-state settlement along Pottawattamie Creek near Lecompton, Kansas, the heart of the proslavery movement in the territory. Brown, a militant abolitionist with visions of crushing slavery by force of arms, entered Kansas with his four sons, intent on "striking terror in the hearts of the proslavery people."[40] On the night of May 24–25, Brown's small force raided three homes, then captured and executed five men with broadswords; several were murdered right in front of their families. While none of Brown's men was ever brought to justice for their crimes, the proslavery attack on Lawrence, followed by the massacre at Pottawattamie Creek, escalated the violence. Over the next eighteen months, more than two hundred people died. Abolitionist forces drove most of the proslavery emigrants, including almost all of Buford's men, out of the territory. Buford's experiment in Kansas ultimately failed, but the bloodshed that took place between abolitionists and proslavery zealots in "Bleeding Kansas" heightened sectional animosity and provided a preview of much deadlier events yet to come.[41]

While sectional violence exploded in Kansas, the gubernatorial and congressional elections of 1855 helped redefine the political landscape back home in the piney woods. Governor John A. Winston was up for reelection. The Democratic Party faithful were so pleased with his leadership that they bypassed the formalities of a nominating convention. The American Party backed Democrat George D. Shortridge, a lawyer, planter, and circuit court judge from Shelby County. Like most statewide elections, local issues often trumped national ones. In this instance, the gubernatorial race became less about Unionism versus states' rights and more about state aid to the railroads. During his first term as governor, Winston had opposed many state-sponsored loans to railroad companies, arguing that such measures benefitted certain sections of the state at the expense of others, entangled the state government with private enterprise, and threatened to send the state into financial dire straits if the loans went bad. Shortridge favored these loans, although as the contest progressed he often moderated his stance, especially when campaigning in anti-aid areas of the state such as the piney woods counties in the southeastern corner of the region. Winston exploited his opponent's waffling on the issue and cruised to a comfortable victory, winning by twelve thousand votes statewide. His victory in the piney woods was even more complete, taking every county except Pike by fairly sizeable margins, and racking up 65 percent of the total regional vote (see Table 4.2). Shortridge did squeeze out a victory in Pike County thanks to a sizeable and influential base of support in Troy.[42]

The 1855 congressional election for the second district, meanwhile, featured Eli Shorter, a prominent member of the Eufaula Regency, and Pike County's Julius Caesar Alford, an old Indian fighter and former Whig congressman from Georgia whose theatrical antics on the floor of the House in Washington won him critical acclaim back home. Back in 1839, for instance, Alford had no sooner taken the oath of office as a congressman when he took to the floor of the house to challenge a Northern congressman who had moments before finished a speech denouncing Georgia's mistreatment of the Indians. "The gentleman from Massachusetts never saw an Indian," he fumed, "never was scalped, never heard the savage war-whoop. I can enlighten him." William Garrett, a contemporary of Alford, recalled that the newly elected congressman gave an energetic "war-whoop in a fine imitation. . . . Then came a tempest of denunciation upon the Northern fanatics, who busied themselves in matters of which they were wholly ignorant; the imaginary sorrows of a brutal Indian outweighed in their tender consciences the misery of innocent women and children whom he had butchered."[43]

Alford's problem in 1855 was threefold. First, he had lived in the region for only about five years, having moved from Georgia to Pike County sometime in 1850, and as such was basically unknown outside of his county. He then had the bad luck to be running in a district gerrymandered by the General Assembly the year before. For years, Democrats had been itching to gain control of District 2, and had removed three large Whig counties—Montgomery, Russell, and Macon—and replaced them with the smaller counties of Lowndes and Butler. The new district, with a weakened Whiggery, more or less guaranteed the seat for the Democrats. Finally, Alford's opponent was a well-known former Whig turned states' rights Democrat with strong ties to communities throughout the southeastern corner of the region. Nevertheless, while Shorter carried Barbour, Coffee, Dale, and Henry, winning 55 percent of the regional vote, Alford was successful in Butler, Covington (by just two votes), Lowndes, and Pike counties, garnering 45 percent of the vote.[44]

Meanwhile, in the Northern states, the Republican Party's surge in popularity after only two years in existence continued with the 1856 presidential nomination of war hero John C. Frémont. The party's presidential slogan, "Free Speech, Free Press, Free Soil, Free Men, Fremont and Victory," left no doubt as to which side of the sectional argument they fell.[45] The American Party chose former president Millard Fillmore as its nominee. Fillmore blamed the Republicans for sowing seeds of agitation and disunion, touted his own executive experience, and promised to "restore sectional harmony by favoring neither North nor South, insisting that 'I know only my country, my whole country, and nothing but my country.'"[46] The Democrats nominated longtime Democratic politician James Buchanan, a Pennsylvanian and former slave owner who, twenty years earlier, had signed manumission papers immediately upon the purchase of two slaves with the caveat that freedom would be postponed; a practice not unheard of among border Northerners. The "gradual emancipator," as historian William Freehling calls him, "was a northern man with southern principles, if one means a Border North man with Border South principles."[47]

Frémont carried ten of fifteen northern states and captured 45 percent of the vote in that section, compared with just 41 percent for Buchanan. Yet Buchanan won the presidency by sweeping the South, taking California, and winning every Northern border state except for Ohio. "Old Buck" garnered 62 percent of the vote in Alabama, similar to the margin of victory gained by the Democratic contender in the governor's race just one year earlier. While Buchanan carried every piney woods county except Butler, he did so in several cases by the slimmest of margins. Coffee, Dale, and Henry, for example, voted solidly and predictably Democratic, whereas Conecuh, Covington, and Pike gave Buchanan the nod by just 117 total votes. Fillmore won Butler County by only fifteen votes (see Table 4.2), and for the first time in a

TABLE 4.2. Governor's race and presidential election, 1855–1856

	1855 governor's election		1856 presidential election	
	Winston (D)	Shortridge (A)	Buchanan (D)	Fillmore (A)
Barbour	1,696	661	1,445	857
Butler	699	632	777	792
Coffee	760	283	703	301
Conecuh	401	390	425	408
Covington	361	140	304	288
Dale	1,232	147	945	419
Henry	1,013	347	966	471
Pike	1,199	1,257	1,262	1,178
Total	7,361	3,857	6,827	4,714

Source: "Presidential Election in Alabama," *Weekly Alabama Journal*, February 5, 1856.

presidential election Barbour County voted Democratic. The evidence suggests that by 1856 a shift in the political winds was beginning to take place. While the Democratic Party had increased its power in the southeastern corner of the region, the demise of the Whigs, the transience of the Know-Nothings, and the growing threat posed by the Republican Party allowed the Democrats to make minor but politically significant inroads into traditional Whig strongholds.[48]

Between 1856 and 1860, a number of momentous events tied to slavery deepened the sectional divide. Just two days after Buchanan's inauguration, the Supreme Court handed down the Dred Scott decision. Seven of the nine justices, including all six Southern jurists, ruled that slaves were not citizens and had no right to bring suit in federal court. The court's ruling effectively nullified the Missouri Compromise and declared that Congress had no right to restrict slavery in any territory. Not only did Buchanan move swiftly to support the court's decision but the administration also defended Kansas's entry into the Union as a slave state, despite the fraudulent circumstances surrounding the Lecompton Constitution. Alabama's General Assembly supported the court's decision and demanded that Congress admit Kansas as a slave state. Both issues undermined national Democratic Party unity, strengthened the Republicans, invigorated the fire-eaters, and ultimately weakened an already-fragile Union.[49]

Two years later, John Brown's 1859 raid on Harpers Ferry, Virginia, sent shockwaves through the South. In the months leading up to the attack, Brown recruited a small force of about fifteen men to assist him in his plans to seize the US armory at the Ferry, foment a general uprising of slaves in the southern Appalachians, and distribute captured weapons to slaves who joined their crusade. The attack on the arsenal was doomed to fail. James McPherson argues that, when Brown finally made his move, "he did so without previous notice to the slaves he expected to join him, without rations, without having scouted any escape routes, with no apparent idea of what to do after capturing the armory buildings. It was almost as if he knew that failure with its ensuing martyrdom would do more to achieve his ultimate goal than any 'success' could have done."[50] Within minutes of the attack, angry citizens surrounded Brown's party and pinned them down with small arms fire until the militia could be organized. Twelve hours later, most of Brown's men were either dead or captured, while Brown himself was arrested and later tried and executed.

The Harpers Ferry raid and the continuing Kansas statehood debacle prompted Governor Andrew Barry Moore—a moderate Democrat elected overwhelmingly in 1859—to take a more proactive approach to stem the rising abolitionist tide and prepare for the worst should the "Black Republicans" gain control of the executive branch. He bolstered Alabama's militia system and supported a resolution "requiring the Governor of Alabama to call a state convention in the event a Republican should be elected President of the United States in 1860." If necessary, this convention would be fully authorized to consider secession and "to advise and consult with her sister states whose interests are similarly affected to bring about concert of action."[51]

The 1860 presidential election finally brought decades of sectional tension to a head. The Democratic Party split into Northern and Southern factions over the issue of slavery. While Democrats in the North nominated Douglas, their prodigal brethren to the South chose Vice-President John C. Breckinridge of Kentucky as their standard-bearer. Former Whigs and Know-Nothings, together with a handful of disenchanted Democrats, coalesced around Constitutional Union Party candidate John Bell of Tennessee. Lincoln, the Republican contender, carried just 40 percent of the popular vote but won the presidency by capturing every Northern state except New Jersey.

Lincoln was not on the ballot in Alabama. Breckinridge carried the state with more than 54 percent of the vote, but John Bell and Stephen Douglas received 30 percent and 14 percent, respectively. Six of eight piney woods counties gave majorities to Breckinridge, while two went for Bell. Breckinridge grabbed 61 percent of the vote, with Bell taking 35 percent. Douglas was a distant third, capturing only five hundred out of 13,425 votes cast in the region. Yet, a closer examination of the data reveals that the race between

TABLE 4.3. 1860 presidential election

County	Bell	Breckinridge	Douglas
Barbour	644	1,715	81
Butler	1,079	918	111
Coffee	394	878	2
Conecuh	338	348	205
Covington	416	404	12
Dale	277	1,280	5
Henry	317	1,109	0
Pike	1,227	1,581	84
Total	4,692 (35%)	8,233 (61%)	500 (4%)

Source: Clanton W. Williams, "Notes and Documents: Presidential Election Returns and Related Data for Antebellum Alabama," *Alabama Review* 2 (January 1949): 72–73.

Breckinridge and Bell was more evenly matched in Butler, Conecuh, Covington, and, to a somewhat lesser degree, Pike (see Table 4.3). The evidence suggests that these counties retained much of their Whiggish allegiance despite recent inroads made by the Democratic Party.[52]

J. Mills Thornton contends that in Alabama the Breckinridge campaign in fact turned the election into a referendum on secession in the event that Abraham Lincoln won the presidency. "The Breckinridge speakers," he notes, "repeatedly proclaimed that, though existing wrongs were not adequate to justify secession, the election of Lincoln would be sufficient cause."[53] Statewide, Breckinridge Democrats defeated their Douglas brethren by nearly three-to-one. While Douglas's supporters were concentrated primarily in the north-central hill counties—an area known for its pockets of robust Unionist sentiment—and a handful of counties in the Tennessee Valley, Breckinridge polled heavily on the flanks to the east and west of that area and in the southeastern corner of the piney woods.

In the piney woods, Thornton's argument appears to be only partially correct. If the counties that delivered the largest number of votes to Douglas truly were antisecession, as he suggests, then the piney woods voters who cast their ballots for Breckinridge were not necessarily opposed to the idea. In other words, if Thornton is correct, many Breckinridge voters believed that secession was a viable option, especially if Lincoln won the election. Douglas received little to no support in the piney woods outside of Conecuh County, where the Little Giant polled about 20 percent of the vote. On the other hand, political party loyalty remained generally intact. Breckinridge's overwhelming victories in Barbour, Henry, Dale, and Coffee suggest that these counties were simply following a long tradition of supporting Democratic candidates (in this case, the only Southern Democrat in the race). There appears to have been an almost even split in Butler, Conecuh, Covington, and Pike counties between those who voted for Breckinridge and those who voted for Bell, the former Whig. It is clear that the Democratic Party siphoned away votes, but the old Whig Party still maintained a loyal following in the southcentral counties.[54]

While many Bell loyalists argued that Southern rights were best protected from within the Union, some warned that a Lincoln presidency not only threatened the delicate political balance between slave states and free, but also would ultimately mean the abolition of slavery itself. For Butler County's Walter Crenshaw—a Bell supporter, Whig Party leader, political moderate, and longtime member of the state house and senate—Lincoln's election changed everything. Writing in the *Montgomery Daily Mail* not long after the election, he renounced his support for the Union and embraced secession:

> It was my love for the *Union of our Fathers* that caused me to support Bell and Everett. I was willing to give the North one more chance . . . and do partial justice to the South. But see how the olive branch of peace was rejected. Our offer of continued friendship was spurned with contempt. You, who were supporting Breckinridge, assured us that such would be the result. But we, animated by a spirit of patriotism, and believing this noble structure which cost our ancestors so much blood and treasure, deserved one more effort to save it from ruin, turned a deaf ear to all such prophecies, and vainly imagined that reason and justice could successfully combat anti-slavery fanaticism. The result proved that you were right, and that we were wrong. . . . As for me, the more I reflect upon the state of feeling existing at the North against the institutions of the South, the more satisfied I am that we ought to separate—and the sooner the better.[55]

Nevertheless, a number of Bell supporters continued to argue that a Lincoln presidency alone was simply not enough to justify breaking up the Union. "Our wiser course," Henry Hilliard insisted, "would be to assert our rights within the Union . . . and we should exhaust every remedy in our power for the maintenance of our rights before we abandon it."[56] Once the election was decided, men like Hilliard were forced to make a decision. Would they continue to defend the Union or would it take more than a presidential election to sway them?

In December, with Lincoln's election finalized, Governor Moore called a special election for delegates to attend a convention in Montgomery for the purpose of debating Alabama's secession from the Union. As it turned out, the only significant difference between the delegates was the disparity between those who supported immediate secession and those who publicly advocated cooperation with other slave states before leaving the Union. Cooperationists did not generally oppose secession, but they did insist that the slave states leave the Union as a unified whole rather than break off piecemeal. Some demanded that any move toward secession must ultimately be voted on by the people. Others argued that unless the Lincoln administration took overt measures against slavery the Southern states had no right to leave the Union.

Despite Hilliard's earlier advice, Lincoln's election appears to have been a turning point. Every piney woods county, except Conecuh where the votes were most evenly divided, elected men who supported immediate secession. In some cases, it is difficult to trace the contests and the candidates involved, but most of the representatives were slaveholders who tended to be well-known lawyers, judges, or former members of the state legislature. Barbour countians sent John Cochran, Alpheus Baker, and John W. L. Daniel. Little is known about their opponents—if there were any. Butler County elected Samuel J. Bolling and John McPherson. In Coffee County, Gappa T. Yelverton soundly defeated cooperationist candidate Francis A. Byars by a vote of 714 to 359, while in neighboring Covington County, DeWitt C. Davis comfortably won out over Albert G. Mallett with 337 votes to 229. It is likely that James McKinnie and D. B. Creech won Dale County with little opposition. In Henry County, Thomas Smith and Hasting Owen won overwhelmingly against George W. Williams. Williams once served as the county's representative in the General Assembly but managed to get only seventy-five votes in the convention race. Andrew P. Love, Eli Starke, and Jeremiah A. Henderson represented Pike County; there is no evidence as to who their opponents were. All three were former Whigs who joined ranks with the states' rights Democrats in the late 1850s.[57]

Conecuh County, on the other hand, gave a slight edge to cooperationist candidate John Green over secessionist Wilson Ashley by a vote of 399 to 372.[58] Green was a thirty-three-year-old planter who owned a 285-acre plantation and fourteen slaves in the Burnt Corn community, about ten miles northwest of Evergreen. He ended up voting against the ordinance of secession, but vowed to "sustain the action of the Convention. . . . He had been elected as a cooperationist; and would now greatly prefer a consultation with the slaveholding States before he severed the bonds of the Union. But, he would not withhold his acquiescence from the will of a majority here, how-

TABLE 4.4. Secession vote turnout comparison

	Cooperation vote	Secession vote	1859 governor's election	1860 presidential election
Barbour	**	1,653	1,656	2,368
Butler	**	695	1,584	2,108
Coffee	359	714	1,013	1,274
Conecuh	399	372	801	891
Covington	229	337	591	832
Dale	195	1,007	*	1,562
Henry	**	763	1,176	1,426
Pike	**	1,571	2,283	2,892
Total	1,182	7,112	9,104	22,457

* No returns from Dale County.

** No cooperationist candidate.

Sources: Lewy Dorman, *Party Politics in Alabama from 1850 through 1860* (Reprint, Tuscaloosa: University of Alabama Press, 1995), 176–177, 192–193, 194–195. Clarence Phillips Denman, T*he Secession Movement in Alabama* (Montgomery: Alabama State Department of Archives and History, 1933), 161–166.

ever much he might be convinced, in his own mind, of the propriety of co-operation."[59] Like most cooperationists, Green hoped that the slave states would move together in whatever course of action they chose to take. He also disapproved of the convention's decision not to submit the document for ratification by the people, which appears to have been his primary motive for voting against the ordinance.[60]

While secession candidates carried the piney woods vote by large margins over the cooperationists, it is important to remember that voter turnout was low, especially compared with the 1860 presidential election turnout (see Table 4.4). From a decline of 13 percent in Conecuh County to a whopping two-thirds drop in voter turnout in Butler, every county in the piney woods saw fewer voters show up for the polls during the secession vote than for the presidential contest. In counties such as Barbour, Butler, Henry, and Pike, secessionist candidates faced no opposition, perhaps making it easier for voters to stay home since there was no doubt about the outcome. It probably did not help turnout rates that the vote occurred on Christmas Eve on a day in which the weather was reportedly cold and rainy. It is also possible that low voter turnout was simply an indication of the region's lackluster support for secession. While this may have certainly been the case for some voters, there does not appear to have been a groundswell of opposition to secession equal to that seen in a number of counties in the northern part of the state. In his memoirs, Henry Hilliard—who himself opposed secession until Lincoln called for thousands of volunteers to put down the Southern rebellion—acknowledged strong opposition to secession in north Alabama but made no mention of similar resistance in the piney woods counties. Indeed, it seems strange that Hilliard would have neglected to mention the existence of a strong antisecession sentiment, if in fact it existed at all, from the very region that he represented and understood so well.[61]

At the convention, every piney woods delegate except Green, unsurprisingly, voted for immediate secession. If William Russell Smith's account of the convention is accurate, the region's delegates rarely made speeches or engaged in direct debate on the floor. Yelverton, one of the wealthiest and most influential citizens in Coffee County, spoke out once in favor of a resolution that would have committed Alabama to defend seceding states from any attempt on the part of the US government to coerce them back into the Union. When cooperationists insisted that the resolution be referred to committee before being voted upon by the full convention, Yelverton defended them:

> The assurances we have from honorable gentlemen of the minority, that the reference is sought only with the great patriotic view of understanding the resolution, and understanding each other, and thus to enable them to vote with us, *for the resolution*, is an appeal all powerful to me. I hold, Mr. President, that it would be exceedingly disgraceful to our gallant State, to have a single vote cast against this resolution; and if I did not go for this reference with the assurances I have, I should feel myself to that extent responsible for that disgrace. Then, I appeal to gentlemen who are already prepared to vote for the resolution, and, as the delay will be but temporary and the result not doubtful, to vote for the reference, that our friends of the minority may have no cause of complaint, and that the resolution may be adopted unanimously.[62]

During the convention, the cooperationists often used delaying maneuvers such as these to postpone or kill proposals they opposed. While secessionists such as Yelverton understood this tactic, they at least wanted to give the impression that the proceedings were fair. In this case, he appears to have believed that the minority was sincere. "I think I hazard nothing in saying that a unanimous report in favor of the resolution would follow such a reference."[63] In the end, the cooperationists won this particular fight; the resolution never came up for a vote.

The convention also debated the question of sending troops to Florida to aid in the seizure of federal installations in Pensacola. Cooperationists argued forcefully that such a measure was unwarranted and potentially reckless. "This unnecessary aggression on our part," one delegate insisted, "will not strengthen our cause in public estimation." Eufaula's John Cochran was among the first to take the floor in defense of the resolution. "There is no necessity for delay," he contended. "To doubt the existence of the necessity for this aid, as requested by Florida, would be an indignity to that State. If the aid is to be granted, let it be granted at once. One day's delay, and all may be lost. In emergencies, such as those which now surround us, all success depends upon the rapidity of our movements." The resolution passed but the roll call for this vote was not recorded.[64]

Much of the debate surrounding the ordinance of secession itself was twofold: first, over whether Alabama should cooperate with other slave states before seceding; and second, whether a measure for popular ratification should be adopted. In both cases, piney woods representatives kept a low profile when it came to the debates. As a member of the minority, John Green's reasoning and opposition to immediate secession has already been noted. Cooperationists such as Green made a gallant stand but their position was ultimately untenable. The same was true for ratification. One delegate argued "that the sovereignty of Alabama remains with the people thereof, and that the result of the convention called by the Governor . . . should be referred back to the people for their rejection or ratification."[65] This, too, failed to win the day. With the exception of Green, none of the region's delegates supported either position.

By February 1861, the convention had taken Alabama out of the Union, voted to send troops to Pensacola, voted down a provision to reopen the African slave trade, and penned a new state constitution. For diehard secessionists such as William Lowndes Yancey, this dream come true was twenty years in the making. For many piney woods residents, both former Whigs and moderate Democrats, the journey from moderation to secession began with the Wilmot Proviso, escalated with the Compromise of 1850 and the subsequent death of the national Whig Party, and reached a plateau during the Kansas civil war and John Brown's raid on Harpers Ferry. Due to their deep devotion to the Democratic Party, which dated all the way back to Andrew Jackson, Henry, Dale, and Coffee counties moved more rapidly toward secession. The Eufaula Regency clearly had an important effect on the entire southeastern corner of the region. Conecuh, Covington, Butler, and Pike counties, where the Whig Party had been strongest, maintained a resilient spirit of moderation until the late 1850s. With Lincoln's election followed closely by secession, the old Unionism began to fall by the wayside as every community prepared for war.

5

"From the Lights before Us I Think War Is Close at Hand"

The War Begins

On November 19, 1860, nearly two weeks after Abraham Lincoln's election to the presidency, more than three thousand people gathered in Clayton, Alabama, to witness a grand military demonstration involving at least six local militia companies from Barbour County. The crowd assembled on the grounds at the recently incorporated Clayton Female College, where students presented a homemade secession flag, and members of the Eufaula Pioneers fired numerous shots from an old smoothbore cannon nicknamed the "Little Fire-Eater." In back-to-back speeches, Jefferson Buford and John Gill Shorter stirred the crowd with calls for immediate secession. Later that evening, the soldiers formed ranks and marched down the town's center street in a torchlight procession complete with drums. The speeches continued late into the night with orations from Montgomery's Samuel Rice, followed by local politicians such as Lewis Cato, Eli Shorter, Henry Shorter, and others. One of Jefferson Buford's friends from Cahaba later wrote: "You do things right in your county. You take the bulls by the horns. Swell the gladsome ring of Barbour thunder, and let the State hear it!"[1]

In many ways, the companies that met in Clayton that day were, like dozens of others organized throughout the piney woods, unique organizations reflecting the values and character of individual communities throughout the region. Company captains were almost always well-respected community leaders, while the rank-and-file tended to be family, friends, and neighbors who identified closely with one another. The men and the communities they represented enjoyed similar social, political, and economic ties, not to mention the bonds of kinship that often ran through their organizations. This chapter looks at the piney woods from Alabama's secession in January 1861 to the Battle of Shiloh in April 1862. It explores the initial enthusiasm for the war effort many communities experienced as they raised and equipped dozens of companies from all over the southeastern piney woods. White men, mostly young and single at first, energetically volunteered for the army while women employed kinship networks to provide everything from uniforms and backpacks to baked goods and boiled eggs for the soldiers. This chapter also explores how the role of the region's soldiers in training and in battle operated as extensions of the home front. Piney woods companies sent to defend coastal fortifications became increasingly bored and frustrated as weeks and months of training and relative inactivity suddenly gave way to the bloodiest battle yet to be fought on American soil. Rather than dampen their spirits, however, Confederate defeat at the Battle of Shiloh actually strengthened the resolve of many piney woods families to redouble their efforts and continue the fight.

On January 4, 1861, Governor Moore ordered a force of state militia to seize the United States arsenal at Mount Vernon, an ordnance-manufacturing center located on the Mobile River about thirty miles north of Mobile. The next day, Alabama troops captured Forts Morgan and Gaines, two federal fortifications guarding the entrance to Mobile Bay. In a letter to President James Buchanan, Moore attempted to justify his actions. "The purpose with which my order was given and has been executed," he wrote, "was to avoid and not to provoke hostilities between the State and the Federal Government."[2] The governor then dispatched an additional six companies, about five hundred men, to Pensacola to aid the Floridians in an ultimately unsuccessful attempt to wrest Fort Pickens from Union control.

The General Assembly, called back into special session in January, further empowered the governor by issuing $2,000,000 in bonds "for the military defence of the state of Alabama." Nearly half was to be appropriated to pay volunteering soldiers. "We seek no conflict; we make no aggressive war," the resolution declared, "but threats of coercion have been made from high quarters, and it is the duty of the Legislature to put the State on a footing for vigorous and successful defense." The measure passed overwhelmingly seventy-five votes to twelve, with every piney woods legislator save Covington County's Alfred Holley voting in support.[3]

Holley—whose strong support for the Union became increasingly problematic as the war progressed—and the other eleven opponents launched a formal protest. They voiced opposition to the bill largely because they believed that portions of it unfairly benefitted the wealthy at the expense of the poor. Money used to purchase bonds, for example, was exempt from taxation, "thus giving capitalists who desire to invest their funds in said bonds an advantage over other citizens who are equally patriotic, but who cannot make such an investment." Critics also contended that the bill's tax incentives deprived the state of much-needed annual revenues that would have otherwise filled the coffers of the state treasury. We "can see no justice or equity in making such discrimination in favor of some and against others of our citizens," they argued.[4] For the moment, such assertions remained a minority opinion.

Alabama's secession convention, held concurrently in Montgomery with the special session of the legislature, meanwhile authorized the governor to recruit and "accept the services of any number of volunteers who shall associate and offer themselves for [military] service."[5] This resolution dovetailed with a similar act passed during the 1860 session of the General Assembly that called for the reorganization of the antiquated state militia system and the formation of new volunteer companies. In the wake of John Brown's raid on Harpers Ferry, a chorus of calls for armed readiness and military resistance to the new administration in Washington echoed throughout the state, including the piney woods. "Every one here looks serious," Barbour County attorney Hubert Dent observed, "but most every one I hope is determined. I shall rejoin the 'rifles' when I return or get up some other Company. I feel like the South now expects every man to do his duty."[6]

Dent's mention of the "rifles" was a reference to the Eufaula Rifles, an organization rooted in the militia structure that had operated to one degree or another in the community for years. Traditionally, the state's militia companies were small, community-based military organizations, composed of men ages eighteen to forty-five who were expected to muster and drill at least twice each year. The rank-and-file elected their own officers, who tended to be affluent, well-known, and well-respected community leaders. As historian Robert Kenzer notes in his study of Orange County, North Carolina, Southern militia companies not only fostered a sense of community and comradeship but they also functioned as training grounds for men who would one day serve as officers in Confederate armies.[7]

Approved in February 1860, the act to reorganize the state's militia sought to establish an all-volunteer force of eight thousand men. The law required company captains to assemble their men "at least twelve times a year, for public parade and instruction, and shall drill and exercise it in the school of the soldier and company."[8] Within weeks, dozens of new volunteer companies sprang up all over the state. Pike County's Orion Blues, Butler's Southern Guards, the Coffee Rifles, and Barbour's Midway Southern Guards were just a few of the units organized in piney woods counties under the new law. In reality, some of these "reorganized" militia companies existed only on paper or disbanded quickly before the war began, but many of them continued to recruit and drill, a few joined the effort to take Fort Pickens from the Yankees, and by the spring and summer of 1861 the members of most of the remaining companies mustered into Confederate service.

Events such as Harpers Ferry, Lincoln's election, the governor's seizure of federal installations, and the state's withdrawal from the Union all triggered a flurry of recruiting activity. The bombardment of Fort Sumter in Charleston Harbor on April 12, 1861, followed three days later by Lincoln's call for seventy-five thousand volunteers to put down the Southern rebellion, prompted a greater sense of urgency and a flood of energetic volunteering. Resolutions adopted at a mass public meeting in Dale County declared that "public feeling is high [and] the success of our arms at Fort Sumter gives new life to all. Dale may be well said to be unanimously sound; ready and willing for any service required."[9] No sooner had the ink dried on Lincoln's call for volunteers, when Thomas Crenshaw of Butler County sat down and penned a letter to his nephew Edward, then attending the University of Virginia. "I am fearful that you will have to leave Virginia before the close of the session," he wrote, "for from the lights before us I think war is close at hand between the North and the South."[10]

Even Henry Hilliard, heretofore strongly opposed to secession and anxiously in hopes that the Union would be preserved, condemned the Lincoln administration's decision and wholeheartedly embraced the Confederate cause. "The situation which confronted the new administration at Washington," he later recalled, "required the adoption of measures in accordance with the spirit of the American government; not a rash and imperious act of usurped authority, such as might have been expected from the absolute ruler of a despotic state."[11] Hilliard soon traveled to Tennessee as an envoy to encourage that state's legislature to secede, and then began recruiting Hilliard's Legion, a large organization of Alabama soldiers, many of whom came from the piney woods.

While an exact count of the number of men from piney woods counties who fought for the South is impossible to determine, the evidence gleaned from surviving muster rolls, payrolls, and other primary and secondary sources suggests that the region contributed approximately eight thousand soldiers to the Confederacy during the conflict. Piney woods communities organized forty-one companies in the months preceding the Confederacy's first conscription act in April 1862. Another fifty-six companies were created after the draft when many of the region's men joined to avoid being conscripted into units not of their choosing. As the war progressed, some companies disbanded, some merged with other companies as manpower dwindled, new companies and regiments emerged as conscription officers

TABLE 5.1. Piney Woods companies created in 1861

Regiment	Date of creation	Company	Army
1st Alabama	March 1861	B, E, F, G	AT*
4th Alabama	May 1861	E	ANV**
5th Alabama	May 1861	A,	ANV
6th Alabama	May 1861	A, B	ANV
7th Alabama	June 1861	E, F	AT
9th Alabama	May 1861	G	ANV
12th Alabama	July 1861	D	ANV
13th Alabama	July 1861	G	ANV
15th Alabama	Summer 1861	B, D, E, F, G, H, I, K, L	ANV
16th Alabama	August 1861	D	AT
17th Alabama	August 1861	B, C, I, K	AT
18th Alabama	September 1861	A, B, F, H	AT
22nd Alabama	November 1861	I, K	AT
23rd Alabama	November 1861	D, H	AT
25th Alabama	December 1861	A, B, K,	AT
58th Alabama	November 1861	E	AT
25th Georgia	December 1861	E	AT

* Army of Tennessee

** Army of Northern Virginia

Sources: Muster Rolls of Alabama Civil War Units, 1861–1940, Alabama Department of Archives and History; *Brief Historical Sketches of Military Organizations Raised in Alabama During the Civil War—Reproduced From Willis Brewer's Alabama: Her History, Resources, War Record, and Public Men, From 1540 to 1872* (Alabama Civil War Centennial Commission, 1962).

rounded up fresh recruits, and many companies attempted to replenish their ranks by appealing to their communities to send additional recruits (see Tables 5.1 and 5.2).

Using the 1860 population census as a gauge, each county contributed anywhere from one-third to one-half of its white, male population ages fifteen to fifty. When the figures are compared to the number of white males ages twenty to forty, the percentages rise even higher (see Table 5.3). Barbour and Pike counties contained the largest white populations in the region and consequently turned out the largest number of soldiers, while Covington County with the smallest population, not surprisingly contributed the fewest. Simply put, piney woods counties contributed an enormous amount

TABLE 5.2. Piney Woods companies created, 1862–1864

Regiment	Date of creation	Company	Army
29th Alabama	February 1862	I	AT*
33rd Alabama	April 1862	A, B, C, F, G, H,	AT
37th Alabama	Spring 1862	A, C, E, F, H, K	AT
38th Alabama	May 1862	E	AT
39th Alabama	May 1862	A, B, C, D, G, H, I, K,	AT
40th Alabama	May 1862	I	AT
42nd Alabama	May 1862	E	AT
45th Alabama	May 1862	A, C	AT
46th Alabama	May 1862	C, H	AT
51st Alabama	August 1862	B	AT
53rd Alabama	November 1862	D, H,	AT
54th Alabama	October 1862	A, E	AT
56th Alabama	Summer 1863	E,	AT
57th Alabama	March 1863	A, B, C, D, E, F, G, H, I, K	AT
59th Alabama	November 1863	A, B, D, E, I	ANV**
60th Alabama	November 1863	A, B, E, G	ANV
61st Alabama	September 1863	D, G	ANV
65th Alabama	July 1864	F, K,	Not Affiliated

* Army of Tennessee

** Army of Northern Virginia

Sources: Muster Rolls of Alabama Civil War Units, 1861–1940, Alabama Department of Archives and History; *Brief Historical Sketches of Military Organizations Raised in Alabama During the Civil War—Reproduced From Willis Brewer's Alabama: Her History, Resources, War Record, and Public Men, From 1540 to 1872* (Alabama Civil War Centennial Commission, 1962).

of manpower to the Confederacy especially compared with the total white population in each community. To be clear, not all of these soldiers served for the duration of the war: some were killed, some suffered debilitating wounds that ended their wartime service, some went temporarily AWOL, and others deserted their units never to return.

Yet, numbers tell only part of the story. In his study of Ashe County, North Carolina, historian Martin Crawford notes that "volunteer companies . . . were direct extensions of the community itself, literally communities away from home."[12] Mark Wetherington similarly argues that, in piney

TABLE 5.3. Number of soldiers by county

County	Number of soldiers	White male population ages 15–50 in 1860	White male population ages 20–40 in 1860	Total white population in 1860
Barbour	1,763	3,536 (50%)	2,118 (83%)	14,629 (12%)
Butler	1,127	2,644 (43%)	1,620 (70%)	11,260 (10%)
Coffee	765	1,827 (42%)	1,024 (75%)	8,200 (9%)
Conecuh	641	1,537 (42%)	940 (68%)	6,419 (10%)
Covington	376	1,210 (31%)	706 (53%)	5,631 (7%)
Dale	824	2,267 (36%)	1,317 (63%)	10,379 (8%)
Henry	816	2,447 (33%)	1,489 (55%)	10,464 (8%)
Pike	1,896	3,580 (53%)	2,170 (87%)	15,646 (12%)
Total	8,208	19,048 (43%)	11,384 (72%)	68,548 (12%)

Sources: Muster Rolls of Alabama Civil War Units, 1861–1940, Alabama Department of Archives and History; *Brief Historical Sketches of Military Organizations Raised in Alabama During the Civil War—Reproduced From Willis Brewer's Alabama: Her History, Resources, War Record, and Public Men, From 1540 to 1872* (Alabama Civil War Centennial Commission, 1962); Thomas McAdory Owen, *History of Alabama and Dictionary of Alabama Biography in Four Volumes* (Spartanburg, SC: Reprint Company, 1978); United States Census, Barbour County, Butler County, Coffee County, Conecuh County, Covington County, Dale County, Henry County, Pike County, Alabama, 1860, Schedule 1.

woods Georgia, "because each company was raised in the same rural neighborhoods or county, it became an extension of the community's economic, social, and political character."[13] Such was the case for dozens of companies formed in southeastern Alabama early in the war.

Capt. James T. Brady's Covington Hunters, for example, exemplified the type of units recruited from small, rural, farming communities. Brady was a thirty-six-year-old local physician from the Rose Hill community, located about ten miles northeast of Andalusia in Covington County. Before the war, he was the town's postmaster, a church deacon, a family man, and a small slaveholder owning just two slaves.[14] The majority of his company's 105 recruits lived in Rose Hill, Red Level, or in nearby Andalusia, all towns that were within just a few miles of one another. Most of the men were young, single, farm laborers between the ages of eighteen and twenty-five who typically resided with parents, relatives, or other families.[15]

5.1. Sgt. Green Berry Dozier, 18th Alabama Infantry (courtesy of the Alabama Department of Archives and History)

Like most companies formed during the first year of the war, kinship and neighborhood ties played key roles in recruitment efforts. Brady's company, soon to be known as Company B, 18th Alabama Infantry, included at least six pairs of brothers and multiple examples of kinship ties between the men. Twenty-one-year-old David Cockcroft and nineteen-year-old James were the last of five siblings still living at home when they joined up. Similarly, brothers Joseph and James Richards, also twenty-one and nineteen-years-old respectively, were the older of eight siblings living with their parents. Next door, twenty-three-year-old William, the eldest of the Richards brothers, left his young wife, Sarah, behind so that he could accompany Joseph and James.

Just down the road, Daniel Dozier, minister of the community's Primitive Baptist Church—the same church in which James Brady served as deacon—watched two of his five sons, Green and Thomas, enlist alongside the Richards and Cockcroft boys. Nearly two years later, Dozier's youngest son, James, who was only fifteen-years-old when the war began, enlisted to fight alongside his brothers and friends. By 1863, four of the five Dozier brothers, including the oldest, Elias, of Company C, 37th Alabama Infantry, were fighting for the Confederacy.

As Brady's company demonstrates, the tangled web of kinship ties was especially important in companies from relatively isolated rural hamlets that dotted the piney woods. William and Emily Moxley of Coffee County's Bullock community provide another case in point. During the summer of 1861, William Moxley worked diligently to raise one of the county's first infantry companies, the Bullock Guards. He was a well-respected local physician and small farmer who owned no slaves and whose modest income would hardly have placed him among the county's wealthy elite. In an overwhelming show of support, nearly every man in the company voted for Moxley as captain.

In addition to enlisting his neighbors and friends, Moxley relied upon an extensive kinship network to recruit family members in Alabama and in Georgia, where most of his immediate family lived. His younger brother Benjamin, who had already joined Company C of the 20th Georgia, requested and received a transfer to the Guards. Moxley convinced three of his wife's cousins, Caleb, William, and John Beck, to join his company along with William, John, and Floyd Babb, three brothers all related to the Moxleys by marriage. All six men were Coffee County residents. Emily even tried to persuade her two oldest brothers, Allen and Tom Beck, who lived just across the line in Pike County, to join the company. Both brothers eventually joined the Pike County Guards, but "Allen says he never will get over not going with you," Emily later reported to her husband. "He done all he could do to get Tom off with him to go in your Company, so Pa says. He rather be with you than any body els."[16]

The volunteers who left their families behind to join the war effort soon found themselves thrown into makeshift military training camps, mustered into Confederate service, and eventually sent to fight alongside thousands of other men on distant battlefields in places that most had never heard of much less visited. Martin Crawford has noted that "for some volunteers enlistment offered an adventure, an escape from private disappointment or economic frustration. For many others, particularly those with young families, the abandonment of home was to prove a searing experience."[17]

Soldiers from the piney woods primarily trained in camps located in Montgomery, Auburn, Mobile, and Pensacola, with a few additional places between. Depending upon time and place, soldiers encountered a wide variety of emotions and experiences, from excitement and eagerness, to boredom, disappointment, sickness, and frequently the death of close comrades.

In early May 1861, the Dale County Greys reported to Camp Hardaway, a temporary encampment located near Glenville in Russell County. Pvt. William Preston recounted that "the citizens for miles around Glenville carried us chickens, eggs, butter, milk, fresh meat, fruit and such things in plenty and without cost. Kind, generous people. We visited in their homes, went to their churches and had a good time there." The men quickly grew frustrated that their pay had been delayed, however, and that they might have to wait months before mustering into Confederate service. Their eagerness to join the fight sooner rather than later prompted many to transfer into other companies. By the fall those who were left went back home; the Greys reorganized a year later with some of the original members joining the new company.[18]

Members of the original Dale County Greys who transferred out were not alone in their frustrations. During the first year of the war, it was not unusual for men to move from one company to another, especially if they believed that doing so would hasten their opportunity to "get off to the war." Unfortunately, not every transfer worked out as intended. Twenty-five-year-old James Cumbia from Coffee County joined the Gulf Rangers sometime during the spring or early summer of 1861. After several months and no sign that the unit would be going off to fight any time soon, he transferred to the Louisville Blues, a company raised in Barbour County. Ironically, within weeks of transferring, Cumbia received word from Capt. Henry Laird that the Gulf Rangers would indeed be leaving for the war. "I got a letter from Laird not long since statin that he would be glad to have me along with him," Cumbia wrote in a letter to the governor requesting a transfer back to the Blues. "No doubt in my mind but what I could strengthen the company some by going with them. If I was to quit this company to join them and by any accident they were not to get off I would return to my same post." The governor denied his request.[19]

That same month, July 1861, Alabama Adjutant General George Goldthwaite ordered Capt. William Moxley's Bullock Guards to report for training at a camp near Auburn. The most obvious route for the company was to travel to Greenville and then take the train. "You will have to get to Greenville the best way you can," Goldthwaite wrote. "I suppose the neighbors will furnish transportation. You will be supplied with tents, arms, and subsistence after you arrive at Auburn." Upon arrival, the Guards became Company A, 18th Alabama Infantry, effectively joining units from Butler, Coffee, Covington, Pike, and several other piney woods counties to form one regiment. The troops drilled, stood in line for inspections, and waited impatiently for their units to be called up for battle. At night, the men gathered around campfires, "some grunting, some playing cards, some fiddling, some dancing, others enjoying them selves as they saw fit."[20] The 18th Alabama spent three long months in Auburn before being sent to bolster Confederate forces gathering at Mobile.

Sickness and disease soon became a growing concern for thousands of men thrown together in training camps for months at a time. Diaries and letters indicate that within weeks of first entering camp the men experienced all sorts of illnesses. In May 1862, Lt. William V. Fleming wrote to his wife that Mobile was a "hell on earth." But getting a furlough was impossible, "unless I was sick and I would rather stay here twelve months than to be sick one week."[21] Historian James McPherson notes that soldiers were most susceptible to sickness during their first year in the military. Childhood diseases such as measles and mumps spread rapidly among men from rural communities, most of whom had never been exposed to such illnesses. He writes, "if soldiers recovered from these diseases and remained for some time at the training or base camp—where by poor sanitary practices and exposure to changeable weather they fouled their water supply, created fertile breeding grounds for bacteria, and became susceptible to deadly viruses—many of them contracted one of the three principle killer diseases of the war: diarrhea/dysentery, typhoid, or pneumonia."[22]

Writing from Fort Gaines, Pvt. Allen Beck of Company B, 25th Alabama Infantry, informed his sister, Emily Moxley, that "we have one of the sarriest Doctors for our battalion you ever saw. He cant tell the chill and feder [fever] from the head ache." Beck explained that two of his closest friends had been sick for more than two weeks. Each morning, the doctor came by, examined the two men, and presented a diagnosis different from the morning before. In Auburn, William Moxley tried to encourage his wife: "My Dear, we have parted before, but under different circumstances. You expect me to return because you did not think of natural death, that is, from disease. Now you fear both." By October, Emily had plenty to worry about as her own husband fell ill and reports of sickness and death in the training camps became more commonplace. Only after several weeks of suffering, "more with my hed than I ever did in my life," did William Moxley slowly begin to recover.[23]

Eighteen-year-old Pvt. Benjamin Adams of Moxley's company was another of the many unfortunate ones. He spent time in the hospital trying to recuperate from the measles and appeared to be improving "untill day before yesterday at dinner," Moxley reported. "They gave him greens to eat that night. He was return worse yesterday morning. News reach me Ben was speachless, but I was not able to see [him] that day, but I did go to day. I found [him] still speachless. I think he is bound to die, and if he does I shall send him home." Benjamin Adams died three days later, one of many soldiers who succumbed to illness in the camp of instruction at Auburn that summer, having never fired a shot in battle.[24]

In early fall, the 17th Alabama Infantry—a regiment that included three companies from Butler County and one from Pike—spent two months in the camp of instruction just east of Montgomery. The unit moved to Pensacola in November where they received additional training and assisted with the occasional bombardment of Union forces at Fort Pickens on Santa Rosa Island. Like Mobile, the port at Pensacola was vital to the economic interests of South Alabama. If the Federals successfully held the harbor and the military installations at Fort Pickens and Fort Barrancas, they would be in a position to launch raids into the lower counties and disrupt the southern half of the state.[25] Each day the soldiers drilled, cleaned their camps, dug latrines, built fortifications, and prepared for an eventual attack against Fort Pickens. As the weather warmed, the already unhealthy conditions worsened. According to Lt. Edward Crenshaw of Company K, it was unfortunate that the regiment was "ordered into camp in a low swampy place on a disagreeable bayou back from the Navy Yard and half a mile distant." In less than three months, Camp Governor Moore (as it was called) turned into a mosquito-infested death trap. Hundreds of men fell ill, nearly one in ten died from disease. While most of the regiment eventually relocated a few hundred yards to higher ground, the two companies that suffered the most, the Pike Rangers and the Butler True Blues, moved to Warrington, a small, recently deserted village just west of the navy yard. "We had a most delightful time during our stay at Warrenton," Crenshaw wrote. "We occupied good comfortable houses and very soon there was a great improvement in the health of our two companies."[26] Despite widespread illness and increasing numbers of sickness-related deaths, volunteers from the piney woods continued to pour into the army. At this stage of the conflict, nothing seemed to dampen their spirits.

Meanwhile, as more and more of the region's young men volunteered, trained, and headed off to war, mothers, wives, sisters, and other female family and friends worked diligently to meet the most basic needs of the soldiers from their towns and communities. Many women formed or participated in ladies' aid societies, also known as soldiers' aid societies. Historian Harold Sterkx explains that "community pride was especially strong among small town and rural organizations, where members went all out to make sure that the local warriors were properly clad."[27] Composed primarily of middle- and upper-class women, these organizations—located primarily in Eufaula, Troy, Greenville, and a handful of other large towns—produced flags, bandages, haversacks, socks, shirts, undergarments, and a wide variety of other clothing and military supplies. In June 1861, a gathering of women met at the Methodist Church in Eufaula to "organize a soldier's relief society to provide clothing for the needy soldiers who have left our own city."[28] Some of the most prominent women in Eufaula joined, including Mary Jane Shorter, the governor's wife, and Wileyna Shorter, the governor's sister-in-law. The women formed both a fund-raising committee and a committee responsible for buying cloth, leather, and other materials necessary for sewing. Edward Young, one of the wealthiest merchants in town, granted the group use of several rooms on the second floor of the building that housed his mercantile business in downtown Eufaula.

Within a week of the society's formation, Capt. Alpheus Baker of the Eufaula Rifles (Company B, 1st Alabama Infantry) left his company at Pensacola, met with members of the committee, and discussed the shortage of adequate clothing among the poorer men in his outfit. Straightaway, the society's purchasing committee bought cloth from Young's mercantile. The next day, Mary Jane Shorter and a handful of other members began sewing items based upon Baker's request. In her diary, Elizabeth Rhodes noted that even though the sewing rooms were hot and dusty and the work conditions difficult, within five days they had produced enough clothing to make an initial shipment. "Mrs. Woods sends for me to go up to the rooms to assist in packing clothing we've finished to send by Capt. Clark to the soldier boys" in Baker's company. There is no indication how many pants, shirts, and socks were sewn, but by the first week of July the aid society sent at least three crates of clothing to the soldiers in Pensacola. In the meantime, Rhodes helped organize yet another soldiers' aid society in Eufaula, which included "a large number of ladies and number of men" structured "upon little different basis to the one organized sometime ago."[29]

By the late summer of 1861, aid societies with limited resources were already running out of both money and supplies, particularly those in sparsely populated piney woods communities. At the same time, many feared that the onset of cooler weather would bring much hardship to scantily clad deep-South soldiers, a few already serving in states in the upper South. The *Montgomery Weekly Advertiser* predicted that "the thousands and tens of thousands of brave volunteers who have left their peaceful homes to endure suffering, privation, and perhaps death . . . will need an immense quantity of clothing to make them comfortable [during] the ensuing fall and winter."[30]

Governor Moore responded by establishing a system whereby the government would supply raw materials to the ladies' aid societies in return for the production of clothing and other finished products. Moore launched the program in August and requested that the women "in each county, city, town, village, and neighborhood, form 'Soldiers' Aid Societies,' and that each society inform him by letter, as early as possible, the number of woolen uniforms, flannel shirts, and cotton-flannel drawers it can make or supply." The society in Manningham, for example, promised to make fifty uniforms for Butler County's soldiers, provided that the governor supply the necessary cloth, thread, buttons, and sewing patterns. "Each suit," they pledged, "will consist of one great coat, one uniform jacket, one pair of pantaloons, one pair of drawers, and one shirt. Be sure to send enough thread and buttons as they cannot be had here."[31] The governor promptly agreed to their request.

The aid society in Troy likewise worked diligently throughout the spring and summer to provide uniforms for three hundred Pike County soldiers then serving in three companies, the Quitman Guards, the A. B. Moore Invincibles, and the Pike Volunteers. By the fall, "their resources for procuring further supplies of cloth [were] exhausted, and they desire to make for these companies the uniform jackets and pants you mention in your recent circular to the aid societies of the state." Society members promised to deliver uniforms, undergarments, socks, and other clothing by late September or October if the governor promptly supplied the cloth. Within a few weeks, the society received "enough material to make 100 jackets and pants to match."[32]

The vast majority of women in piney woods counties did not participate in ladies' aid societies or any such formal organizations. While women in towns such as Eufaula, Greenville, and Troy enjoyed a greater pool of resources and laborers, those who lived miles from town in the remote corners of the region—especially the communities in the southernmost counties—were forced to work alone or in small, independent groups of family and friends. Mary Love Fleming remembered that, in Dale County, the people in her neighborhood "had no sewing circles or any other kind of aid societies as were common in towns and in some communities in the South. . . . But almost every family worked hard to supply clothing and other necessaries for the soldiers, and these things were usually collected in the community and shipped together to our men in the army."[33]

About twenty miles east of Greenville in Butler County, Mary Bigbie worked hard to provide clothing for her husband, Thomas, a member of Company G, 33rd Alabama Infantry, then serving near Chattanooga, Tennessee. She routinely sent items by way of furloughed soldiers returning to the unit. On one occasion, she sent several pairs of socks and a pair of woolen pants with John, a soldier in Bigbie's company. Thomas later informed Mary that even though the socks were a bit too large, "I was very pleas with my pants. I want won more pair of pants and a good coat and I want it lind good and made as warm as you can for this is a mity cold windy country here. Be shore and send my vest and I want them wooling under shirt and drawers."[34] On another occasion, Mary's sewing was apparently not up to par with her earlier work. This time the socks and shirt fit just fine, "but my pants was way to little. I put them on and ever time I stoop down they busted. I could stand up in them but I could not stoop down in them."[35]

Like Thomas Bigbie, most of the soldiers fully understood and usually appreciated the hard work of the women back home. When Capt. Pierre D. Costello of Company K, 25th Alabama, offered to share his wife's cakes with Col. John Loomis, "the Colonel tried some of them & wrote at once to his wife to follow your example." These little tastes of home boosted morale and "has raised your wifely qualities to the highest mark," Costello acknowledged.[36] Examples such as these demonstrate that the work previously confined solely to the domestic realm now proved essential to helping meet the physical and psychological needs of the men fighting the war. As historian LeeAnn Whites argues, "these men may have gone to war initially in defense of what they perceived to be their prerogatives as free men, but the actual demands of fighting the war made them conscious of their own dependence upon women's love and labor in ways that had hitherto been obscured by the latter's subordination within the household."[37]

While piney woods women worked diligently to meet the needs of increasing numbers of soldiers, the war's first major battle gave everyone a glimpse of the horrors yet to come. Indeed, the First Battle of Bull Run, or First Manassas as the Southerners called it, changed the way Alabamians perceived the conflict. On July 21, two opposing armies, made up almost exclusively of men who largely had never fired a shot at another human being, clashed near Manassas Junction, Virginia, about twenty miles southwest of Washington, DC. Throughout most of the day, Brig. Gen. Irvin McDowell's untested Union soldiers performed well until Confederate reinforcements arrived, collapsed the Union right flank on Henry Hill, and routed the entire Federal army.[38]

Four piney woods companies fought with the Confederate army at First Manassas. Three companies of the 5th and 6th Alabama Infantry regiments were attached to Brig. Gen. Richard Ewell's brigade. It spent most of the day at Union Mills only to be ordered forward late in the afternoon when most of the fighting had subsided. The day went much differently for the Conecuh Guards, officially known as Company E of the 4th Alabama Infantry. The 4th Alabama was one of five regiments in Brig. Gen. Barnard Bee's brigade. On the morning of the battle, Bee's brigade, along with the brigade of Col. Francis Bartow, confronted an overwhelming Union force at Buck Hill, just north of the Warrenton Turnpike. The Confederates fought hard but were unable to hold. By noon, the Alabamians were on their heels and headed toward the relative safety of Henry Hill. It was there that Confederate reinforcements led by Brig. Gen. Thomas J. Jackson counterattacked and drove the Federals back in disarray.

In the early fighting, forty of the 4th Alabama's soldiers died, including Col. Egbert Jones, and 157 were wounded, a shocking number for any regiment. In his after-battle report, Gen. P. G. T. Beauregard praised the regiment's sacrifice: "The Fourth Alabama also suffered severely from the deadly fire of the thousands of muskets which they so dauntlessly confronted under the immediate leadership of Bee himself. Its brave colonel (E. J. Jones) was dangerously wounded, and many gallant officers fell."[39] First Manassas was a wake-up call for Southerners who realized that their war for independence would be costlier than many could have imagined. Families of the Conecuh Guardsmen who had died at Bull Run understood the full impact of this new reality. Nevertheless, the region's communities continued their efforts to recruit new soldiers and support local companies as more and more men headed off to war.

As news of the battle spread and the reality of war began to sink in, piney woods citizens pondered their choices for the state's next war governor. Two of the region's most prominent sons, Eufaula's John Gill Shorter and former Butler County resident Thomas Hill Watts, were in the running. Andrew Moore's second term would come to an end in December 1861, and by law he was prohibited from seeking another term. Five candidates for the governor's seat eventually emerged. Thomas Judge of Montgomery and Tuscaloosa's Robert Jemison Jr. were unable to generate much enthusiasm outside their local communities and withdrew relatively early in the process. John E. Moore of Florence was the candidate of choice for many in the northern part of the state. He was particularly popular with several newspapers which, after his withdrawal from the race, accused Democratic politicians in South Alabama of neglecting northern counties and violating an unwritten agreement that the governorship would alternate between the two sections of the state. As the August election drew near, only Watts and Shorter remained.[40]

Thomas Watts spent at least part of the summer recruiting men from Butler and surrounding counties for service in the 17th Alabama Infantry, a regiment he would soon lead as its colonel. Even though he had lived in Montgomery since 1848, he spent most of his early life in Butler County. He served three terms as a legislator from Butler County in the 1840s and later, after moving his law practice and residence to Montgomery, represented Montgomery County as well. A staunch Whig, Watts frequently clashed with members of the Democratic Party and strongly opposed the Yanceyite doctrine of secession. Yet, his belief that Southern rights were safer inside the Union than out came to an end with Lincoln's election. "Why delude ourselves with the futile hope of obtaining new securities . . . within the present Union," he wrote shortly after the election.[41] Watts was a delegate to the secession convention, where he opposed the cooperationists and played a key role in the passage of the ordinance of secession. Shorter, in the meantime, served in the Confederate Congress where he played an important role in drafting the Confederate Constitution.

As the campaign for governor got under way in late spring, many of the state's political leaders realized that politics as usual threatened to reopen old wounds. Immediate secessionists and cooperationists had clashed at the secession convention just a few months prior. Some believed that a political bloodbath between old party rivals—especially at a time when thousands of Alabamians were preparing for war—would be detrimental to the fragile but strengthening unity that existed throughout much of the state. The *Montgomery Weekly Advertiser* urged its readers to shun partisanship and avoid any activity that might be regarded by the Northern press as a sign of weakness or vacillation: "Let us do nothing or say nothing which can lead our enemies to suppose we have a party in our midst . . . which could in any event be induced to consent to a reconstruction of the Old Union on any terms whatever."[42]

Despite the *Advertiser*'s warning, the press and the citizenry generally crystallized along old party lines. Both candidates enjoyed a substantial home base of support. Along with members of the Eufaula Regency, hundreds of prominent citizens from Barbour and surrounding counties endorsed Shorter, as did the newspaper that had served as the beacon for the Democratic Party in the area, the *Spirit of the South*. Watts, on the other hand, found strong support in his home county of Butler, where he expressed thanks "to those who have known me from my boyhood, and who on many occasions have entrusted me with their dearest interests." Neither candidate officially campaigned, believing that doing so might be seen as undermining the war effort. Watts went so far as to temporarily withdraw from the race: "As I hope and surely trust the slumbering embers of party may never again be rekindled . . . I am unwilling to do anything which may have a tendency to elicit the recollection of bygone party conflicts."[43]

Malcolm McMillian notes that the August 8 election returns "typified most of the elections held in Alabama since the rise of the party system in Andrew Jackson's day."[44] By a vote of 37,849 to 28,121, Shorter carried the state in the same way that his Democratic predecessors had—by winning large majorities in northern Alabama and in the southeastern counties near the Chattahoochee River. Watts won most of the Black Belt counties and traditional Whig strongholds in southcentral and southwestern Alabama. One could certainly argue that piney woods counties simply supported their fa-

TABLE 5.4. 1861 gubernatorial election

	Shorter (Democrat)	Watts (Former Whig)
Barbour	1,524 (80.3%)	373 (19.7%)
Butler	369 (22%)	1,311 (78%)
Coffee	778 (90.6%)	81 (9.4%)
Conecuh	194 (22.4%)	671 (77.6%)
Covington	309 (45.8%)	365 (55.2%)
Dale	1,225 (96.1%)	51 (3.9%)
Henry	1,552 (96.9%)	49 (3.1%)
Pike	1,380 (60.7%)	893 (39.3%)
Total	7,331 (65.8%)	3,794 (34.1%)

Source: Michael J. Dubin, *United States Gubernatorial Elections, 1861–1911: The Official Results by State and County* (Jefferson, NC: McFarland and Company, 2010).

vorite sons, but it is equally compelling to note that old party alliances largely carried the day for both candidates in the region as well. Shorter won resoundingly in the Democratic strongholds of Barbour, Coffee, Dale, Henry, and Pike, while Watts carried his home county of Butler along with Conecuh and Covington, traditional Whig territory (see Table 5.4). Although Watts lost the election, his supporters predicted that he would occupy the governor's mansion soon enough. "He will be elected Governor or Senator before many years," wrote Butler County representative Walter Crenshaw to his son Edward, then serving in Watts's 17th Alabama, "unless the Yankees kill him which it is hoped they will not succeed in doing."[45]

When Shorter took office in January 1862, he faced an impending Federal invasion of north Alabama and the growing threat of a Union naval attack on the port city of Mobile. Like his predecessor he also was worried that Confederate authorities would abandon Pensacola and give the Union a formidable staging area from which to launch raids into the southern part of the state. Writing to Secretary of War Judah P. Benjamin, the governor pointed to the importance of the port city to both the state and the Confederacy and "opposed the abandonment of Pensacola so long as there was the slightest hope of holding it."[46]

Gen. Braxton Bragg, commander of the Confederate Department of Alabama and West Florida, had at that time more than eight thousand men at Pensacola, including two full regiments of Alabamians, and another nine thousand at Mobile, nearly all of whom were in-state volunteers. The majority of companies raised in piney woods counties during the spring, summer, and fall of 1861 served either with the Army of Pensacola or the Army of Mobile. By the end of 1861, many of them were within a few months of seeing their twelve-month enlistments expire. Some had no intention of reenlisting. Writing to his wife from Pensacola, Lt. Hubert Dent of Eufaula's Company B, 1st Alabama Infantry, noted that "the freshness and first excitement of the war has worn off and men, many of them at least, are tired of the service. Many troops will be entitled to their discharges in the next six months and it will not be easy to supply their places unless the men reenlist."[47]

While some men had no intention of reenlisting, many were simply tired of the inactivity. Despite a handful of minor engagements, including a small attack on Union-held Fort Pickens in early November, the vast majority of Confederates serving on the Gulf Coast expressed frustration that their service had amounted to little more than drills, dress parades, picket duty, and erecting breastworks. Most of them had never fired a shot in battle. One study of the soldiers who fought at the Battle of Shiloh contends that recruits during the war's first year had no intentions of becoming permanent, professional soldiers; they enlisted to fight as soon as possible, defeat the Yankee invaders, and return to their homes. As historians Joseph Frank and George Reaves observe, "How was it that after all these months, after the mobilization of such enormous armies of volunteers, they had not yet been used?"[48] Writing to his sister from Fort Gaines, Pvt. Tom Beck sarcastically remarked that his nine-year-old nephew, George Moxley, "must come to the ware and learn to shoot yankees, though I am afraid we will never have to shoot them heare."[49] There were so many false alarms associated with Union naval activities and erroneous rumors of impending attacks on Fort Pickens that many of the men simply began to ignore them. "Bragg has an idea that the fight is going to come off," Dent observed, but "it makes very little impression on me because I have heard it so often."[50] Even Secretary of War Judah P. Benjamin acknowledged the "self-sacrificing spirit displayed by [Bragg] and the gallant spirits that are now chafing in hateful inaction on the sands of Pensacola Harbor."[51] Hundreds of piney woods soldiers no doubt felt that their time and energy were being wasted on picket duty and drills. They had volunteered to kill Yankees and win the war, yet their role as soldiers had so far been meaningless.

In a circular issued in late November, Bragg encouraged the men to reenlist immediately, promised generous furloughs to those who did so before their current enlistments expired, and vowed to employ the troops in more active roles as soon as practicable. Three weeks later, Bragg reported dismal results in his enrollment efforts. He now tried to stimulate reenlistments by offering furloughs to *all* of the men. Bragg believed that the ultimate cure for his enlistment woes was to get the men involved in combat. If the veterans were assured that they would soon face the enemy, "I am satisfied it would have a happy effect in causing many to re-enlist 'for the war.' Without such assurance and a short furlough to visit their homes but few can be secured. It would be a great misfortune to lose them, for they are the best troops I have ever known."[52]

In December, the Confederate Congress offered bounties and furloughs to every man who reenlisted, and moreover allowed the troops to reorganize their companies and elect their own officers. While Bragg vehemently opposed this last provision—believing that it would seriously undermine combat effectiveness and lead to unnecessary confusion—his earlier predictions of massive departures never materialized. "From what I can see and learn," he wrote in mid-January, "there seems to be a prospect of reaction taking place, and our success may yet be greater than anticipated when I last wrote."[53] Hubert Dent was one of many who took advantage of the opportunity to secure what he hoped would be a better command with higher rank. He joined with Texan Felix Robertson to create an artillery battery made up of soldiers from south Alabama and Florida. "The temptation of going in with Robertson with his light artillery was so great that I have concluded to go in with him," he informed his wife. "I am busy trying to raise the company or assisting to do it."[54]

Unfortunately for the Confederacy, but luckily for the troops serving along the Gulf Coast hoping for more active duty, Union victories in February 1862 at Mill Springs in eastern Kentucky and Forts Henry and Donelson near the Tennessee-Kentucky border forced the Confederates to abandon the Bluegrass State, retreat from Nashville, and give up much of middle and western Tennessee. On February 28, Bragg withdrew ten thousand men from Pensacola and Mobile and headed north to Corinth, Mississippi, to rendezvous with Confederate troops under Gen. Albert Sidney Johnston and Gen. P. G. T. Beauregard. Five weeks later forty-four thousand Confederates converged on Federal forces under Gen. Ulysses S. Grant in Tennessee about fifteen miles northeast of Corinth, Mississippi, near a small country church named Shiloh.

The Battle of Shiloh provided the first real taste of combat for most of the companies raised in piney woods counties during the first year of the war.[55] Brig. Gen Adley Gladden's brigade included five companies from the region, two in the 22nd Alabama Infantry and three in the 25th Alabama Infantry. Eight companies from the 17th and 18th Alabama Infantry regiments, of Brig. Gen. John K. Jackson's brigade, included soldiers from Butler, Coffee, Covington, and Pike counties. On March 10, while most of the men had already disembarked at Corinth, Beauregard sent Gladden's brigade a few miles north to intercept a detachment of Union troops rumored to be heading toward Bethel Station, Tennessee. Drenching rains and ankle-deep mud made life miserable for several of the regiments who arrived without tents or cooking supplies. One of those regiments, Col. Thomas H. Watts's 17th Alabama, bivouacked for nearly two days before finally receiving their supplies.

After rumors of Federal troop movements proved false, Beauregard sent for Gladden's brigade to return immediately to the main body. Watts's exhausted regiment refused to budge, a decision that led to his arrest and the arrest of several of his officers. As one soldier later recalled, "here they were in chilling rains and deep mud without shelters of any kind, separated for a time from their baggage [and] cooking utensils. It was in this state of distress that Colonel Watts and the officers of the regiment refused obedience to orders . . . and were put under arrest."[56] According to Capt. Edward Crenshaw, Watts protested "that his men had been without their tents and cooking utensils for several days in consequence of which more than half the regiment were then sick and that they had just received the cooking utensils and had commenced to cook their rations."[57] Within days, the arrested Watts learned that he had been appointed by Confederate President Jefferson Davis to the post of Attorney General. Watts left immediately for Richmond, his officers were restored to their units after issuing a formal apology, and the regiment was reassigned to Gen. John K. Jackson's brigade.[58]

With Ulysses S. Grant's Army of the Tennessee encamped and waiting for reinforcements at Pittsburg Landing, Beauregard and Johnston saw an opportunity to attack Grant before Maj. Gen. Don Carlos Buell's Army of the Ohio arrived. Although incessant rains delayed the attack by two days, on the morning of April 6 the Confederates were ready to strike. At daybreak Maj. Gen. William J. Hardee's corps slammed into the Federal left flank. Gladden's brigade and Brig. Gen. James R. Chalmers's troops painstakingly advanced through rough terrain to attack the extreme left of the Union line. Gladden's Alabamians, along with the 1st Louisiana Infantry, poured volley after volley into the Blue line, forcing them to retreat across Spain Field and into the woods on the opposite side. There they hastily regrouped and waited for the Rebels to appear (see Figure 5.2).

Just to the right of the reformed line, two Federal batteries unlimbered and opened up with both canister and solid shot, every gun firing as rapidly as possible across the field now almost totally obscured by smoke. According to one soldier, "the bullets passing through the trees above us cut the half grown leaves which fell on us in a continuing shower." As the Confederates emerged from the woods, they ran headlong into a storm of small arms and artillery fire. When Gladden rode ahead to get a better look and survey the situation, a blast of artillery knocked the general from his horse, nearly ripping off his left arm and rendering him mortally wounded.[59]

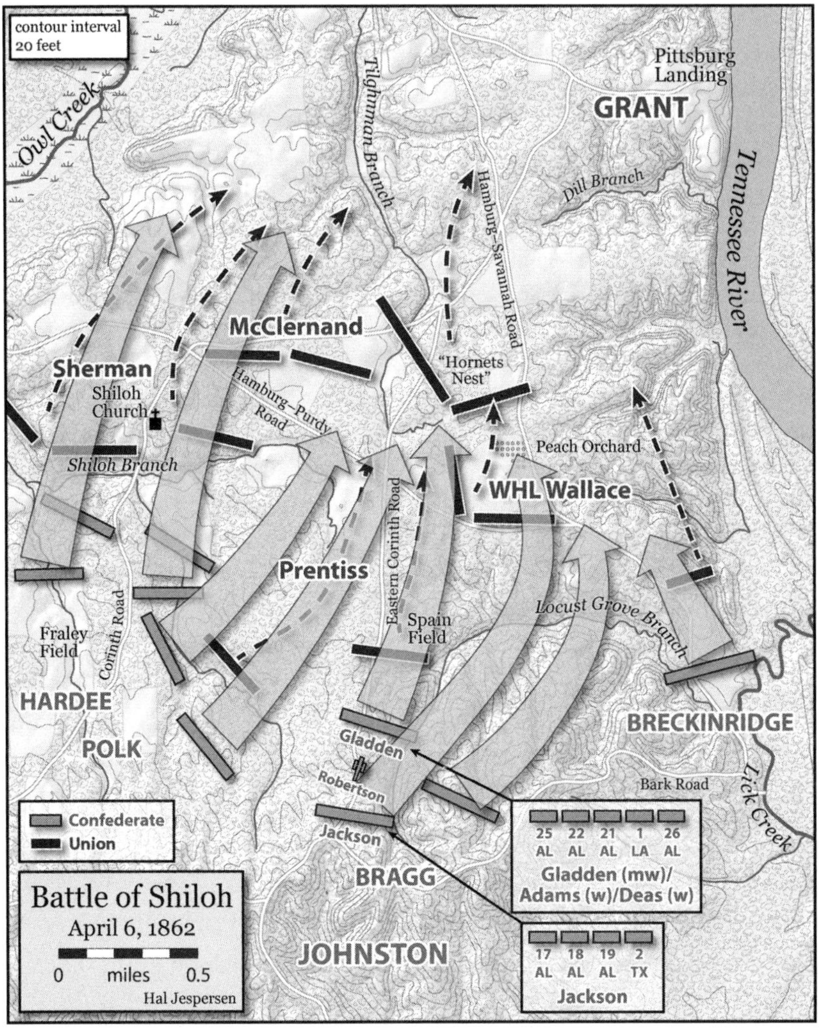

5.2. Battle of Shiloh, April 6, 1862

The artillery and small arms fire devastated Gladden's advancing columns (now commanded by Col. Daniel W. Adams) and forced a temporary Confederate retreat back across the field. Adams quickly rallied his men and led a second charge across Spain Field, sending shockwaves up and down what was left of the Federal left flank. Hundreds of Confederates re-crossed the field, still partially obscured by the smoke, and emerged right in front of the Federal position with fixed bayonets, yelling at the top of their lungs. Union Capt. Andrew Hickenlooper later recalled that hearing the high-pitched shrieks of the Rebel yell for the first time "caused an involuntary thrill of terror to pass like an electric shock through even the bravest hearts."[60] Federal batteries tried desperately to quell the oncoming attack by spraying the field with double canister shot. Yet the massive shotgun-like blasts caused only temporary pauses to the unrelenting Confederate assault.

At about the same time, Capt. Felix Robertson and Lieut. Hubert Dent of Eufaula moved their battery into position to support the Confederate advance. Their primary objective was to silence Federal artillery on the opposite side of the field. What happened next was nothing short of a nightmare for Union artillerists. As they frantically attempted to limber their cannons, "there comes a crashing volley, that sweeps our front as with a scythe. . . . Every horse in our left section goes down in one . . . mass of struggling horses, wounded men and defenseless guns. The supports break and give way in wild dismay."[61] Col. Adams later reported that Robertson's artillery "returned the enemy's fire with such promptness and great effect, that it drove them from their guns and caused them to abandon their battery."[62] The Federals fell back and regrouped in an area of the battlefield that came to be known as the Hornet's Nest.

In the meantime, the 17th and 18th Alabama of Jackson's brigade were in a firefight with several Illinois regiments from Brig. Gen. William H. Wallace's division just east of the Hamburg-Savannah Road. At one point, the Alabamians came under a deadly crossfire from three different directions, taking heavy casualties. Isaac Taylor Tichenor, the 17th Alabama's "fighting chaplain," walked up and down the line encouraging the men to stand fast: "I called upon them to stand there, and die, if need be, for their country."[63] For two hours, the fighting continued until the Confederates launched an attack that finally broke the Union line. For the rest of the afternoon, the Rebel army drove the Federals back toward the river, capturing thousands of prisoners in the process. "The officers . . . and men of the regiment conducted themselves throughout the several engagements with much gallantry and spirit," Col. Eli Shorter of the 18th Alabama later reported.[64] As the daylight began to fade, Jackson's Alabamians launched one last attack against fortified Federal positions along a ridge less than a half mile west of the Tennessee River. The attempt failed.[65]

The next morning, Grant's reinforced army launched a multipronged counterattack over the same ground they had abandoned the day before. Due to the chaos from the previous day's fighting, Confederate regiments were scattered all over the place. The 17th Alabama had moved back all the way to their original staging area more than a mile and half from Pittsburg Landing. The 18th Alabama was en route to Corinth with one thousand five hundred Union prisoners under guard. Gladden's bloodied command, which had passed from Gladden to Adams to Lt. Col. Zachariah Deas, contained only "fragments of regiments, numbering together less than 500" men.[66] This unit was involved in the day-long fighting that occurred along the Hamburg-Purdy Road slightly northeast of Shiloh Church. Deas had two horses shot from underneath him and suffered wounds severe enough that by mid-afternoon he was unable to walk. Still, after the battle, he had nothing but praise for his shattered brigade: "The indomitable courage and perseverance of the officers and men of this brigade; the willingness and gallantry with which they advanced to the attack when called upon, after having endured almost superhuman fatigues in the desperate and long-continued struggles of Sunday and Monday, are deserving of the highest encomiums."[67] In two days of fighting, Gladden's brigade suffered more than seven hundred casualties and Jackson's brigade lost more than four hundred killed or wounded.[68]

By late afternoon, all of the brigades in Bragg's division were slogging down the muddy roads leading away from the battlefield toward Corinth. As the rain pummeled the retreating masses, one of Bragg's men took shelter under a tree, "but was so exhausted that I actually fell asleep in that position. . . . When I awoke I was lying in water."[69] As night fell, the Confederates must have wondered how the elation of the previous day's victory had turned so quickly into the misery of defeat. Yet, by all accounts, soldiers from the piney woods fought gallantly. Months of inaction along the Gulf Coast gave way to two furious days of bloodletting at Shiloh. The dead and wounded would soon be replaced by new volunteers as the region continued to support the Confederate war effort.

For decades, historians have debated the motivations of the soldiers who fought in the Civil War. With only a handful of sources from piney woods soldiers, it is difficult to determine with certainty what motivated the men at Shiloh, but there are clues. Joseph Frank and George Reaves argue that duty and patriotism were the primary motivators for the men who fought at Shiloh, while Gerald Linderman maintains that soldiers were driven primarily by courage. Both duty and courage were motivating factors for piney woods soldiers at Shiloh. Certainly, Isaac Taylor Tichenor appealed to the troops' sense of duty when he rallied the 17th Alabama. Of course, it could just as easily have been Tichenor's courage in walking up and down the line, himself wounded and bleeding, waving his hat in the air to inspire the men to continue the fight. It is likely that both played a role in the regiment's actions that day. "The effect was evident," Tichenor noted, as "every man stood to his post—every eye flashed and every heart beat high with desperate resolve to conquer or die."[70]

What is certain is that the men in Bragg's army were itching for a fight, and many of them believed that it would take just one desperate, bloody battle to end the war. According to Frank and Reaves, "they sought battle so that they could get it over with in one fell swoop. Then having at last decided the issue, the soldiers would return home heroes. They had enlisted for a great cause; they wanted to be direct principals in deciding its outcome."[71] Duty and bravery were the keys to getting back home for the piney woods soldiers who crossed Spain Field, drove the Federals through the woods just east of the Hamburg-Savannah Road, and attacked the Union left near the Hornet's Nest.

For the people of the region, the first year of the war began with the recruitment of hundreds of young, single men. Companies raised in the area trained in a handful of places, from Montgomery and Auburn to Mobile and Pensacola. Soldiers stationed along the Gulf Coast spent month after month in grueling inactivity, plagued with boredom, and visited all too often by disease and death. Back home, the women formed ladies' aid societies or worked in small informal groups to provide adequate clothing for the poorer soldiers from their communities. On the political front, the region largely supported Democrat John Gill Shorter as the state's next governor while Thomas H. Watts managed to win solid majorities in several former Whig counties. In April 1862, the soldiers finally got their baptism by fire at the Battle of Shiloh. The troops fought well on the first day only to be forced into retreat the very next day. Meanwhile, the Confederate government in Richmond was about to adopt a policy that would change the very nature of recruitment and the way in which the South fought the rest of the war.

6

"I Have No One to Assist Mee on Earth"

The Piney Woods War, 1862

On June 18, 1862, thirty-eight-year-old Sarah Driggers of Coffee County wrote to Governor John Gill Shorter pleading for help. "With an acheing hart and trembling hand," she explained, "I attempt to address you with a few lins in humble recuest to you for your helpe and your assistence most noble sir as I am left here alone in this world without husban or child." At the time of the letter, her husband, Pvt. Charles Driggers, was within four days of serving the first year of a three-year enlistment with Company A, 18th Alabama Infantry. Such a plea would have been unimaginable a mere two years earlier. Before the war, Charles and Sarah, along with their fifteen-year-old son, Benjamin, worked a small thirty-five-acre farm just outside of Elba. In 1860, with the help of a sturdy horse and matching pair of oxen, the Driggers' family produced four bales of cotton, seventy-five bushels of sweet potatoes, and one hundred bushels of corn. The family's three milk cows produced enough milk to make one hundred pounds of butter, while the twenty hogs rooting around in the lot next to their home and in the woods nearby provided a hundred dollars' worth of meat for household consumption with plenty left over for market.

The condition of the Driggers farm was drastically different by 1862. Sarah spent the summer alone and destitute. Charles was still in the army. Benjamin had run off and joined the 33rd Alabama Infantry, without his mother's permission. With no male laborers, the farm suffered, production stalled, and the once-thriving homestead declined rapidly. Like many of her neighbors, Sarah found herself on the county's list of indigent soldiers' families—though she must have realized that the state's beneficence was sorely insufficient. Inflation already was on the rise. Under these circumstances Sarah pleaded with the governor to "have mercy and compashion on a pore disconsolate mother and have my poor son sent home most noble sire I am a pore woman I have no one to assist mee on earth and my son is not 17 years of age till the first day of September next being born in the year 1845." Even though the governor's office forwarded the letter to the secretary of war, the evidence suggests that Benjamin remained in the Confederate army until the end of the war.[1] Aside from a handful of furloughs, Charles stayed with the 18th Alabama, where he was promoted to the rank of sergeant in 1864. He appears to have returned home for good in March 1865.

A few miles north of the Driggers farm, Zachariah and Christine Blackman's circumstances were somewhat different. Their eight hundred–acre farm, of which only sixty was improved, was worth over $2,500. They owned no slaves but employed a farm laborer named John Betterton. It is possible that Betterton joined the army in 1861 but the evidence is too ambiguous to determine with certainty. As for Zachariah, he became one of many to be drafted into the army under the Confederacy's 1862 conscription act.[2] This chapter explores the war in the piney woods from Confederate conscription to the end of 1862. The draft changed the dynamic on the home front, especially for families who owned no slaves and found themselves without enough manpower to keep their farms producing. Consequently, women began looking to the state government for help. Since they had sent their sons, husbands, brothers, and fathers to fight, the least the government could do would be to provide financial assistance to poor families and release those men from military service who were absolutely essential to their communities. Alabama's governor responded, taking measures to expand grain supplies, outlaw grain distillation (except for medical purposes), increase the salt supply, and provide direct aid to the indigent families of Confederate soldiers. It is remarkable that the piney woods continued to produce recruits, considering that so many men had already volunteered for Confederate service. For the men left at home, some joined out of devotion to the cause, others signed up out of obligation to brothers or friends already in Confederate service (including boys initially too young to volunteer who came of age later in the war), many were caught up by the new conscription policy, a few were legitimately exempted from the service, and some claimed exemption status simply to avoid going to war.

By 1862, it was clear that the Confederate policy of manning its armies solely with volunteers was not working. Most of the men serving out twelve-month enlistments would soon be eligible to return home. Back in December, the Confederate Congress tried to promote reenlistments by granting generous furloughs, allotting a $50 bounty, and providing opportunities for soldiers to reorganize their units and reelect new officers. Confederate commanders such as Braxton Bragg and Robert E. Lee opposed this strategy, arguing that it would weaken the army at precisely the time that the Federals were threatening major portions of the South. The effort ultimately fell far short of expectations.

For his part, Lee supported a conscription policy that placed Richmond firmly in control of enrollment efforts and guaranteed an adequate fighting force for the duration of the war. In this way, the Davis administration could bypass the states and draft men directly into Confederate service. Ironically, this position was totally at odds with the principles for which many Southerners claimed they were fighting, namely the idea that centralized power should be limited with sovereignty retained primarily by the states. But for the majority of Confederate politicians, pragmatism took precedence over principle when it came to filling the ranks. As Senator Louis Wigfall of Texas contended, "the enemy are in some portions of every state of the Confederacy. Virginia is enveloped by them. We need a large army. No man has any individual rights which come into conflict with the welfare of the country."[3]

Supported by Lee and other commanders, Jefferson Davis presented his case to the legislature in March 1862. The overly complex volunteer system then in place, he argued, would never produce the kind of numbers that the Confederacy needed to win the war. As historian Albert Burton Moore has observed, Davis "had early become an exponent of a simple and uniform military system with a centralized control, and he urged it with fervor upon Congress from the beginning of 1862."[4] Davis also intended to use conscription as a means to enlist thousands of men who were less than enthusiastic about the war. "It is necessary that in a great war like that in which we are now engaged," he reasoned, "all persons of intermediate age not legally exempt for good cause should pay their debt of military service to the country, that the burdens should not fall exclusively on the most ardent and patriotic."[5]

In April, the Confederate legislature passed overwhelmingly the first of three conscription laws designed to provide a steady supply of troops for Southern armies. Officially known as An Act to Further Provide for the Public Defence, the first enrollment act or conscript act stipulated that every able-bodied white male between the ages of eighteen and thirty-five was subject to military service. Those already in the army on short-term enlistments were required to serve an additional two years; the furlough and bounty program adopted four months earlier remained in place for their benefit. The law still allowed draftees to hire substitutes, but only from the pool of men not subject to conscription or specifically prohibited by statute. It also continued to provide bounties and a thirty-day grace period for men to volunteer on their own, thus allowing men to avoid the stigma of being drafted.

Five days later, Congress approved a supplementary bill exempting from the draft certain professional and industrial laborers. The legislature believed that some jobs were vital to the overall war effort and recognized that while many of these men would otherwise be subject to conscription, some had little means by which to secure a substitute. The provision included exemptions for Confederate and state officials, mail carriers, telegraph operators, railroad workers, miners, college presidents and professors, nurses and attendants, ministers, teachers, pharmacists, and "superintendents and operatives in wool and cotton factories." For the moment, Congress declined to exempt overseers, an issue they would revisit soon enough.[6]

In Alabama, Governor Shorter initially opposed the new law, believing that such a move violated the spirit of the Confederate cause and threatened to undermine morale on the home front. "If we are to depend upon [conscription] to maintain the liberty of the South," he complained, "I should almost despair of our ultimate triumph."[7] Within weeks of the law's passage, Shorter implored Richmond to postpone implementation in northern Alabama, the state's breadbasket, in order to give poor and yeoman farmers enough time to harvest their crops. Having received numerous letters from local citizens, the governor was well aware that the manpower shortage in many neighborhoods threatened to further destabilize whole communities. In some places, wives, sisters, and mothers were "left to plow and sow and reap and mow on the principle of 'root hog or die.'"[8]

Although the Davis administration denied Shorter's request, once the law was implemented, the governor gave it his full support, despite whatever personal reservations he might have had. Shorter nonetheless anticipated problems in the hill counties of northern Alabama, where support for the Confederacy was unenthusiastic and pockets of Unionism flourished. Within months, armed resistance broke out in Randolph and several other counties as hundreds of vigilantes reportedly hid out in the woods to escape the enrollment officers. In some neighborhoods, Confederate officials were in constant danger of being attacked. An armed mob stormed the Randolph County jail, for example, and freed an unspecified number of deserters and draft evaders. Shorter advised Secretary of War George Wythe Randolph—who apparently wanted to avoid any bloodshed and sought out the governor's advice—to meet resistance with force. "Entertaining . . . the firmest conviction as to the policy and necessity of a prompt, rigid, and equal execution of the act in every part of the State, I am of opinion that . . . a cavalry force should at once be ordered out sufficient to put down resistance and arrest the ringleaders. This I have but little doubt could be effected without bloodshed, but the law should be enforced at every hazard."[9]

While the governor focused his attention on conscription problems in north Alabama, piney woods residents experienced difficulties of their own adjusting to the new law. Before the law's enactment, families large enough, wealthy enough, or able to retain enough able-bodied relatives to keep their farms going could afford to send one or more of their men off to war. Historian Martin Crawford observes that in Appalachian North Carolina's majority white communities, "informal support systems may have offset the effects of absentee labor. Farm households who could rely on familial or neighborly assistance . . . could more easily adapt to wartime demands, although over time such compensation would have been insufficient to sustain economic activity at prewar levels."[10] This seems to have been true in the piney woods as well. Pike County resident James Hill, for instance, was better off than many of his China Grove neighbors. When his two oldest sons, Samuel and Benjamin, joined Dowdell's Volunteers, 37th Alabama Infantry, Hill relied upon his own labor, his fifty-year-old male slave, and his young teenaged son Charles to work the farm.[11]

The Riley boys, on the other hand, were members of an extensive kinship network of lower- and middle-class farming families in Dale County. Brothers Edward, George, Gillum, and John, along with their cousins Samuel and Daniel, joined the Henry Pioneers, 15th Alabama Infantry, in August 1862. At least three other close relatives fought with the Dale County Greys, 33rd Alabama Infantry. Although several of them left wives and young children behind, they relied upon the Riley men who were either too young or too old for the army to take care of their families while they served. Unfortunately for the family's patriarchs, they shouldered a much heavier burden than they could have ever imagined, as five of their sons soon died from disease, several others were captured in battle, and two suffered debilitating wounds.[12]

The Hill and Riley families are just two examples of the hundreds of kinship networks, both extensive and limited, that allowed many piney woods residents to support the war effort while maintaining some semblance of economic security. To be sure, poor families with limited resources lived on the edge of economic ruin even during the best of times, so it goes without saying that these families were less than enthusiastic about giving up their most precious human resources to the Confederacy. The evidence suggests that the Conscription Act changed the dynamic that existed during the first year of the war and forced many of the region's communities to try and adjust to the economic challenges they faced. The most significant effect, especially in poorer communities and neighborhoods in the southernmost counties, was that hundreds of men, previously counted upon to deliver various goods and services or perform certain tasks, were now subject to the draft. In addition, the conscription of physicians, millers, and blacksmiths, men already in short supply, threatened to undermine economic stability further in neighborhoods strained by the loss of so much manpower. Many citizens accordingly wrote to Montgomery and Richmond, requesting that these men either not be drafted or receive special exemption from the service. As historian Stephanie McCurry notes: "from the very moment that officials began to make demands on the population for the manpower and materiel with which to wage war, requests for relief and revision of government policy poured into the offices of state governors and the various Confederate secretaries of war."[13]

Within weeks of the law's passage, for instance, fifty-eight women from Pike County sent a petition to Governor Shorter imploring him to "exonerate Dr. James Reynold from servise in the Confederate army under the late law now in forse as a Conscriptive soldier as all of the Phisicians are gon and is going which will leave our familys Destitute of Medical ade and hope you will Release him from going to war."[14] Residents of nearby Orion similarly asked the governor to "release Dr. B. F. Adams – a conscript, who is now in camp at Camp Wood Notusulga, to us." The petitioners were quick to inform the governor that their section of the county was "thickly populated especially with women and children. Our brave men are nearly all in the army, but their poor families are here without any medical aid."[15] In like manner, more than 150 residents from Butler and Covington counties petitioned both the governor and the secretary of war for the return of Dr. John Balden, "as our section of [the] country is left without any medical Physician within any reasonable distance and consequently great suffering there by."[16]

Physicians were not the only citizens whose absence adversely affected small communities. Alvin May and F. M. Walker were the proprietors of a blacksmith and carriage shop in Elba, Coffee County. Sheriff James T. Moody wrote the governor on behalf of the citizens of the town and surrounding communities, inquiring as to the status of the two men, whether or not they were liable to conscription and, if so, how the town might be able to hold on to them. "The farmers and citizens generally around here are anxious for them to stay at home," he noted. "The fact is, we don't know what we will do if they are taken. The farmers cant get along with their farms unless their plows & wagons are kept up."[17] In Henry County, twenty-six-year-old William C. Capps, another blacksmith and carriage maker from the Woodville community, signed up with the 3rd Alabama Infantry to avoid being conscripted. State Senator William H. Wood, who represented Dale and Henry counties, joined nearly two dozen citizens petitioning the governor for Capps's release. He is a "blacksmith and mechanic located where such workmen is much wanted," they argued, "and if taken away will cause much disadvantage to the Farmers of his vicinity in cultivating there Farms."[18]

In Butler County, seventeen poor and middle-class soldiers' wives petitioned the governor for the relief of William H. Capps, a local farmer who had spent considerable time and energy helping the families in his community. Sally McLean, the wealthiest and perhaps most educated of the group, penned the letter to Governor Shorter: "We the undersign petitioners wives of soldiers now in the service of [the] Confederate states are in a destitute condition with familys of little children to support." She made it clear that Capps's assistance was a godsend: "for the last eight months he has done every thing that a man of his circumstances could of done . . . and is ready and willing at all times to assist us." Stephanie McCurry has suggested that women such as these grew increasingly bold as the war progressed, exercising their political power as "soldier's wives" in letters and petitions to government officials. Unfortunately for Sally McLean, Nancy Clancey, Martha Amos, Sarah Combs, and seventeen other women, the governor refused to intervene on their behalf.[19]

Another example of piney woods citizens petitioning the government for the release or exemption of certain individuals from conscription occurred in Coffee County. About 1860, a wealthy twenty-nine-year-old Polish immigrant and merchant named Hyman Yaretzky moved to Elba with his younger brother, Julius, and two business associates, Elias Fitzkosky and Morris Alkus. The elder Yaretzky opened a general store and hired his brother and two partners to help run the business. By the fall of 1862, Alkus was fighting with the Little George Matthews Friends, later Company K, 25th Alabama Infantry, while Julius Yaretzky served in Company A of the 33rd Alabama. Hyman Yaretzky continued to sell much-needed goods at reasonable prices in a community already feeling the pinch of inflation not to mention the hardships caused by the absence of so many men fighting in Confederate armies.

When the conscription act made Yaretzky eligible for the draft and indirectly threatened to close his store, Coffee County's enrolling officer, H. W. Henry, advised several prominent citizens to petition Montgomery on Yaretzky's behalf. A local lawyer named William D. Roberts wrote to the governor, requesting that Yaretzky receive an exemption on the grounds that he "is the only man that is doing any business of any consequence in this county and I must say that he has been as charitable to the poor class as any man. . . . He furnishes the people of this county such articles as they need cheaper than they can buy the same in any market." Indeed, Yaretzky often sold spools of sewing thread, needles, cloth, and other items in high demand to poor citizens at or below cost. "If Mr. Yaretzky leaves," Roberts added, "then his business will close greatly to the misery and probably I might say to the distress of a large number of good citizens and mostly the soldiers families who are depending on him." The governor agreed, consulted Confederate authorities in Richmond, and secured Yaretzky's exemption.[20]

In other cases, families were confused about the law and how conscription worked. Some were more than a little disappointed when they discovered that soldiers whose age exceeded the maximum age limit would not be automatically discharged from the service. Men from Henry, Dale, and Barbour counties serving with the 25th Georgia in Savannah, for example, were frustrated to learn that the older soldiers would not be allowed to return home. Writing on their behalf, Private Joel D. Holt, a forty-seven-year-old farmer from the Green Mill community in Henry County, asked Governor Shorter to explain the law to him and his friends and to intervene if possible. "If I under stand it corectley all the men over thirty five and under eighteen yars was clare of the cirvice on the 16th, wish has past and no one has bin made to lett us go home. . . . Most of the old men in captans Holmes company from Alabama are pore men and has left sufering famaleys and sum of them sick and we are not aloud to go home and see them." Holt's letter demonstrates the confusion surrounding the law's implementation, and illustrates the mounting problems that poorer families faced back home. Indeed, the letter reveals the soldiers' expectations when it came to the state's responsibility to their families: "We apele to you for protection in our trubels about our sick & sufering famleys."[21]

Other men petitioned the governor and the secretary of war on their own behalf. In Dale County's Skipperville community, thirty-two-year-old conscript John Munn informed the governor that he was physically unable to fight in the army and suggested that his skill as a blacksmith would be more helpful to the cause than his service in the military. "I live in a poor settlement," he argued, "and thare is not anough a men left here to take Sebastopal [Sevastopol] if thay were to try and thare is so many soldiers familes to attend to and thare is several of them that looks to me for thair blacksmith work without wich they could not till thair little farms." Munn hoped to receive an exemption but also expressed a desire to do whatever was necessary "for the independance of our beloved South." In the end, he left his wife and three young children behind, joined the 15th Alabama Infantry, and went on to fight in some of the bloodiest battles of the war including Gettysburg, Chickamauga, and Cold Harbor.[22]

The conscription act presented unique challenges for the men who had already served out their twelve-month enlistments and decided not to reenlist. Some of them believed that they had fulfilled their duty to the Confederacy. Twenty-two-year-old Angus Stewart, for example, was among the first to join the Clayton Guards in early 1861. He left the service a year later when his temporary enlistment expired. Stewart then was elected as a lieutenant in the local militia but did not receive his commission until *after* he had reenlisted in the Confederate army in Capt. R. F. Kolb's battery, Hilliard's Legion, a decision undertaken "more to avoid enrollment than from the impulse of feeling. When I returned home," he declared to the governor in August 1862, "I did not intend on going into the service again for if I had I could verry easily have received a Lieutenancy in Captain Hargrove's Company 39th Ala Regt." His letter reveals a man who felt all but betrayed by both the governor and the Confederacy. In his view, he had served in the army, was duly elected as an officer in the state militia, and was now being pressed back into Confederate service against his will. "Believing then that I was exempt by your protection . . . I want to know now of you whether it is in your power or not to release me. If it is I demand it and appeal to you for it and if done I will return the bounty and all the funds I have drew from the government." In response, the governor scribbled a note to his clerk on the bottom of the letter that read, "he is a volunteer and therefore I can't relieve him." Like it or not, Angus Stewart was stuck in the army.[23]

Of all of the examples mentioned above, only one man, Hyman Yaretzky, ultimately received an exemption from conscription prior to the law's revision in October 1862. The rest joined new or existing companies, most likely to avoid being drafted into units not of their own choosing. Historian Kenneth Noe labels these soldiers "later enlisters" to distinguish them from the men who made up the initial wave of volunteers during the first year of the war. Noe describes several reasons for these later enlisters, but as none of the men presented here left behind diaries or letters, outside of their correspondence with the governor, it is difficult to ascribe any particular motivation other than avoiding conscription for their enlistment in the army. Tracking their lives through the end of the war can also be frustrating. Yet by all indications men such as Joel Holt (the only known substitute in the group), William Capps, and John Munn served out their terms of enlistment with as much commitment as any soldier. Noe explains that later enlisters "largely proved to be willing soldiers, driven to defend their kin, homes, and property in an acceptably manly fashion not so unlike their comrades of the class of 1861."[24]

Nevertheless, the evidence demonstrates that piney woods communities, already strained by the loss of so many men to the army in 1861, risked even greater economic difficulties as conscription drained more manpower from the region. Poor families struggling to make ends meet wrote letters (if they were literate), signed petitions, or expressed their concerns indirectly through local sheriffs, judges, or wealthy neighbors who might have more influence. Throughout the spring, summer, and early fall of 1862, the volume of letters flooding into the governor's office as well as that of the Confederate Secretary of State in Richmond had the desired effect. In October, Congress amended the original conscript act and added several new categories of exemptions. Even though many restrictions and conditions remained, the new law generally exempted factory owners, shoe-makers, tanners, blacksmiths, wagon-makers, salt-makers, miners, physicians, newspaper editors, and certain other classes of artisans and manufacturers. There was also a provision, the so-called "twenty-negro law," which exempted one white man for every plantation with twenty or more slaves and one man for "every twenty negroes on two or more plantations within five miles of each other . . . on which there is no white male adult not liable to military duty."[25]

The conscription act and the modifications passed in October invited numerous opportunities for evasion, despite the fact that the revisions were supposed to close loopholes in the original law. Covington County, with its relative isolation, high levels of poverty, and comparatively few slaves, along with the influence of Unionists such as Alfred Holley and the growing propensity among many to oppose the Confederacy, represented one of the greatest challenges conscription officers faced. Local attorney James Little—who narrowly lost an 1863 bid to unseat incumbent Alfred Holley in the state legislature—notified the governor that "the disposition to evade the law is so manifest in this (Covington) county, that, I judged it proper to inform you of the same." Apparently, men who had never shown an interest in teaching, law enforcement, or other exempt positions were "taking the Deputy Clerks office, some the Deputy Sheriffs office, and some are taking schools—all to keep from going to the war."[26] As the war progressed, the problems in Covington County grew increasingly worse.

In Eufaula, meanwhile, Lewis Cato, a member of the vigilance committee in Barbour County, likewise informed the governor that one of the local citizens—who appears to have been under arrest at the time for evading conscription—positively refused to join the army. According to Cato, the unnamed man boastfully declared that he "would see every woman and child in the South killed & every negro freed before he would go to the war!" He furthermore hoped that the next time the Confederate Congress met they "might all be captured." Cato believed that the man was a legitimate threat and asked the governor if there were any legal penalties or charges that might be brought against him. There is no indication of the governor's response or the final disposition of the case, but given the violence sometimes meted out to those considered disloyal, one can only imagine the extralegal recourse committee members could have taken.[27]

Butler County's Zechariah Bush was at least honest when he told the governor, of whom he claimed to be an old acquaintance, of his plans to escape the draft by becoming an overseer. "I cant stand camp life," he acknowledged, "and I wont to do somting for the Southern confederat states." Bush wanted nothing to do with the fighting, but it appears he had little if any actual experience as an overseer. "I have folard overseeing a grate deal of my time an as they is a grate cal for overseers I would like ta be detail for that buisness." Shorter actually recommended that he locate a plantation with "20 negroes" that did not already have an overseer and try to get a job there. Otherwise there was nothing he could do.[28]

Along with modifications to the conscript act, Congress added the "twenty-negro law," as it was commonly called, to the list of exemptions after large planters complained that there were not enough able-bodied men to serve as overseers. Women worried that conscription would leave them vulnerable to slave rebellions as more and more white men were drafted into the army. Sixty-two-year-old Thomas Richards, a plantation owner whose extended family owned hundreds of acres of land and dozens of slaves in both Barbour and Henry counties, had four sons and multiple family members serving in Confederate armies. If Richard's account is accurate, his young nephew, Benjamin Franklin Richards, must have worked himself to a frazzle trying to take care of three family farms. In May 1862, twenty-four family members and neighbors including twelve women and two soldiers petitioned the governor on his behalf: "If he has to leave under this conscript act his family and these others that he has had in [his] care are bound to suffer as thare childring are small, fer the most of the men have heartofour voluntered an are gon before the pasing of this act." Their efforts were in vain; Richards joined the 37th Alabama Infantry later that month. He was killed at the Battle of Iuka on September 19, 1862, just weeks before revisions to the conscript act might have aided his father's efforts to get him out of the army.[29]

In Pike County, meanwhile, John Blair Sr. was eager to use the "twenty-negro law" to get his son Leonard, one of four sons who fought during the war, out of the army. Leonard and brothers Needham and Zephaniah joined the 53rd Alabama Partisan Rangers back during the summer of 1862, ostensibly to avoid being drafted. Zephaniah served nine months with the 4th Alabama Cavalry Battalion before receiving a disability discharge. Levi, the youngest of the four brothers, was a private in the 15th Alabama Infantry until he died of typhoid fever in January 1862. In November, John Blair requested that the governor release Leonard from the army "to act as an overseer and agent for me [as] I am getting very old and not able to do the business on my plantation." Shorter responded that the "affidavit shows no cause of exemption from conscription." Within two months Leonard was dead as well.[30]

Meanwhile, as the home front struggled to comply with the new law, conscription came as something of a welcome relief to Confederate armies starved for manpower. Thousands of new recruits, such as the Blair brothers, were either drafted or volunteered to avoid the humiliation. Yet the majority of newly formed piney woods companies missed the bloody battles in Virginia and Maryland during the summer and early fall. While new recruits trained in Auburn, Montgomery, Mobile, and other locations, veteran regiments such as the 15th Alabama Infantry, made up almost exclusively of men from the piney woods, participated in Maj. Gen. Thomas J. "Stonewall" Jackson's Shenandoah Valley Campaign, playing a key role in the Confederate victory at Port Republic. There, on June 9, 1862, the 15th Alabama "regiment made a gallant resistance," impeding the Union advance just long enough for the Rebel army to move into place, occupy the best ground, and ultimately win the fight.[31]

East of the Blue Ridge Mountains, piney woods soldiers fought in a series of battles that came to be known as the Peninsula Campaign. From March through July of 1862, Maj. Gen. George B. McClellan's Union Army of the Potomac attacked up the Yorktown Peninsula with the goal of capturing the Confederate capital of Richmond and ending the war. A dozen piney woods companies from eight infantry regiments participated in some of the campaign's bloodiest engagements.[32]

At the Battle of Seven Pines, for instance, Confederate Gen. Joseph E. Johnston attacked two Federal corps at Fair Oaks Station about five miles east of Richmond. Rebel assaults were initially successful but Union reinforcements prevented a clear-cut victory. In an eastward attack running parallel with the Williamsburg Road, the 6th Alabama Infantry suffered more than three hundred casualties, fully 60 percent of its effective fighting force. Capt. Thomas H. Bell of the Henry County Blues (Company A, 6th Alabama) lost nearly every man in his command. "In a sheet of fire . . . this company stood until the last officer and non-commissioned officer, except 1 corporal, and 44 of the 56 men carried into action, had fallen."[33] Lying mortally wounded, Bell carefully loaded his revolver and fired round after round into the Blue line less than fifty yards from his position.

About four hundred yards to the right, Capt. Eugene Blackford's Barbour County Grays of the 5th Alabama Infantry fought through a barrage of canister fire and musketry to capture one of the Federal batteries. "Thick as hail fell the shot around us," wrote one Alabamian, "some burst as they struck, others a fluttering noise, and then the keen whistle of the minnie ball."[34]

Along that same line of attack, the 12th Alabama's Coffee Rangers pushed through the Yankee encampment and a second line of abatis only to find themselves pinned down by enfilading fire. The men dropped to the ground, loaded their rifles, and raised up just long enough to take aim and fire. "I saw him fall!" shouted several of the Rebels whose slugs found their marks.[35] Sixteen Rangers were wounded during this exchange, including Capt. Exton Tucker, Pvt. Edward Roads, and Cpl. Michael Horn, all from the Buzbeeville community in Coffee County. Pvt. William Cardwell, a poor farmer who lived just a few houses down from Tucker, and Pvt. Franklin Winslow, the son of the wealthiest planter in the community, were killed alongside six of their comrades from the same neighborhood. Seven Pines turned out to be a costly affair for the small community of Buzbeeville.[36]

During the Seven Days' Battles—a series of six major engagements fought on the outskirts of Richmond at the climax of the Peninsula Campaign—piney woods soldiers saw the most action at Gaines' Mill and Malvern Hill, the two bloodiest days. On June 27 at Gaines' Mill, Capt. Eugene Blackford's Eufaula boys performed admirably when their regiment, the 5th Alabama, spearheaded an assault on the Union right that led to the capture of a Yankee battery. In less than three hours, the regiment lost forty-five wounded and twenty-one killed, including the regimental colonel, Christopher Pegues.[37] About a mile to the west, the Greenville Guards (8th Alabama Infantry) and the Jeff Davis Rangers (9th Alabama Infantry), both raised in Butler County, were heavily engaged alongside the 10th and 11th Alabama Infantry in the attack on the Union left. Under a murderous fire, 1,800 Alabamians crossed an open field, fought through a creek bed that the Yankees used as a makeshift rifle pit, overran two lines of breastworks, and swept the Federals over the back side of the hill. Lt. Col. Hillary Herbert later recalled that "in spite of brush, briars and ditches and under the concentrated fire of two lines, our men drove the enemy's first line back pell mell upon the second, and charging up the heights it too broke and fled in confusion, leaving us the masters of the strong position" at the crest of the hill.[38] "The victory is complete," reported Brig. Gen. Cadmus Wilcox, "the enemy is repulsed and pursued at every point, and those that escape falling into our hands do so under the cover of the darkness of the night."[39] The 8th and 9th Alabama lost nearly three hundred men killed or wounded, including Rangers' captain Edward Young Hill, who died early in the assault, evidently the victim of a Union sharpshooter.

Meanwhile, about five hundred yards northeast of the Watt farm, the 15th Alabama hammered the Federal center. Nineteen-year-old Pvt. Thomas Burke, the only son of one of the wealthiest planters in Eufaula, was among the first to fall. Fatally shot through the "pit of the stomach" and writhing in pain, he tried to stop the gushing blood by plugging the wound with his canteen cork. Pvt. Samuel Dickerson from Dale County was shot through the chest and died almost instantly. Cpl. Gus McClendon was nearly shot in the head by one of his own men. "The stinging about my neck," he later recalled, "was caused by grains of powder" penetrating his skin. McClendon remembered that the weather that day was so hot and humid that several men died from heat exhaustion. Despite suffering more than one hundred casualties, the 15th Alabama captured a battery of seven guns and helped push the Federals off the hill into full retreat. Gaines Mill was a disaster for the Union and convinced McClellan to abandon his effort to capture Richmond.[40]

McClellan's unsuccessful Peninsula Campaign led to the creation of a new Union Army under Maj. Gen. John Pope. In late August, Pope's Army of Virginia clashed with Robert E. Lee's Army of Northern Virginia at the Second Battle of Bull Run, known to Confederates as Second Manassas. On the night of August 28, the 15th Alabama joined in Stonewall Jackson's attack against Brig. Gen. John Gibbon's brigade about two miles west of Bull Run Creek, near Brawner's Farm. For the 15th Alabama, this bloody night raid resulted in at least fifteen dead and thirty-eight wounded. Some of the men were so terrified that they hugged the ground "like a frightened squirrel lay upon the branch of a tree."[41] Pvt. John Sauls from Henry County was shot in the head, "the ball entered between his left eye and his nose . . . and came out behind his right ear." Sauls miraculously survived but suffered permanent blindness in one eye, facial disfigurement, and a lifetime of mental disability. No one thought Cpl. Lott McMath's head wound was too serious until a day later when his fever spiked. He soon began showing signs of insanity, escaped from the field hospital, and died alone in the woods.[42] For two days, Stonewall Jackson's three divisions held off repeated Federal assaults until Maj. Gen. James Longstreet's corps arrived at noon on August 29. The following day, fresh off their victory at Thoroughfare Gap, Longstreet's five divisions shattered the Union left flank and routed Pope's army. The 15th Alabama helped repel the Federal attack of August 29 with few losses and participated in the rout of the Union army the next day.[43]

Following his victory at Second Manassas, Lee launched an invasion onto Union soil. On September 17, 1862, the Army of the Potomac, essentially back under the command of George B. McClellan, clashed with the Rebel army just outside the town of Sharpsburg, Maryland. Piney woods companies were involved in several phases of the Battle of Antietam, a battle that soon earned its place as the bloodiest single day of the war. With fewer than sixty men present for duty, the Conecuh Guards (Company G, 4th Alabama Infantry) lost about half its strength in the vicious early morning fighting that occurred on the Confederate left, an area known as the Cornfield. One soldier recalled that "it was the severest clash of arms in which the 4th Alabama ever participated."[44] About two hours later, several companies of piney woods soldiers from the 5th Alabama, 6th Alabama, and 12th Alabama, all part of Rodes's Brigade, were heavily engaged in the fighting at the Sunken Road—a wagon-worn, weather-beaten side road off the Hagerstown Pike known afterwards as Bloody Lane. John B. Gordon was wounded five times before being carried off the field and replaced by his twenty-two-year-old second-in-command, Lt. Col. James Lightfoot. In the chaos, Lightfoot—a store clerk from Abbeville whose gallantry during the war earned him several promotions—misunderstood an order from Gen. Rodes and mistakenly pulled his entire regiment out of the line, a move that caused other units to retreat and ultimately resulted in the Rebel abandonment of the Sunken Road.[45] By nightfall, the Confederate Army was on its heels, badly outnumbered, while the Federals controlled nearly every part of the battlefield. Still, McClellan failed to take advantage of the situation and allowed Lee's army to retreat back across the Potomac River into Virginia.

While thousands of Americans were fighting and dying in Virginia and Maryland, Confederate General Braxton Bragg's Army of the Mississippi was on a collision course with Maj. Gen. Don Carlos Buell's Army of the Ohio in a struggle to determine Kentucky's fate in the war. The two sides met on October 8, 1862, at the Battle of Perryville, the first major battle to include significant numbers of conscription-related recruits from the piney woods. At Perryville, the 33rd Alabama, raised almost exclusively in southeastern Alabama with companies from Dale, Coffee, Butler, and Covington counties, took part in its first major engagement of the war. Attached to Brig. Gen. Sterling Alexander Martin Wood's Brigade, the regiment participated in the bloody fighting just before sunset at the crucial Dixville Crossroads. The plan was to take the intersection, isolate Maj. Gen. Alexander M. McCook's I Corps on the Union right, and cut him off from the main body. At first the Rebels gained the upper hand but fresh Union reinforcements soon drove the Alabamians back with heavy losses. Sgt. George D. Bush from Company G, the Daleville Blues, explained the carnage to his father: "Our Companey went in with 14 men and thare was 6 wounded and 1 kiled. D. A. Thomas was kiled dead on the field A.J. Nobling was wound very bad L. W. Bigbie was shot in the sholder with one ball and in the neck with another . . . J. M. P. Talley shot in the leg Henrey McCulough shot in the knee and broke his knee all to smash Jas. M. Ellis slitley threw the belley W. G. Waren struck with a peace of a bum on the sholder."[46] Col. Samuel Adams from Butler County was shot in the foot, thrown from his horse, and dragged for some distance before his foot untangled from the stirrup. Adams, Lt. Col. Robert Crittenden from Coffee County, and Maj. James Dunklin from Butler had their horses shot from underneath them—which prompted them to lead their men on foot in subsequent battles. Capt. Robert E. Ward fell, mortally wounded. As he lay dying after the battle, he instructed his slave, Jesse, to return home to Dale County and inform his family of his death. All total, the 33rd Alabama suffered 167 casualties out of fewer than four hundred engaged.[47]

As the sun set, the battle ended. Despite setbacks late in the day, the Rebel army managed to push the Federals back more than a mile from their original positions. Many Confederate soldiers were thrilled that they had won a great victory and were understandably frustrated when orders came to abandon the field. "The army are terribly disappointed at the result of the Kentucky Campaign," Pierre Costello later complained, and "accuse their generals of bad management in not fighting the Yankees at various points in Ky."[48] Bragg, on the other hand, rightly concluded that he was overwhelmingly outnumbered and feared the Yankees would get in behind him and cut off his escape route. In the end, the Confederacy's hope of holding on to Kentucky was all but lost when Bragg retreated back into Tennessee.[49] Nevertheless, for piney woods soldiers the loss of Kentucky was only a temporary disappointment. Pierre Costello later reported that troop morale remained remarkably high despite battlefield setbacks and the freezing winter cold that arrived early that year.

Back in Alabama, on October 27, just days after Bragg's army moved through the Cumberland Gap out of Kentucky into Tennessee, the General Assembly convened in Montgomery for a special session. The conscription act had exacerbated the economic problems that had been mounting since the fall of 1861, and Governor Shorter needed the legislature to address the growing crisis. In majority-white areas such as the piney woods, the hardship began for poor families as soon as the men went into the army. Historian Bessie Martin has estimated that 10,263 families received state aid in 1862, roughly 10 percent of the total number of families for the whole state—and these figures are based upon reports submitted by the counties before conscription. In 1863, the number tripled to 31,915, an increase of more than 200 percent. The 1863 reports further suggest that, with the exception of Barbour, at least one-third of the families in the piney woods received at least some support from the state.[50]

The initial 1861 legislation that set aside funds "for the aid of the indigent families of absent volunteers" failed to adequately meet the needs of the state's impoverished families.[51] Each county maintained a list of needy families and made periodic reports to the governor suggesting the amount of funds that it would take to help each family. In the summer of 1862, for example, Judge E. W. Teague of Henry County reported that 170 families consisting of 831 individuals required at least some help from the state and, of that number, 392 were entirely destitute.[52] But not everyone felt that they were being treated fairly. Just weeks after Teague's report, several women complained. "They say they are upon sufferances," one man wrote on their behalf, "and they think very hard of it, knowing that the women of Barbour [County] fair very different from what they do, for they get more every month than [the women of Henry] get for the year."[53]

In Coffee County, Lucretia Simmons wrote to the governor on behalf "of some of the soldiers wives in this settlement. Some of them is living on bread alone without salt we have understood here that thare was some appropriations made for the releaf of them if it is so its not attended to here." Simmons added that Nancy Rudd, whose husband had been in the army for almost a year, "was left quite distitute of the means to live on and she has never recd but 12 buoshel of corn and 30 lbs meat." Rudd did not yet know that her husband, Francis Marion Rudd, had been killed a few weeks earlier at Gaines' Mill. The governor could only inform her that indigent funds were administered by the local officials and complaints needed to be handled on the local level if possible.[54]

At the governor's urging, the special session of the legislature that met in October 1862, appropriated an additional $2,000,000 to support indigent families of soldiers and conscripts; the families of substitutes and deserters were disallowed from receiving assistance. To pay for the program, the assembly empowered the governor to sell bonds. Funds would be distributed by county probate judges under the direction of the local courts of county commissioners. Stiff penalties would be imposed on county officials convicted of embezzling or misusing indigent funds. The legislature later revisited this issue twice, once in 1863 and again in 1864, each time appropriating more money as the ranks of the poor increased.[55] For piney woods families struggling to survive, the state's indigent funds may not have been entirely sufficient, but at least it was something. And it demonstrated the state's good will toward helping the families of Confederate soldiers.

One problem closely associated with poverty was the dwindling grain supply. By 1862, commodity prices throughout the Confederacy were at record highs, due partly to the Union blockade, but also to drought conditions in several parts of the state that nearly wiped out the 1862 wheat crop and contributed to significantly lower yields of corn. In addition, as historian Ben Severance observes, "planters often persisted in growing cotton despite the official embargo, while small farmers pursued the greater profits of distilled spirits. As a consequence, food shortages led to inflation and gradually pushed the state to the brink of starvation."[56] To combat shortages, inflation, and the increasing likelihood of widespread poverty, Shorter issued a proclamation in March 1862, exhorting Alabamians to "plant not then one seed of cotton beyond your home wants, but put down your lands in grains and every other kind and description of farm product, and raise every kind of livestock which may contribute to the support of your own families and the needy families of your brave defenders."[57] Shorter further threatened large producers with a cotton tax if he felt that the state's farmers were not planting their fair share of grain crops.

The governor's efforts appear to have worked to a certain extent. While wheat yields remained depressed, the number of acres devoted to corn and other provision crops increased to such a degree that overall production numbers multiplied. "Owing to the largely increased quantity of land planted in corn," the governor affirmed in October, "there is an abundant supply for all the people of the state, and a heavy excess to spare for the use of our troops in the field."[58] Nevertheless, he recommended that the legislature tax the cotton crop in anticipation that the additional cost would encourage planters to grow even more corn. The tax on cotton was part of a much larger revenue bill passed by the legislature in November 1862. The law imposed a 10-cent tax on every pound of seed cotton harvested in excess of 250 pounds per hand. Every pound of ginned cotton was equal to four pounds of seed cotton, which meant that farmers and planters were allowed only a bale and a half before the new tax kicked in. The legislative journals do not reveal specific voting patterns on this issue, but the debate appears to have been more about the size and scope of the tax than whether the tax should be levied in the first place.

The General Assembly also took up a prohibition bill outlawing the distillation of whiskey that originated with an executive military order issued by the governor in March. Earlier in the year, Tennessee and Georgia restricted the manufacture and sale of whiskey, a move that prompted many distilleries to relocate across state lines into Alabama. In several parts of the state, distillers bought up corn so rapidly that poorer families were priced out of the market. This was particularly true in remote areas in the southernmost piney woods, where converting corn into whiskey was more profitable than hauling cumbersome grain crops to market. In the past, of course, making whiskey was not a problem, but the demand for grain brought on by the war created a situation whereby the need for animal feed and human consumption took precedence over whiskey production. The governor also hoped that his order would discourage inebriation on the part of the troops in training camps throughout the state. "The baneful effects of intemperance among our troops," he argued, "were daily seen in the demoralization and wild excesses of a large number who, for the first time, had thrown off the restraints of peaceful pursuits and devoted themselves to the arts of war."[59]

While the governor's antidistillation order was clearly intended to preserve corn supplies for human and animal consumption, it appears to have had the unintended consequence of severely limiting medicinal alcohol. From the moment the order was issued, requests from distillers all over the state poured into the governor's office, including numerous requests from piney woods distillers. Some of these operators clearly saw this as an opportunity for financial gain. Shorter tried to be careful to differentiate between those who wanted to distill for medical purposes and those who were interested in manufacturing and selling their wares for recreational consumption. Requests made by ordinary citizens were almost always denied. Thomas Bement from Greenville in Butler County, for example, sent an affidavit to the governor signed by two prominent Butler County citizens, Judge Samuel Bolling and Benjamin F. Porter, requesting a contract to provide "pure whiskey" to the state. Shorter insisted that "the state has made no contract for whiskey and is not in the market."[60] Hosea Bailey's bid to distill up to one thousand gallons of whiskey for Barbour County's druggists and physicians was similarly denied; the governor informed Bailey that his offer would be forwarded to the legislature in October. These types of requests were usually rejected.

On the other hand, Shorter quickly approved requests submitted by physicians. In July, Drs. Charles Pickett and W. A. Andrews of Fort Browder, Alabama—a small community located about twenty-five miles west of Eufaula—sent word to the governor that their stockpiles of medicinal whiskey were nearly exhausted. Their letter sums up candidly the situation that existed in many piney woods communities:

> You are aware of the scarcity of the article and the enormously high price of it in our county. Now in view of the approaching summer and fall sickness, what are the physicians to do. We know of no substitute that we can bring in, in cases of typhoid fever, dysentery and a number of others. Also we are compelled to have alcohol or good whiskey in preparing [most of our] tinctures. We now ask you the privilege of having H. Baily of our county to still us as much as sixty gallons of good whiskey, which spirits shall be used for medical purposes. We pledge ourselves that no person shall have any unless his condition absolutely requires it.[61]

Pickett and Andrews's letter verified what the governor already knew to be true. Just four months after the ban, doctors were already running out of an important and necessary remedy. While Shorter approved this request and others like it, it was clear that he needed and preferred the support of the legislature to continue the program, strengthen his ability to provide for the medical needs of the state, and limit the manufacture of illegal whiskey.

When state House and Senate members convened in October, they supported Shorter's proposal by wide margins. From the piney woods, eight of the eleven house members present at the time voted in favor of the legislation.[62] While it is difficult to determine with certainty the motives of the men who voted, whether for or against, the evidence suggests that several of those who opposed the bill may have believed that the law did not go far enough to restrict the manufacture of illegal whiskey. Pike County senator E. L. McIntyre, for example, proposed an amendment that removed the reference to "spirituous liquors" altogether and provided instead "that nothing but alcohol shall be distilled . . . and that of 95 percent strength," an indication that distillation should be utilized exclusively for medicinal purposes.[63] Although his amendment failed, he ultimately supported the bill, believing perhaps that doing something was better than doing nothing. Barbour County's Charles Parker, on the other hand, voted against the legislation. Parker was a wealthy planter, slaveholder, and Primitive Baptist minister whose religious convictions may have convinced him that the law was not strict enough. DeWitt Davis from Covington County was another Primitive Baptist minister who refused to support the bill. As a middle-class farmer who owned no slaves and whose net worth was based almost entirely in land and livestock production, he would have had a keen understanding of the importance of feed corn to the farmers in his county, many of whom relied solely upon livestock for their livelihoods; of course, it was just as probable that he disagreed with prohibition altogether.[64]

The legislation passed by the General Assembly in October strengthened the governor's proclamation and gave it the force of statutory law. Shorter determined that twenty counties, including Conecuh and Covington, would not be eligible for contracts due to insufficient supplies of grain. Yet contract offers came from many of the other counties. Butler County's James R. Yeldell, who had been producing legal spirits for physicians in the surrounding area for at least five months, applied for a license to continue to make up to sixty gallons of whiskey per week. Judge Walter Crenshaw endorsed the application, arguing that because Yeldell's operation was located in the fertile northwest corner of the county, where corn was plentiful, there would be more than enough grain to meet the county's needs. "All of the practicing physicians for 15 miles around him," he added, "think it is very necessary that this distillery should not be closed up, for if it is, they will be put to very great inconvenience in getting alcohol for tinctures and other uses in their practices."[65]

Coffee County's probate judge, Benjamin Starke, meanwhile, wrote to the governor on behalf of Joseph Blue, a local physician who wanted to set up his own still. "His chief object," Starke wrote, "is to get whiskey enough for medical purposes, that the county is entirely distitute of that article and he knows that his patients have greatly suffered for want of it and there is no way to get it." The judge further insisted that the corn mash produced from the manufacture of whiskey was just as effective for feeding and fattening up livestock as an equal amount of grain. Starke assured the governor that intemperance would not be an issue since most of the county's young men were already in the army and "if the 45 year men are called into service, as I have no doubt they will shortly, there will be but few left in the county but women and children."[66] Joseph Blue received the contract.

Despite the state's efforts, prices for almost everything continued to rise. By late 1862, corn was selling for more than $2.00 a bushel. One planter observed that in some parts of the state flour was selling at $40 a barrel, whiskey $16 a gallon, and eggs 25 cents per dozen. Yet few other economic problems aroused the interest of state authorities more than the rising cost of salt. While it is an important nutritional supplement for both humans and animals, salt is essential for the proper development of beef cattle. Sodium deficiency in cattle leads to reduced feed intake, inhibits growth, limits milk production, and exposes the animal to numerous diseases. In addition, salt was absolutely essential for preserving meat, especially pork products. Governor Shorter became so concerned over the threat of a potential "salt famine" that he devoted more than one-third of his 1862 General Assembly address to the subject. His wartime correspondence contains so many items related to salt that one wonders how he found time to deal with any other issue with equal enthusiasm.[67]

In Alabama, the price of a bushel of salt rose from less than $1 in 1860 to nearly $20 in 1862. Before the war, salt was abundant and cheap, but the Union blockade prevented salt-laden European ships from entering Southern ports.[68] As early as November 1861, the General Assembly passed a series of bills aimed at curtailing speculators, building salt reserves, and ensuring that the salt produced within the state remained in Alabama. Through a series of executive orders and legislative mandates, the governor continued the process of procuring domestic salt. The state leased a portion of the salt reservations in Clarke County and advanced $10,000 to John P. Figh and Company to construct on-site furnaces and provide salt directly to the people at reduced prices. Alabama's salt commissioner, A. G. McGehee, traveled to Virginia, studied the salt-making process at Saltville, and returned to oversee the construction of a state-owned salt mine in Clarke County known as the Upper Works.

Shorter took the additional step of opening up all of the state's salt reservations to Alabamians who wished to come and make salt for their own families. On at least one occasion, the governor threatened to seize a company for lack of adequate production. "I, as executive of the state will feel it my duty to seize your works as a military necessity, that the same may be made completely subservient to the public welfare." Indeed, the state's involvement in salt procurement became so direct that Malcolm McMillan has suggested that it "created a veritable revolution in the economic affairs of Alabama, . . . actions unthinkable to antebellum Alabamians." William C. Davis takes it a step further by referring to the intervention of Confederate state governments as "salt socialism."[69]

Given the circumstances, piney woods counties fared relatively well when it came to salt resources, particularly when compared with counties in the northern part of the state. Butler, Conecuh, and Covington were all reasonably close to the salt works in Clarke County, while the eastern counties relied upon works that dotted the Gulf Coast from Pensacola to Apalachicola. Salt companies shipped their product by railroad or wagon to county seats all over the region. Local justices of the peace in partnership with probate judges distributed salt to the citizens either free of charge, for indigent families, or at a reduced cost based upon the needs of each household. Residents had to sign affidavits swearing that purchased salt would be used for household purposes only and would not be resold or bartered. On April 28, 1862, Eliza Coleman of Butler County traveled twenty-four miles roundtrip, from Armadillo to Greenville and back, to buy three bushels of Figh and Company salt from Justice of the Peace Coleman O'Gwynn. Eliza's husband, Jesse, was off fighting with the Confederate Army of Mississippi in Company B, 17th Alabama Infantry, a regiment that only three weeks earlier lost 125 men at the Battle of Shiloh. It is entirely possible that even at this point Eliza may not have known that her husband survived the battle, but one thing is certain, the salt that she purchased that day was essential to the well-being of her two young girls, Rachel and Sarah, and the small herd of livestock she attended on the family's sixty-acre farm in the southwestern corner of the county.[70] Stories such as this became all too familiar as the war dragged on.

While the scarcity of salt was a challenge for piney woods families for much of the war, dwindling salt supplies during the winter of 1862–1863 proved particularly troublesome. Ella Lonn argues that for the Confederacy as a whole the "clamor for [salt] rose in a mounting crescendo during the first two years, probably striking the most strident note during the packing season of 1862–1863."[71] In fact, the evidence suggests that while hogs were readily available in most piney woods counties that winter, the scarcity of salt threatened to undermine the usual production of cured pork. James Darby, a merchant and planter from Troy, proposed that the farmers in his area would gladly provide meat to the Confederate army if the governor would guarantee the requisite amount of salt for the upcoming curing season. "My neighbors could spair a few thousand lbs of bacon," he wrote in June 1862, "provided they can git salt in lieu of it. If not they cant do it as they have not salt to salt their butter, poltry, beef nor preserve their pork next winter, but by gitting salt they can spair bacon now." Darby promised to deliver "good country cured sides . . . clear sides and sides with ribs in it" to Montgomery as soon as the governor approved the trade in salt. Unfortunately, Shorter's response is not included in the administrative files but given the nature of feeding the armies it is hard to believe that he did not take advantage of the offer.[72]

As early as October 1862, Florida Governor John Milton warned Confederate officials about the exposed condition of salt works along the entire panhandle region. He suggested that a force of five hundred troops and two or three cavalry companies would aid in protecting "the arrangements for making salt by citizens of Alabama, Georgia, and Florida, which will otherwise be defeated [by Union raiders] and cause much suffering among citizens and soldiers for the want of beef, bacon, and pork."[73] In fact the Union Navy routinely attacked salt works along the coast but the effect, while significant, was only temporary as most were up and running again within days or a few weeks. Indeed, the Union never effectively stamped out the flow of salt from the gulf coast into the piney woods.

As the year 1862 came to a close, it was clear that the war was taking a toll on families in the piney woods. The conscription act had changed the socioeconomic dynamic on the home front. In majority-white communities, especially those in the southernmost piney woods, the new law drained even more manpower into the army. Poor families already strained by the realities of war experienced even greater hardships than most. Nevertheless, state and county officials took measures to alleviate some of the effects of poverty especially among destitute soldiers' families. The state appropriated millions of dollars in direct aid to the poor, opened or expanded salt works, and took steps to increase the production of grain crops. Piney woods soldiers fought with distinction in both the eastern and western theaters. Despite growing problems on the home front, the morale of many of the region's fighting men remained remarkably high; Kentucky's fall to Union forces and the growing list of dead and wounded did not dampen their spirits.

7

"I Feel Like We Are Almost Ruined"

The War Takes Its Toll, 1863–1865

According to legend, one night in February 1865, former Confederate-soldier-turned-outlaw John Ward murdered Columbus Holly on his plantation near Kinston in Coffee County. One source claims that no one actually knew who had killed the wealthy plantation owner until years later when Ward confessed to the crime on his deathbed. Some suspect that Holly was murdered because he strongly supported efforts to hunt down outlaws like Ward, and may have even participated in several manhunts against deserters in Coffee and surrounding counties. Several of Holly's slaves also reportedly collaborated with Ward. Not only did they provide critical information about their owner's whereabouts and habits but they also carried Ward on their shoulders from his horse to the main house and back in order to fool the bloodhounds. The myth and mystery surrounding the death of Holly, and Ward's involvement in the crime continues to the present day, but the internal violence that occurred during the war's final years was a growing problem for Alabama officials and the Confederate war effort.[1]

This chapter explores the Civil War in the piney woods during the final two years of the conflict. By 1863, the deprivations of war began taking their toll on the region's families. Desperation and poverty, especially in the southernmost counties, led to increased numbers of deserters and stragglers who had remained at home purportedly to protect and provide for their families. Certain communities within the region became hotspots for desertion, drawing the attention of both Union and Confederate authorities who sought either to exploit or curtail such activity. Raids by both armies often gave residents the feeling of being besieged by friend and foe alike. Bands of outlaws gathered together and carried out raids of their own in the lower counties. The most severe home front disruptions generally occurred during the final year of the war, especially in communities in the southernmost counties. For piney woods soldiers and Confederates in general, morale plummeted in 1863, following the losses at Gettysburg and Vicksburg, only to rebound later that year and continue well into 1864. Indeed, it is remarkable that Confederate soldiers participated in suicidal frontal attacks against fortified Union earthworks in battles such as Franklin and Nashville so late in the war knowing that their cause was all but lost. For the soldiers from southeastern Alabama, the war's final two years proved to be the most challenging. Desolation and poverty on the home front caused many to question their loyalty to the Confederacy—to the extent that some put thoughts into action by deserting their units and returning home. Yet those who remained, whether out of loyalty to the Confederacy or devotion to their comrades, demonstrated their courage through some of the bloodiest battles of the war.

By 1863, the depravations of war began taking their toll on piney woods families. Perhaps more than any other group, women faced some of the greatest challenges. Conscription had stripped nearly every able-bodied man from the countryside, and women were left with little if any support raising children, attending slaves, and working farms. Women were now relied upon more than ever to take care of livestock, plow up and plant fields, harvest crops, keep plantation records, and attend to all of the financial aspects of running their farms. Husbands wrote letters home advising their wives when to slaughter hogs and how many, which crops to plant in which fields, and to whom they should turn to if things went wrong. Capt. Pierre Costello encouraged his wife in Coffee County to "take the best care you can of our little stock of cows & hogs as they will be scarce articles if this war continues. Increase them all you can they will be more valuable than negroes. Keep my tax paid so that none of my lands may sell, & keep the store house & other houses rented out to the best advantage."[2]

Writing from Vicksburg, Mississippi, Pvt. Elisha Flournoy was anxious to learn all he could about his wife, Martha, and their farm: "Write me how your garden is your cane potatos fruit fence pasture cows calves hogs and horse and dogs emily [Emily was most likely a slave hired to help Martha with the farm] chickens you and everything else is getting along." He later instructed her to purchase a sow from a nearby neighbor. "You must pay him the money," he wrote, "and put her in that field at the house with the fatening hogs so she will stay at home or cary some corn over there to fead her . . . I had rather have hogs than money at this time."[3]

While women such as Cordelia Costello and Martha Flournoy were better off than many, even *their* confidence began to wane as the war dragged on. "From what I learn there is less dissatisfaction in the army than at home," Pierre Costello wrote. Cordelia, who must have felt completely overwhelmed by the added responsibilities, urged her husband to resign and return home. Pierre conveyed his displeasure in a sternly worded reply. "Where was the use of commencing this war," he insisted, "if we did not intend to continue it until we achieved our independence & to accomplish this there must be no resigning, deserting, holding back, or backing out." After a few patriotic pronouncements, he brazenly answered her question. "No Delia! Don't ask your husband to resign & abandon a crowd of gallant boys who left home to remain with him during the war. Let him continue with them who can't resign & when their work is done if it be Gods will to spare them, they can return as they left together."[4]

Some women encouraged their husbands to hire substitutes, despite the fact that such men were becoming more and more difficult to find. Writing from her home in Henry County in April 1863, Sarah Terry assured her husband that she could raise the money that it would take to buy a substitute. "I am perfectly willing my self to give it," she wrote. "I think I could rase it by putting your horse and sadle in at 5 hundred dollars . . . it is warth that much to try and get it if they is any chance for I want to se you worse then I ever did." She ended her letter with a pointed reminder of her discontent: "nothing more at present I remain your unhappy wife untell death pray for me and the poore little farther less children."[5] Nimrod Long from Pike County encouraged his wife to abandon any ideas of hiring a substitute. "You are in the notion of hiring a sub," he wrote, "yet I do not want one and if I did there would be no chance to get one into this regiment." Long, a wealthy planter from Perote, Alabama, who served in Company B, 51st Alabama Cavalry, insisted that Col. James D. Webb would not allow any substitutes to join the regiment. He explained that, on one occasion, an officer hired a substitute, brought him to the front, and was forced to send him back home. "Web had no objection to the man but said he would not receive a substitute for any body."[6] These women clearly wanted their husbands home, even if it meant hiring expensive substitutes to fight in their place.

For many piney woods families, the growing sense of desperation became even more pronounced in April 1863, with the passage of the Confederate "tax-in-kind" law. The "tithe," as some called it, was a 10 percent direct tax on everything from potatoes, beans, and corn to sugar, molasses, cotton, wool, tobacco, and peanuts. As was to be expected, farmers did everything they could to evade the new taxes. Sarah Terry wrote to inform her husband that she hoped to avoid the tax by limiting her cane production for the upcoming year. "I shal not sell no more surup," she noted, "they say that the tenth of all we make we have to give it for the support of the army."[7] Ironically, the tax came at precisely the time when the ranks of the destitute on the home front were swelling and the state was trying to meet the needs of its poorest citizens. By the summer of 1863, the situation was so desperate in southeastern Alabama that authorities suspended the collection of produce in Pike, Henry, Coffee, Dale, and Covington counties. Indeed, the tax fell so heavily upon majority-white neighborhoods that the General Assembly petitioned Richmond to completely exempt soldiers' families "whenever the support of such families is derived entirely from the proceeds of white labor."[8] The law was amended later that year, and again in 1864, giving the Davis administration more flexibility in its enforcement. These actions helped to alleviate some of the pressure that poor families faced but came nowhere close to solving the problem entirely.

Another issue facing piney woods communities, particularly those in the southernmost counties, was the growing problems associated with armed bands of deserters, shirkers, and Unionists. These outlaws hid out in the swamps of southeastern Alabama and northern Florida robbing homes and occasionally raiding unsuspecting neighborhoods. To be sure, discontentment did not arise overnight but evolved slowly beginning with relatively small numbers of "tories" and conscription evaders in 1862, and ending with violent guerilla forces "no longer committed to the Confederacy, not quite committed to the Union . . . but fully committed to survival" in 1864 and 1865.[9] The trouble began in December 1862, when a Union raiding party from Pensacola (which had fallen into Union hands back in May of that year) attacked and burned several buildings in Geneva, Coffee County. Florida governor John Milton wired John Gill Shorter that a number of "Tories, deserters, and Negroes" had joined the party and was heading north toward Elba. Governor Shorter immediately dispatched Col. James H. Clanton with orders to raise a force of thirty-day volunteers from Coffee, Covington, Dale, Henry, Pike, and Barbour counties "adequate to drive out the enemy and protect for the present that part of the state."[10]

A few days later, the Davis administration approved Shorter's request to enlist conscription-age men, some of whom had managed to escape the enrollment officers, for a period of six months. "Reluctance to leave their unprotected families . . . is an excuse of some speciousness," the governor wrote, "which they make and accompany with a profession of readiness to take up arms for the purpose of local defense. While some of them are disloyal, many of them have, on account of their unprotected families, availed themselves of the facilities which their territory, generally poor and sparsely populated, affords for escape and concealment."[11]

By the end of January 1863, Clanton's command took the fight into northwest Florida, arresting suspected Unionists, destroying their property, and rooting out deserters.[12] Two months later, Shorter confidently, if prematurely, reported to Secretary of War Seddon that the temporary policy allowing draft dodgers to "join Colonel Clanton's organization has had a most happy effect in silencing all clamors against the conscript act in those counties, and in inducing many who were hiding to come into the service."[13] Unfortunately for the governor, a sizeable number of Clanton's new recruits grew increasingly disgruntled with the war. Many of these men had "entered the army very reluctantly," Maj. Gen. Dabney Maury later reported. "Unusual influences and inducements have been used to recruit them and to keep them. They have been kept near their homes, have received many indulgences, and have never been in real field service." From his headquarters in Pollard (Conecuh County), Clanton desperately attempted to isolate and quell the rebellion before it ruined his entire command. In a letter to Clanton in December 1863, Capt. W. G. Swanson of the 61st Alabama acknowledged that there was "a general disposition upon the part of the poorer class of men, foreigners, and substitutes to lay down their arms, yield up the cause, and accept the best terms the Yankee Government will grant. Their object is to close the war as they have little to fight for." When dozens of soldiers mutinied in early January 1864, Clanton arrested the ring leaders and sent seventy prisoners "in irons" to Mobile to stand trial. "Nearly all of them ought to be shot," he responded in anger. Confederate officials promptly transferred several of Clanton's regiments to commands out west and in Virginia, far from their homes in South Alabama and much closer to the fighting. Ironically, the two transferred regiments—the 57th Alabama and the 61st Alabama—went on to fight with distinction in battles such as Franklin, Nashville, Spotsylvania, and Winchester.[14]

Some of Clanton's problems stemmed from the fact that he had recruited a number of men from piney woods communities where desertion and evasion had become a serious and growing problem. Back in July 1863, word reached Governor Shorter that a dozen deserters hiding out in the Pea River swamps in southern Coffee County were harassing the local citizenry. "These men and all who are harboring them should be forthwith arrested," he wrote to Col. Sevard Lee in Clanton, "and I am surprised that our people who are at home and can as easily circumvent and arrest them do not do it."[15] Suspected deserters in Henry and Dale counties likewise prompted Shorter to send in a small force of home guards to investigate and make arrests. Capt. Thomas Armstrong's Henry Rebels, a home guard unit in Abbeville, captured a handful of deserters and arrested several old men "who have aided and abetted the deserters in that section." The governor directed Armstrong to join with other militia companies in the region, including a small contingent of Confederates operating near Campbellton, Florida, to "keep the woods and swamps constantly scoured, and use your most earnest endeavours to rid your county and the community of these outlyers."[16] A few weeks later, Armstrong's men arrested six deserters, but the squad escorting the captured men to Abbeville was ambushed, the prisoners set free, and one of the guards seriously wounded. Not only were the outlaws becoming more violent but rumor had it that furloughed troops out of Campbellton were supplying them with weapons and ammunition.

The governor also believed that Confederate defeats at the Battle of Gettysburg and at Vicksburg, Mississippi, earlier that summer, had eroded public confidence and threatened to swell the ranks of deserters in the southernmost counties. By September, having largely failed to dislodge them, Shorter complained to Gen. Dabney H. Maury that if these bands are "permitted to remain with impunity, their numbers will soon be largely increased by the paroled men from Vicksburg who are already evading their duty under pretext of their obligations of their parole."[17] It is unclear whether the governor's prediction concerning Vicksburg parolees fully materialized, but the evidence suggests that all of the regiments containing piney woods companies were back with the army in Demopolis, Alabama, by the end of August.[18] Indeed, many of the soldiers captured at Vicksburg and paroled eventually returned to duty and went on to fight in the Army of Tennessee until the end of the war.

For some soldiers, overstaying furloughs or slipping home did not necessarily translate into disloyalty. Pvt. Elisha Flournoy was not with his regiment, the 46th Alabama Infantry, when it surrendered at Vicksburg. He had been captured at the Battle of Port Gibson several months earlier, exchanged in June, and hospitalized in Virginia until his release in mid-July. "I intend to go by home if I go back to Miss. whether I get a furlough or not," he wrote to his wife a few days before leaving the hospital. "Every one of the people tells me to come by my home a few days and they never will bother me for it. Go by home and see how my business is going on and then go on to my command and all will be right. A private soldier is cared no more for than a sheep killing dog. . . . I intend to come by home and that will be no killing crime."[19] Not only did Flournoy go home but he apparently remained there for several months. Back with his unit, he penned his next letter to Martha from Demopolis on October 11, 1863. "My eating so much when I was at home," he wrote, "must have been the cause of my [recent] sickness, for we get nothing hearty to eat here and my health is improving. If I ever get home again you must not give me so much to eat."[20] Of course not every soldier returned to duty; some decided that protecting and providing for their families took precedence over the army.[21] Yet for Flournoy and many like him, a temporary period of desertion did not translate into disloyalty.

In some cases, zealous officials went too far in their dealings with suspected deserters and draft dodgers, which only made matters worse. On October 22, 1863, a group of prisoners captured in Coffee County stopped in Troy en route to Montgomery. Four of the men requested to see a local attorney named Benjamin Gardner, but when he arrived, the post commander, a Capt. McKay, turned him away. Within an hour, all of the prisoners "started for Montgomery under a strong guard." Even though he did not know the men personally and had never spoken to them, Gardner found out that two of them should have been exempt from the service; one was a Baptist minister and the other a shoe maker who claimed to have exemption papers signed by the previous enabling officer. In a letter to the governor, Gardner admitted, "I know myself nothing about the men referred to above—they may not have been entitled to relief—but they certainly were entitled to have their complaint heard by an attorney."[22] Governor Shorter promptly fired off a series of letters to administration officials, including Gen. Gideon Pillow, head of the Confederate Volunteer and Conscript Bureau, insisting that "in all cases where the citizen claims the right of an appeal to the judicial tribunals to determine his status and liability to conscription, before he shall be forced away from his home and into the army, will mollify the harshness of the law if he be allowed every reasonable facility to test the legality of the claims made upon him."[23] By the time this letter was written, the four men were already on their way to join the Army of Northern Virginia.

Capt. McKay was soon replaced, but the conflict between state and Confederate officials continued and at times worsened under Alabama's next Civil War governor, Thomas Hill Watts. The 1863 governor's race between Watts and Shorter was in many ways a repeat of the previous contest two years earlier, but with a drastically different outcome. Following his defeat in 1861, Watts organized the 17th Alabama Infantry, served with that unit until a few days before the Battle of Shiloh, and resigned to take the job as attorney general in the Davis administration. As attorney general, he used the power of his office to strengthen the supremacy of the central government, authored over one hundred opinions—four times more than both of his predecessors combined—and even challenged organizations and businesses in his home state. As the August election approached, Watts was determined not to actively campaign for the job, deciding instead that he would "accept the governorship if the people so desired."[24] Both Watts and Shorter remained in their respective jobs, allowing their friends in the newspaper business to campaign for them. The election was a landslide for Watts,

TABLE 7.1. 1863 gubernatorial election results

	Watts (Former Whig)	Shorter (Democrat)
Barbour	826	447
Butler	797	42
Coffee	507	73
Conecuh	388	62
Covington	438	40
Dale	434	115
Henry	422	227
Pike	966	229
Total	4,778	1,235

Source: *Journal Called Session, 1863, and the Third Regular Annual Session, of the Senate, of the State of Alabama, Held in the City of Montgomery, Commencing on the 17th August and the Second Monday in November, 1863* (Montgomery, AL: Saffold and Figures, 1864), 109.

who captured 74 percent of the statewide vote, and four out of five ballots in piney woods counties (see Table 7.1).[25]

There are several possible explanations for Shorter's defeat. Throughout his administration, he rarely took steps to defend or explain his political decisions to the general public. Historian Malcolm McMillian argues that he "was an able and energetic war governor [and] statesman who made difficult decisions while ignoring political expediency."[26] Moreover, Shorter's impressment of slaves for state and Confederate work projects angered so many slave owners that he all but lost his planter base. Impressment was the "strongest element which carried the state so largely against me," he later admitted.[27] To make matters worse, Union occupation in northern Alabama, raids in the southeast, and deepening depravation impacted large segments of the population that increasingly blamed Shorter for their plight. To be sure, unpopular politicians often suffer the electoral consequences while their opponents reap the benefits. According to McMillan, Thomas Watts and other former Whigs were "fortunate to be the 'outs' in a war situation that had become deplorable and intolerable."[28] Perhaps most damaging, Shorter's loss came on the heels of two of the Confederacy's worst defeats. "I have good reason to believe," he predicted just days before the election, that the disasters at Gettysburg and Vicksburg "will have a prejudicial influence over our approaching elections."[29] He seems to have been right.

As for Watts, he certainly benefitted from the overall dissatisfaction Alabamians had experienced, but his victory should in no way be construed as the result of a general peace movement to end the war on the part of the people in the piney woods. As a secessionist who served in the Confederate army and spent several years as Jefferson Davis's attorney general, Watts was an unlikely choice for voters who desired peace. Even McMillian concedes that Watts was a "war man all over."[30] Because he was a household name to piney woods families, and had come close to winning the governorship in 1861, it is reasonable to suggest that the region felt comfortable that his leadership would surpass that of his predecessor.

During the spring and summer of 1863, while Alabamians back home focused on the governor's race, Confederate and Union armies in both the east and the west clashed in a series of battles that arguably altered the trajectory of the war. On May 1, 1863, the Union Army of the Potomac, now under the command of Gen. Joseph Hooker, attacked Gen. Robert E. Lee's Army of Northern Virginia about two miles east of Chancellorsville, Virginia.[31] Despite his numerical and tactical advantage, Hooker withdrew his army to defensive positions closer to his headquarters, located in the home of Francis Chancellor. That night, Lee decided to split his own force, sending Stonewall Jackson's corps on a risky but ultimately successful twelve-mile flanking maneuver around the Union right the next day. At around 5:00 p.m. on May 2, Jackson's tattered veterans slammed into Gen. Oliver Otis Howard's Union XI Corps, driving them back over a mile until confusion and Federal artillery finally forced the Rebels to stop. Men from the piney woods were there. During the attack, the Coffee Rangers and other soldiers from the 12th Alabama Infantry "received a heavy volley from the enemy . . . passed over two formidable works, and assisted in taking several pieces of artillery."[32] Over on their right flank, Col. James Lightfoot from Henry County commanded the 6th Alabama Infantry. His brother, Capt. Thomas Lightfoot of the Henry Blues, "was the first to plant the colors of the regiment on the artillery captured." The regiment captured 105 prisoners that afternoon and feasted on Yankee rations later that evening. "My officers and men all acted so very gallantly," he reported. "I had 5 color-bearers shot down, 2 of whom were killed, besides 1 color-corporal killed and 1 wounded."[33] Not too far down the line, the Barbour Grays of the 5th Alabama Infantry anchored the left flank of Robert E. Rodes's entire brigade. After taking a line of breastworks, the whole unit was nearly cut off and surrounded, losing its regimental flag in the process and leaving behind one hundred men as prisoners of war. With the help of Confederate artillery, the 5th Alabama regrouped, charged, and recaptured the ground.[34]

The next day, Lee launched a dawn attack against the Federal center, routing the Yankees and ultimately forcing Hooker to withdraw his army a day later. Meanwhile, Maj. Gen. Jubal Early's division, which had been fighting a rearguard action in Fredericksburg[35] to prevent Maj. Gen. John Sedgwick's VI Corps from reinforcing Hooker, was finally overwhelmed and forced to try to link up with Lee at Chancellorsville. Brig. Gen. Cadmus Wilcox's Alabamians delayed Sedgwick's advance at the Battle of Salem Church, buying time for reinforcements to arrive. Historian Ben Severance notes that "Lee's Alabama boys not only held but successfully counterattacked against heavy odds, thereby making the battle at Salem Church arguably Alabama's finest hour of the war."[36] Lt. Col. Hilary Herbert of the 8th Alabama Infantry, former captain of the regiment's Greenville Guards, recalled later that the Alabamians not only boldly attacked the Yankees but also "followed the enemy between one-half and three-quarters of a mile, with a very deadly fire."[37] While the brigade suffered 495 casualties, reinforcements soon arrived and defeated Sedgwick. Lee noted in his report that "Brigadier-General (now Major-General) Wilcox is entitled to especial praise for the judgment and bravery displayed in impeding the advance of General Sedgwick toward Chancellorsville, and for the gallant and successful stand at Salem Church."[38]

While Lee's piney woods soldiers celebrated their victory in Virginia, Maj. Gen. Ulysses S. Grant's Union Army of the Tennessee had crossed the Mississippi River at Bruinsburg, skirmished with the Rebels at Port Gibson, and marched east toward Jackson, Mississippi. Grant's ultimate objective was to destroy the Confederate garrison at Vicksburg, one of the last major impediments to complete Union control of the Mississippi River.[39] The Federals took Jackson on May 14 and then defeated the Army of Mississippi at the Battle of Champion Hill two days later, a mere twenty miles from the outskirts of Vicksburg. During the battle, the Union army captured hundreds of Confederate soldiers, including most of the 46th Alabama Infantry. The assault against Col. Michael L. Woods's position was so rapid that he never received orders, sent just minutes before the attack, to withdraw his regiment. Nearly all of the officers were killed or captured. Capt. Ley L. Croft from Henry County was taken prisoner along with most of his men, as was Pike County's Capt. Alexander McCaskill. He was severely wounded, his company was captured, and he died a few days later from pneumonia.[40]

The Union army that had fought and maneuvered so brilliantly for nearly three weeks now prepared to take Vicksburg. For the next six weeks, Grant besieged the city. By the end of June, half of the Confederate army defending Vicksburg was suffering from scurvy, the population had been reduced to eating rats and squirrels, and troop morale reached its lowest point of the war. In a stroke of irony, the Rebel garrison finally surrendered on July 4, Independence Day. Years later, Grant wrote in his memoirs that the "fate of the Confederacy was sealed when Vicksburg fell."[41]

While Vicksburg was surrendering, the Union Army of the Potomac was fighting for its life at Gettysburg, Pennsylvania. During the first three days in July, the Federals battled Lee's Army of Northern Virginia in a brutal struggle that began with the Confederacy's second invasion of the North. Back in June, as his army marched northward through western Virginia, Lee hoped that a major victory on Northern soil would strengthen the antiwar factions in the North, secure recognition of the Confederacy from European states, and possibly end the war. Fresh off its victory at Chancellorsville, the Rebel army, now seventy-five thousand strong, was at the pinnacle of its power. Spirits were high as the men marched through Pennsylvania farm country passing hundreds of Yankee civilians curious to get a glance at the "Johnny Rebs." One attractive young woman sat on the front steps of her home glaring derisively at the soldiers, "her bosom covered by a jaunty little Union flag." Upon seeing her, Martin Riley, a young private from Greenville, Alabama, with a penchant for humor, yelled out, "Madam, you had better be particular how you flaunt that flag—these boys are in the habit of charging breast-works wherever they see that flag flying."[42]

By the end of June, Lee's army and the Union army, now under the command of Maj. Gen. George Meade, converged upon Gettysburg. On the first day of battle, the Confederates drove Union cavalry and the leading elements of Meade's army out of Gettysburg onto the hills south of town. Four companies of soldiers from the piney woods, men from Butler, Henry, and Barbour counties, participated in the Rebel assault against Brig. Gen. John C. Reynolds Union I Corps northwest of town. At first, the 5th Alabama, 6th Alabama, and 12th Alabama of Col. Edward O'Neal's brigade did not have enough manpower to break through. Reinforcements soon arrived and gave the Alabamians the upper hand. The Yankee counterattack against Maj. Eugene Blackford's Henry County sharpshooters "drove in my men there posted behind the trees. These retired, firing from tree to tree until they met Gordon's brigade advancing, after which they were rallied on the center at the sound of my bugle."[43]

The next day, the Confederates launched simultaneous attacks against the Union right flank on Culp's Hill and against the left flank just east of the Emmitsburg Road, an area encompassing the Peach Orchard, Wheat Field, Devils Den, and Little Round Top. Divisions from Lt. Gens. Ambrose Powell Hill's and James Longstreet's corps launched attacks against the Union left at around 5:00 p.m. Amid all of the bitter fighting that afternoon, the role the 15th Alabama Infantry played in the struggle for Little Round Top became the stuff of legend. The vast majority of the regiment's soldiers came from piney woods companies, with a greater portion of those from Barbour and Henry counties, including the regimental commander Col. William C.

Oates. Born in 1835, Oates had spent his boyhood years on his family's small farm in Pike County. With a reputation for being a boisterous young troublemaker, he left home in his late teens and traveled from Alabama and northern Florida to Louisiana and Texas, taking on odd jobs to support himself. He moved back to Alabama in 1854, settled in Henry County, took a job as a school teacher, and within two years began studying law in Eufaula. By 1860, he owned a small law firm in Abbeville, Henry County, and supplemented his income as a newspaper editor. He not only supported secession, but raised and outfitted one of the county's first infantry companies, the Henry Pioneers.[44]

At the Little Round Top, the 15th Alabama was in position on the extreme right of the entire Confederate army.[45] Ordered to find the Federal left flank and do as much damage as possible, the regiment moved up the western slope of Round Top hill, down the other side, and up the smaller hill slightly to the northeast. There, they encountered Col. Joshua L. Chamberlain's 20th Maine, a regiment that had arrived at their position just fifteen minutes beforehand and hastily piled up rocks to create a strong defensive position. "From behind this ledge, unexpectedly to us," Oates recalled, "they poured into us the most destructive fire I ever saw."[46] After multiple charges, the Alabamians finally broke through the Blue line, but only temporarily. In fierce hand-to-hand combat, the men shot, stabbed, punched, bayonetted, and clubbed one another. At one point, Sgt. Patrick O'Conner from Eufaula thrust his bayonet through the head of a Union soldier who was attempting to grab the 15th Alabama's colors. The intensity of the fight finally forced the Confederates back down the hill, where they prepared for yet another charge. Knowing that his men were almost out of ammunition, Chamberlain rallied the Mainers and led a bayonet charge of his own. Whether Oates ordered a full retreat, as he later insisted, or Chamberlain's men swept them down the hill, the Rebels "ran like a herd of wild cattle" before the onrushing Federals.[47]

The 15th Alabama's losses were severe. Out of four hundred men, the regiment suffered 161 casualties. Col. Isaac Feagin from Barbour County was shot in the leg (which later required amputation). Captain Henry C. Brainard, a twenty-three-year-old school teacher from Henry County and "one of the bravest and best officers in the regiment," fell mortally wounded. "Oh God! That I could see my mother," he exclaimed only moments before he died.[48] Just before the regiment's movement up the hill, Oates had tried to convince his younger brother, Lt. John Oates, to remain behind. "If I were to remain here," John replied, "people would say that I did it through cowardice; no, sir, I am an officer and will never disgrace the uniform I wear; I shall go through, unless I am killed, which I think is quite likely."[49] He suffered multiple gunshot wounds and died three weeks later from his injuries. Pvt. John Keels was shot in the throat, his windpipe mutilated, and he died the next day. Oates recalled that the blood from the dead and wounded "stood in puddles in some places on the rocks; the ground was soaked with the blood of as brave men as ever fell on the red field of battle."[50]

On the final day of the battle, thirteen thousand Confederate soldiers attacked the center of the Union line on Cemetery Ridge, an action that came to be known as Pickett's Charge.[51] Brig. Gen. Cadmus Wilcox's brigade of Alabamians, including the Greenville Guards and the Jeff Davis Rangers—the only piney woods companies on the field that day—watched the bombardment and the attack, having been drawn up in reserve to the right of Pickett's original starting position. About thirty minutes into the fight, Wilcox's men moved forward, crossing the same ground that Pickett's men had crossed just a little while before. As they neared the stone wall, they encountered the same destructive fire as their comrades had, yet Wilcox could see none of the units that he was ordered to support. It is probable that by the time Wilcox arrived, there were few, if any, of Pickett's men left to support along that section of the line. He rode back to the artillery and requested support, but they had already used up all of their ammunition. "Not getting any artillery to fire upon the enemy's infantry that were on my left flank . . . and knowing that my small force could do nothing save to make a useless sacrifice of themselves, I ordered them back."[52] Pickett's Charge failed. After three days of hard, bloody fighting Lee's army retreated back into Virginia. Longstreet, Pickett's commanding officer, recalled years later: "that day at Gettysburg was one of the saddest of my life."[53]

The devastating losses at Vicksburg and Gettysburg weighed heavily upon the army as well as the Confederacy. James McPherson maintains that the loss of Vicksburg was an even greater blow to the men of the Army of Northern Virginia than their own defeat at Gettysburg. Jason Phillips similarly observes that "much of the grief in the summer of 1863 did not derive from a fear that the war was lost. Instead many men lamented that setbacks prolonged the conflict. Vicksburg crushed their dreams of an early peace." At least one piney woods soldier agreed. "I fear the War will last for the next 50 years," Lt. Joshua Callaway of the 28th Alabama infantry wrote just after the city's fall. "The future does indeed look dark and gloomy. Oh, when will the end be!"[54]

To make matters worse, in early September, Confederate Gen. Braxton Bragg abandoned Chattanooga without a fight, leaving one of the South's most important railroad hubs in Union hands. Later that month, however, Southern optimism lifted with the Confederate Army of Tennessee's victory at the Battle of Chickamauga in northern Georgia. On September 19,

Bragg attacked Maj. Gen. William S. Rosecrans's Union Army of the Cumberland just west of Chickamauga Creek. The early morning attack began on the Union left in the woods north of Brotherton Road, but by mid-day the fighting had spread south along a two-mile front running roughly parallel with the Lafayette/Chattanooga Road. Around 2:00 p.m., Brig. Gen. Henry D. Clayton's Alabama brigade was among the first that afternoon to engage the Union center about two hundred yards southeast of Brotherton Farm in woods and undergrowth so thick that many of the men could not see twenty feet beyond their position. One hour later, the brigade fell back, cut to pieces by Union artillery and small arms fire. The 18th Alabama Infantry, including four companies of piney woods soldiers, suffered 35 killed and 175 wounded, about 40 percent of its strength. Yet, their day was not done. Thirty minutes later, while the brigades of Brig. Gens. William Bates and John C. Brown pushed through the same woods, Clayton's men reengaged and helped drive the Federals back (see Figure 7.1). The men "moved forward in good order," Maj. Peter F. Hunley of the 18th Alabama later reported, "passed General Bate's line, and, having broken the enemy's line, drove him about 1 mile or more, capturing a battery."[55]

About a mile away Brig. Gen. Sterling Wood's Brigade prepared to attack the Federal left, an area already strewn with the bodies of dead Confederates repulsed hours earlier. With only a half hour of daylight left, the brigade's 33rd Alabama Infantry—soldiers from Butler, Dale, Coffee, Covington, and Montgomery counties—took position on the far left of the formation. Under a hailstorm of bullets and shrapnel, which Maj. Gen. Patrick Cleburne later reported "was the heaviest I had ever heard," the grey line edged forward through the woods and over an open field, pushing the enemy before them (see Figure 7.1).[56] In the fading twilight, soldiers from both sides relied upon the orange flash of musketry to guide them. Hundreds fell behind, confused, disoriented, or downright terrified. Stragglers from the 33rd Alabama accidently fired into the backs of their own friends. "In advancing and fighting in the dark, some laggards persisted in shooting from the rear," Pvt. William E. Matthews recalled. "Such a one of our men killed Adjutant Alfred M. Moore . . . shooting him in the neck accidentally from the rear."[57] Moore's personal slave accompanied the body back to Alabama, where it was received by a grieving father, the former governor.

While Wood's Brigade had pushed the Yankees back about three hundred yards, the issue was far from settled. That night, Longstreet's two divisions arrived from Virginia. About mid-morning the next day, Wood's Brigade, Clayton's Brigade, and several units from Longstreet's command attacked the Federal line near the Poe Farm. From behind makeshift breastworks, the Yankees poured a deadly mixture of canister and small arms fire into

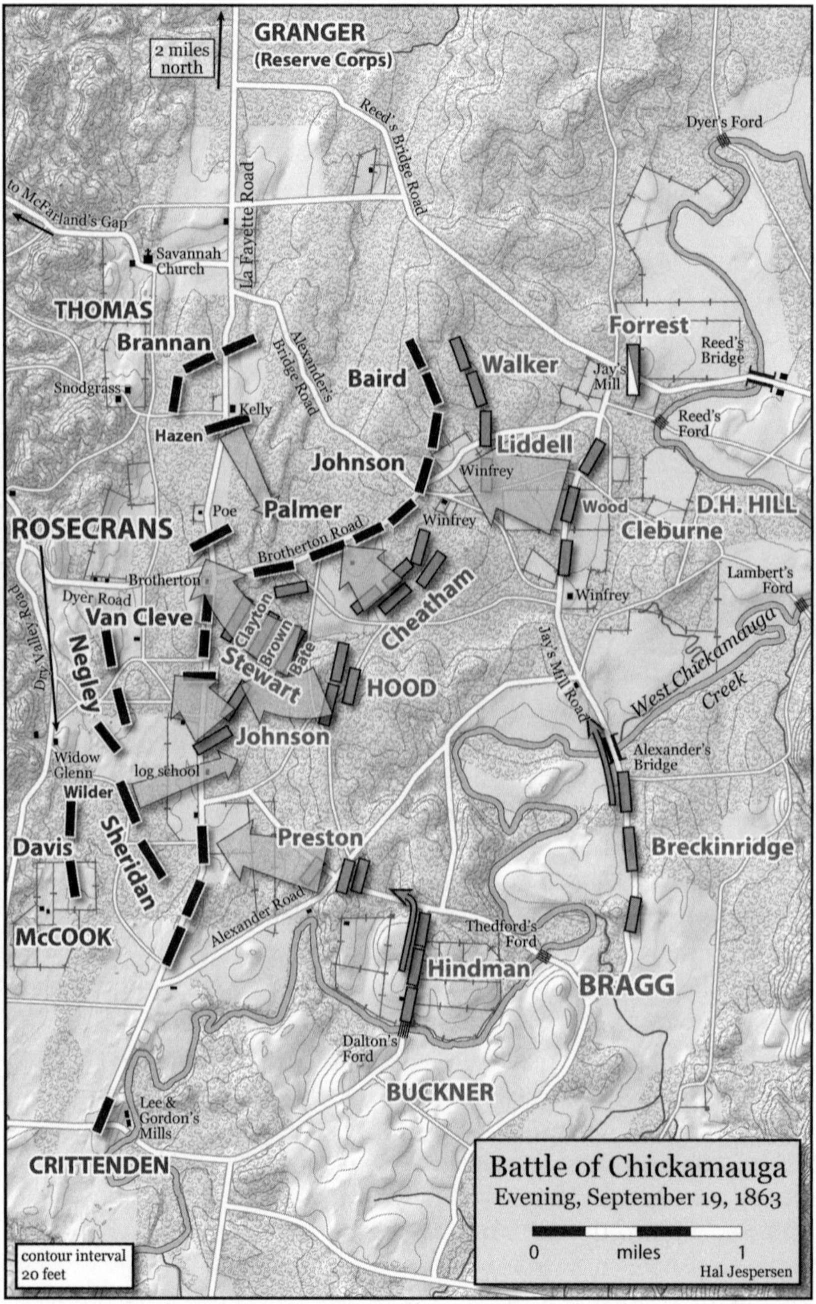

7.1. Battle of Chickamauga, evening of September 19, 1863

7.2. Col. Samuel Adams, 33rd Alabama Infantry (courtesy of the Alabama Department of Archives and History)

the Confederate ranks. Col. Samuel Adams led his piney woods regiment across Poe Field and past the burning farm house to within forty yards of the Blue line. There he grabbed his regiment's colors and tried in vain to rally the fewer than one hundred nonstragglers who were still with him. In less than an hour, no fewer than five brigades had been repulsed.

After this failed attempt, Longstreet orchestrated a massive, concentrated attack that broke the Union line, sending two-thirds of the Federal army into full retreat.[58] Pvt. Thomas Bigbie of Company C, 33rd Alabama, wrote to his wife the day after the battle: "on sundy wee [attacked] their brest work and faild to take them the first time. late in the evening wee drove them back from the brest works and they left that night. wee have advanced five or six miles and it is said that they are in full retret and I am in hops that is so and I think that wee will keep them a going. we have got a reinforcement from

Verginia and I think that wee will push them [though] we lost a heepe of men and they lost a heep."[59] The Union army fled back to Chattanooga in disarray, giving the Army of Tennessee its most significant victory of the war. Bragg soon occupied the heights on Lookout Mountain and Missionary Ridge, cut the supply lines to the city, and prepared to starve the Yankees into submission. By the end of November, however, fortunes turned as Confederates suffered numerous setbacks and reluctantly retreated into northern Georgia. For soldiers and civilians alike, the brief season of hope and jubilation following Confederate victory at Chickamauga had once again turned to defeat and despair.

As the Army of Tennessee went into winter quarters near Dalton, Georgia, the situation back home in the piney woods went from bad to worse. For women in the region, inflation, depravation, and the toils of labor, even among some in the upper classes, continued to take their toll. The situation was so distressing to Martha Flournoy that, by February 1864, she seriously considered abandoning her Pike County farm and moving back with her parents. Celia, the rented slave who had helped her for almost two years was now gone, as was Martha's teenage brother Jimmy, who had taken care of the farm until January 1864, when he left home to join the 45th Alabama Infantry, leaving his sister all alone and desperate for help. Writing from Dalton, Georgia, Elisha Flournoy of the 46th Alabama admitted that the possibility of Martha "breaking up house" was more upsetting than anything he had experienced since the war began—which was amazing considering that he had fought in some of the war's bloodiest battles. "Just think for a moment what will become of our stock and everything else," he wrote in February 1864. "I feel like we are almost ruined now and if you do break up and leave home you will find that it is the worst thing you ever done in life I am sorry to think you ever had such a notion it is the most distressing thing that has ever crossed my mind." He encouraged Martha once again to try and find someone to stay with her and help out on the farm. "I know it seems lonely and hard for you to stay there but . . . there is no other place so good as your own home."[60] Elisha's handling of this situation suggests that, while he was well aware of Martha's predicament, he was unwilling to leave his company and return home.

For Martha Flournoy and her neighbors, the final year of the war brought the conflict closer to their doorsteps than they could have imagined three years earlier. At times, the citizenry must have felt that they were under siege from the Yankees as well as their own government. Confederate cavalry operating mostly in northwest Florida occasionally ventured into South Alabama foraging or hunting for deserters. A force of about three hundred infantry and cavalry from Col. Orlando S. Holland's 37th Mississippi Infantry marched through the region in April 1864, rounding up deserters and confiscating the property of suspected Unionists. The regiment traveled by rail from Pollard to Sparta, then on foot southeast to Brooklyn, through Covington County, and down into Florida. At Sparta, according to one report, "we met with a most hospitable reception; the ladies manifesting their joy and sympathies for our cause by an invitation 'to trip the light fantastic toe' at an evening party. Our soldiers accepted the honor with becoming grace. . . . Our next march brought us to Brooklyn, on the Sepulga river, where we were welcomed amid bright faces, the waving of white kerchiefs and miniature flags."[61]

Despite the writer's glowing account, other communities were not at all happy to have Confederate cavalry in their neighborhoods. Thomas P. Cottle, Covington County's enrollment officer, informed Governor Watts that Lt. Needham Cannady's cavalry was terrorizing the citizenry. They "went to the house of an absent solder and insulted his wife and dauthers and threattened to ravish them," arrested men suspected of desertion without proper authority, and stole private property without compensating the owners. When Cottle demanded the prisoners' release, Cannady angrily responded that he "would be d—d if he did not send them to the army." The ensuing argument became so heated that Cannady arrested Cottle, only to free him a short time later when cooler heads prevailed. "Our most loyal responsable and upright citizens say that they do not feel safe while they are in the county and ernstly desire that they may be ordered a way and others sent in their place," Cottle wrote. The governor sent letters to both Richmond and to Gen. Dabnay Maury, commander of the District of the Gulf in Mobile, condemning the actions of overzealous cavalry and protesting what he believed to be flagrant violations of the conscript laws.[62]

Meanwhile, in Richmond, the Confederate Congress amended the conscription laws again in February 1864. The new law expanded the pool of recruits to those between the ages of seventeen and fifty, finally eliminated substitutions, reduced the number of exemption categories by half, gave the president more authority over the exemption process, and changed the "twenty negro law" to a "fifteen negro law" with added restrictions. The legislation also allowed states to recruit younger men between ages seventeen and eighteen and older men between forty-five and fifty to serve completely within the confines of their respective states.[63] In many respects, Richmond was not only responding to the growing manpower crisis but also reacting to public pressure to change a system perceived to be wholly unfair. Importantly, by developing a system of state reserves, Congress hoped to encourage the men who remained at home, regardless of the reason, to get involved in the war.[64]

Some piney woods communities responded to the new law by raising new companies for local defense.[65] In Greenville, former Confederate soldier David Gaffney requested permission from the governor to raise a company in Butler County. Judge Samuel J. Bolling and state Representative S. F. Gafford endorsed the idea: "We think if you would give him authority to raise a company that he would be able to do so in a few days. We will use all our influence in assisting him." Two weeks later, the company appeared to have enough volunteers but lacked the necessary weapons. "Can you let us have guns and ammunition," Gafford requested, "and when you furnish us with these articles I think we can make a pretty good fight."[66] In Clayton, meanwhile, Capt. Lovard Lee wanted to send a portion of his company to help protect Selma—one of the South's major manufacturing centers and a prime Federal target—and then raise additional men at home to replace them. "I have some forty men who would be pleased to receive orders for proper authority to report at Selma to give all the aid in our power in driving back [the Yankees] from our beloved state."[67] The governor endorsed the plan.

By the spring of 1864, while home guard units attempted to fill their ranks with teenagers and older men, piney woods Confederates in Virginia and Georgia continued to slog it out with Federal armies more than twice their size. In sheer intensity and brutality, the fighting during Ulysses S. Grant's Overland Campaign eclipsed that of previous operations. From early May until late June, Confederates inflicted nearly sixty thousand casualties on the Federal army. "Great confidence is felt in Grant," wrote Union Secretary of the Navy Gideon Welles, "but the immense slaughter of our brave men chills and sickens us all."[68] Lee learned quickly that Grant, unlike previous union commanders, would not run away or disengage for months at a time after getting his nose bloodied in battle.

On May 5, two corps from Lee's army clashed with three Federal corps in a thickly wooded area about five miles west of Chancellorsville. The Battle of the Wilderness raged back and forth in woods so dense and smoke so thick that men at times could not see five or ten feet in front of their faces. Embers from artillery and small arms fire ignited the woods, engulfing the wounded in horrifying deaths. Brig. Gen. Cullen Battle's Brigade participated in the ferocious fighting that took place in Saunders Field, a relatively small clearing along the Orange Turnpike. Battle personally led the brigade's newest regiment, the 61st Alabama Infantry. Although the regiment had been organized in Pollard in 1863 as part of Gen. James Clanton's brigade, mutiny within the ranks prompted Confederate officials to transfer the unit from South Alabama "to more active fields of service, as the natural remedy for the discontent supposed to exist."[69] When the 61st Alabama took the field for the first time on May 5, they inflicted massive casualties on the 104th

New York Zouaves, in addition to capturing a battery of six guns. The regiment "loomed up in magnificent proportions . . . and its men were the first to place their hands on the captured guns," Battle reported. Capt. Archibald McCaskill, a twenty-seven-year-old merchant from Buzbeeville, was one of several piney woods soldiers killed during the assault.[70] The next day, both armies launched attacks and counterattacks but neither side gained a tactical advantage. This time, however, the Union Army did not retreat back across the Rappahannock River but regrouped and moved south toward Richmond.

At Spotsylvania Court House, piney woods soldiers fighting with Brig. Gen. Abner Perrin's brigade helped save the Confederate Army from being completely overrun by Federal assaults at a place called the Bloody Angle. Less than a week after disengaging at Spotsylvania, Confederate and Union forces began constructing a series of parallel trenches and earthworks near Cold Harbor. On June 3, three Federal corps launched a massive attack against fortified Confederate entrenchments in one of the most ill-fated attacks of the war. The night before, piney woods soldiers and others from the 15th Alabama worked all night building up their defensive works. As the sun began to rise, Noah Feagin's Barbour County boys, who had been sent out a couple of hours earlier as skirmishers, came running back toward the trenches with the advancing Yankees in close pursuit. As the Alabamians fired volley after volley, Rebel artillery poured double canister into the bluecoat lines as fast as the men could load and fire. "The blaze of fire from it at each shot went right into the ranks of our assailants and made frightful gaps through the dense mass of men," Col. William C. Oates wrote. The Federals regrouped and charged again, only this time they met both direct and flanking fire. "I could see the dust fog out of a man's clothing in two or three places at once where as many balls would strike him at the same moment. In two minutes not a man of them was standing."[71] Seven thousand Union soldiers fell in about six hours that day, while Rebel losses amounted to fewer than fifteen hundred. "I have always regretted that the last assault at Cold Harbor was ever made," Grant recorded in his memoirs.[72]

While Grant and Lee were slugging it out in Virginia, Mag. Gen. William Tecumseh Sherman's army group—three separate Union armies fighting together under Sherman's generalship—executed a series of flanking movements around the Confederate Army of Tennessee from Chattanooga south to Atlanta.[73] Sherman was not interested in bleeding his army to death by launching suicidal assaults against fortified Confederate positions. Each time Johnston moved his army onto advantageous ground, Sherman simply moved around the flanks, threatened Johnston's railroad supply lines, and forced the Rebels to retreat.

In early June, Sherman's end-around campaign literally bogged down less than twenty miles from Atlanta. For three weeks, drenching rains, coupled with Johnston's ever-expanding defensive fortifications around Marietta, frustrated the Union high command and prompted Sherman to launch an attack against Confederate entrenchments at Kennesaw Mountain in hopes of breaking the stalemate. On June 27, the Federals feigned an attack against Kennesaw Mountain while launching the main assaults several miles south at Pigeon Hill and Cheatham's Hill.[74] Nearly all of the three thousand bluecoats who fell that day perished in front of the "Dead Angle," a point on Cheatham's Hill where the Rebel earthworks made a sharp turn southward. "The ground was piled up with one solid mass of dead and wounded Yankees," wrote Pvt. Sam Watkins of the 1st Tennessee Infantry. "I learned afterwards from the burying squad that in some places they were piled up like cord wood, twelve deep."[75] To the right of the Dead Angle, the 33rd Alabama Infantry of Patrick Cleburne's Division, a regiment raised almost entirely in the piney woods, participated in the slaughter. The division killed or wounded an estimated one thousand Yankees in their front while suffering only two dead and seven injured. One of the two soldiers killed in Cleburne's Division was Capt. William E. Dodson, a twenty-nine-year-old merchant from Greenville.[76] The battle was a much-needed victory for the Confederates but, true to form, Sherman's flanking movements forced the Confederates to retreat yet again.

Jefferson Davis grew tired of Gen. Joseph E. Johnston's slow, demoralizing retreat and replaced him with Lt. Gen. John Bell Hood, a commander known for his aggressiveness in battle. Although historians have debunked the phrase once attributed to Robert E. Lee that Hood was "all lion and no fox," the reality may have actually come closer to the truth than the mythical statement. "When we learned Hood was in command," wrote Pvt. William E. Matthews of the 33rd Alabama, "all agreed that we had hard work in front of us."[77] On July 20, just three days after taking command, Hood launched an attack against Sherman's army two miles north of Atlanta at Peachtree Creek. At first the Rebels caught the Federals off guard but the bluecoats quickly rallied, held their ground, and inflicted twenty-five hundred casualties on their attackers. For the soldiers of the 57th Alabama Infantry, a regiment of later-enlisters from Coffee, Dale, Henry, Pike, and Barbour counties, this was their first real taste of battle. "Our men acted bravely, drove the enemy out of their first line of fortifications but were unable to hold their position, and were driven back by force of numbers," wrote Joel Dyer Murphree to his wife the day after the battle. "The last [I] seen of Baily he was retreating from the enemy in the rear of his Company exposed to the fire of the enemies shot and shell. . . . He may have laid down behind something to protect him and was captured."[78] In fact, Baily M. Talbot, a thirty-year-old grocer from Troy and close neighbor to the Murphrees, was killed that day along with Maj. William R. Arnold, while Lt. Col. Richard Bethune and Lt. Alexander Faison, Talbot's second in command, were seriously wounded.[79] The regiment lost 157 out of just 330 men at Peachtree Creek, nearly 50 percent of its effective fighting force. Capt. Augustus L. Milligan from Dale County later reported: "The long list of casualties in this regiment in the engagement of the 20th instant will be sufficient evidence of its deep devotion to the cause of Southern liberty and independence."[80]

During the next four weeks, Hood tried again and again to strike a significant blow against the Union army, but each time his plans were foiled and his soldiers defeated. This strategy wreaked havoc on soldiers from the piney woods. "The change in commanders no doubt caused the death or capture of those near and dear to us," Joel Murphree lamented, "but I do believe it was the best for the success of our cause."[81] The 33rd Alabama, for instance, suffered seventy-nine casualties at the Battle of Peachtree Creek, including the death of Col. Samuel Adams. Shot dead by a Union sharpshooter, "this true patriot and Christian hero—a perfect specimen of a soldier and gentleman—who had distinguished himself on many well-fought fields, fell at his post, leaving his gallant regiment to feel as orphans, and many other friends and comrades in arms to mourn an irreparable loss."[82] Two days later, the same regiment was under fire in the Battle of Atlanta when Pvt. William Matthews witnessed a ghastly site. "One of the regiment wondered among us with a minie ball in his forehead and a knot of brains as big as a hen's egg over the hole. Occasionally we could hear another ball strike him. He did not appear to mind, and we not caring, thinking the sooner he died, the better."[83] Hood ultimately abandoned Atlanta to avoid being cut off and surrounded. As the victorious Yankees marched into the city, Sherman wired President Lincoln: "Atlanta is ours, and fairly won."[84]

Back home in the piney woods, desertion had become especially problematic after Confederate defeats at Mobile Bay in August and Atlanta in September 1864. Judge Gappa T. Yelverton of Coffee County estimated that there were some two thousand deserters between southeastern Alabama and the Florida Gulf Coast.[85] At this late stage of the war, many of the disaffected were not just deserters trying to take care of their destitute families, or draft dodgers hiding out in the woods close to home to avoid the war, but organized bands of heavily armed ex-soldiers who continued to prey upon the local citizenry. Historian Malcolm McMillan has suggested that "all were outside the law after deserting and thus were forced to become bushwhackers to sustain themselves and their families."[86]

In Evergreen, Andrew Jay, one of the wealthiest planters in Conecuh

County, created a company of mounted reserves to protect the southern portion of the county from both Federal raiders and local bushwhackers. In Jay's estimation, this was the only way to respond effectively to such emergencies. "I have not the confidence in the reserve militia force," he wrote to Governor Watts. "Scattered as they are throughout the county it must be a tedious business to gather them, and then the tardiness of movement will render them in my opinion of little avail." He assured the governor that the men would provide their horses and shotguns but needed some help procuring ammunition. "I don't want a better weapon than my own double barrel," Jay wrote, "but give us good heavy blue whistlers and good [percussion] caps and we will try and take care of Conecuh."[87]

Perhaps the most interesting episodes involving the disaffected occurred in Henry, Dale, and Coffee counties. Stories about anti-Confederates such as "Speckled" John Ward, Joseph Sanders, and Bill Sketoe attained near mythological status in the annals of Alabama's post–Civil War history. To be sure, the counties of Dale and Coffee were so volatile that the circuit judge refused to hold court without a military escort during the final two years of the war. Back in April 1864, a band of deserters, reportedly led by John Ward, slipped into Elba late one night and burned down the courthouse. According to legend, Ward had been discharged from the Confederate army in 1863, only to be conscripted back into the military a year later. He reportedly murdered the conscript officer who tried to arrest him and became an outlaw deserter hiding out in the swamps in the extreme southeastern corner of the region. The torching of the courthouse, where all of the conscription records and tax records were kept, was an attack upon the system that Ward and his men believed to be unfair. Fortunately for the citizens of Elba, a group of Masons meeting nearby rushed into the burning building and saved most of the county's records.[88]

In September, the outlaws hit the town again, this time at one in the morning. Three buildings were soon ablaze; one housed the new conscript office, the others were temporary offices being used by county officials. A group of slaves who lived and worked at a nearby sawmill extinguished the fires, thus saving the town square from certain destruction. Meanwhile, a ten-man posse rounded up a pack of bloodhounds, hunted down the perpetrators, and caught up with them seventeen miles south of Elba. The ensuing skirmish, known locally as the Battle of Fairview, resulted in the deaths of three posse members: a Confederate tax assessor, a local tax collector, and the deputy sheriff. Several deserters also were killed or wounded. In response, twenty-five influential citizens petitioned Montgomery for the return of a company of reserves recently called up by the governor. According to O. G. Payne, the local enrolling officer who endorsed the petition, I "feel that my own life is in danger. If some protection is not afforded now, I will be unable to discharge the duties of my office."[89]

The governor's response is not recorded, but several soldiers returning home on furlough or permanent discharge were eager to help. Col. James Lightfoot of the 6th Alabama Infantry spent a few weeks on furlough at his home in Henry County. He learned that the county had six or seven reserve companies and suggested to the governor "that it would be a good idea to station one or more companies in the lower portion of the county in that region mostly affected with deserters & Tories and relieve them every week or ten days. By doing this I think it would effectively break them up and no person would be absent from his business longer than a week or ten days."[90] Pvt. Charles H. Reading, who lost an arm in the battles around Atlanta, hoped likewise to raise a company of mounted infantry in Henry County. "I have made application to be retired," he wrote. "I purpose (when I get my retired or discharge papers) to raise a company of boys (under seventeen) to remain in the 8th congressinal dist for the purpose of hunting up deserters."[91]

Another soldier who attempted to solve the desertion problem in the extreme southeastern counties was Capt. John C. Brown, part of the posse who fought in the Battle of Fairview. He later served as captain of a home guard company in Maj. Joseph Barbiere's Cavalry Battalion.[92] Sometime in January 1865, he hatched a plan to organize a regiment or possibly even a brigade of disaffected citizens and ex-soldiers to fight solely under his command, with guarantees that the unit would not be divided and would not be sent into the Confederate army. According to both Judge Yelverton and Alabama Attorney General Marvin A. Baldwin, Brown was the perfect man for the job. As a middle-class merchant, farmer, and small slave owner from Buzbeeville in southern Coffee County, he understood that section of the state and knew many of the deserters and their families personally. "As to Captain Brown," wrote Solicitor James Arrington, "I have been well acquainted with him for years, and take pleasure in saying that I know of no one better fitted than him for such an undertaking. He is an experienced officer, bold, firm, intelligent, and of unswerving integrity."[93] As far as some of the deserters were concerned, Baldwin summed up their grievances:

> What private griefs they have to take their present status I know not, except they are generally poor men, and there was much difficulty in the way of having their families provided for in their absence. This, added to the fact that they were assigned to companies in the service not of their choice, and the fact that they resided near the coast of Florida, from whence were occasional raids by the enemy, partly

> prompted them to take the position as deserters. Considering that they had perhaps forfeited their lives, and their characters ruined, many of them, I understand, have been giving the enemy not only aid and comfort, but actually fighting against us. Many of them desire to return if they can be allowed to join in an organization by Captain Brown, whom they all know. He lives among them and they know him well, and know that he is a high-minded, brave, and generous man.[94]

While there is no record that Brown's plan was put wholly into effect, Baldwin's assessment of the growing bands of outlaws in the southernmost counties demonstrates three things. First, some men were eager to serve but would not sacrifice the safety of their homes or families to do so. Second, and perhaps more important, the Confederacy had failed to protect families on the home front. If the state and national governments could not provide for and protect their families then they would, even if it meant collaborating with Union forces in northern Florida. Finally, if Baldwin was right, then as late as January 1865 some individuals continued to demand the right to choose their own companies. In many respects then, the southernmost piney woods counties in Alabama were similar to certain areas in piney woods Georgia late in the war. "Although deep within the Confederate interior," Mark Wetherington observes, "wiregrass Georgia was not clearly under Confederate control. In many respects, the landscape resembled a no-man's-land." Some soldiers decided to return home, "in essence deserting a front-line war with the Yankees to face another threat within the Confederacy's deteriorating interior."[95] As for John C. Brown, the evidence suggests that his company served out the rest of the war defending the central part of the state, surrendering with Barbiere's Battalion at Citronelle in May 1865.[96]

The problems in the southernmost counties worsened as increasing numbers of men began collaborating with the Union army in Pensacola. Perhaps the most well-known Unionist in the piney woods, or infamous depending upon one's perspective, was Alfred Holley of Covington County. Before the war, Holley served multiple terms in the lower house of the state legislature. During that time, he focused almost exclusively upon helping his constituents and supporting his county while avoiding the sectional issues of the late 1850s. Yet in the months leading up to war, Holley declared his opposition to secession and voted against every piece of legislation that he believed would weaken the Union. He lost his bid for reelection in 1861 but ran again two years later, successfully winning a fifth term in office. True to form, he opposed a bill to reorganize the militia system and attacked proposals that would have made it easier for officials to hunt down deserters and Unionists. His opposition to this last measure may have been an attempt to protect his own self-interest.

During the war, Holley and his oldest son, Calvin, frequently sold cotton, cattle, and horses to the Federals in Pensacola. Col. Orlando S. Holland's cavalry raid in March 1864, exposed these activities. Holland's men seized one thousand head of cattle; confiscated thousands of dollars' worth of tobacco, horses, and mules; and sent Holley fleeing toward the coast. On April 1, a party of Confederates attacked Holley and five members of the Bass family as they tried to escape by boat from present-day Niceville, Florida, through Boggy Bayou, down to Union-held Santa Rosa Island. The next day, he reported to Union officials that three members of the family were killed and two wounded in the attack. He and Calvin spent the remainder of the war in Pensacola helping the Union army in every way that they could.[97]

Meanwhile, in mid-November 1864, Gen. William Sherman decided to cut his supply lines near Atlanta, live off the land, and move his army south to capture Savannah. John Bell Hood's strategy, which James McPherson has called a fantasy "scripted in never-never land," was to disengage Sherman's army, move northward through Tennessee and Kentucky, pick up twenty thousand recruits, defeat a Union army almost twice the size of his own, and link up with Lee in Virginia.[98] This plan came crashing down after the Battle of Franklin, an ill-advised and reckless attack that cost the Army of Tennessee nearly seven thousand soldiers, at least a dozen generals, and over fifty regimental commanders.[99] In the late afternoon hours of November 30, twenty thousand Confederates, including hundreds of piney woods soldiers, attacked fortified Union entrenchments in the bloodiest, most violent engagement of the war west of the Appalachian Mountains. The assault lasted for almost six hours and often involved brutal hand-to-hand combat. "When we got to their works, our ranks were so thin that our boys could not get over," Pvt. William Matthews of the 33rd Alabama later recalled. "Many were shot in the attempt. Among them was our color bearer, Neal Godwin, and the flag was seized by the enemy. But we did not need any colors since the regiment was almost annihilated."[100] Brig. Gen. Zachery Deas's Brigade, which included eleven companies from the piney woods, entered the fray right as the sun set and was cut to pieces (see Figure 7.3). "Their dead were mostly in the trenches and on the works of the enemy, where they nobly fell in a desperate hand-to-hand conflict."[101]

The 17th Alabama Infantry, which included about two hundred soldiers from Butler and Pike counties, entered the battle with Brig. Gen. Charles Shelley's Brigade (see Figure 7.3). According to Maj. Gen. Edward Walthall, while these men were "terribly torn at every step by an oblique fire from a

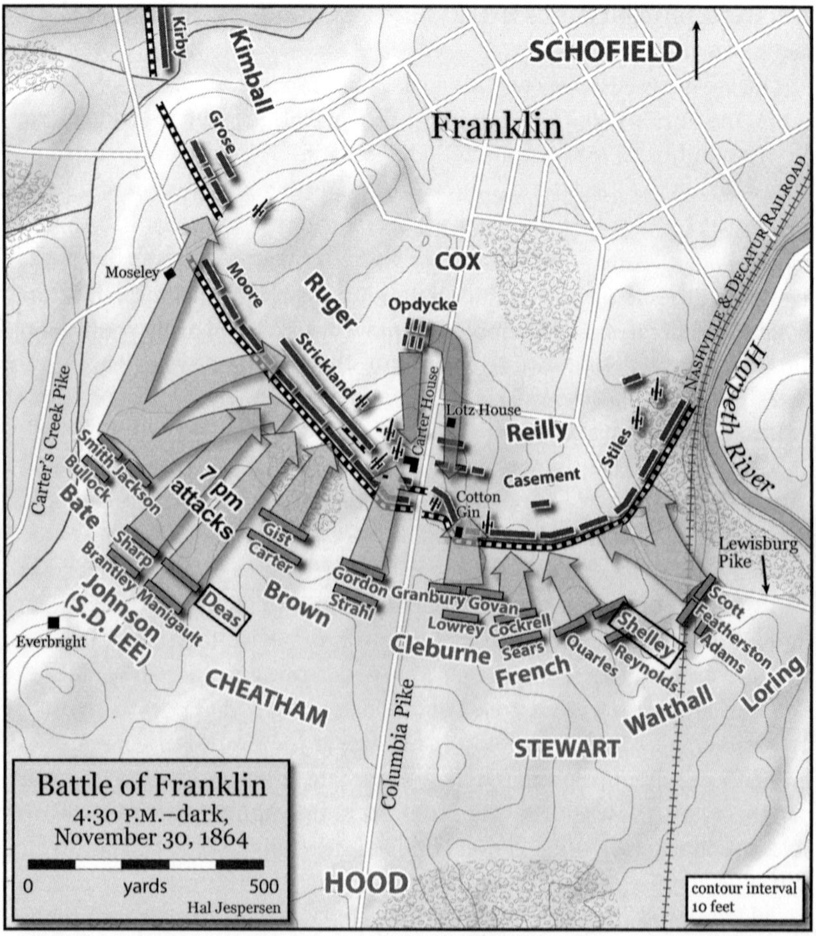

7.3. Battle of Franklin, 4:30 P.M. to dark on November 30, 1864

battery advantageously posted at the enemy's left, no less than by the destructive fire in front, the line moved on and did not falter till, just to the right of the [Lewisburg] pike, it reached the abatis fronting the works." The 17th Alabama lost two-thirds of its men trying to drive the Federals from their fortifications. Capt. Thomas A. McCane from Butler County was captured, along with Col. Virgil S. Murphey, Capt. William W. McMillian, and dozens of others.[102] "The men bounded over like infuriated demons," Murphey wrote in his diary, "and were either shot down on the summit of the works or were [bayoneted]. The conflict was brief, bloody, and decisive. I was a prisoner."[103] Most of what was left of the regiment was either killed or captured at Nashville two weeks later. Years after the war, Lt. Col. Isaac R. Sherwood of the 111th Ohio Infantry noted in his memoirs that "Franklin dug the grave of the Confederacy. . . . At midnight on the battlefield of Franklin, the finger of destiny was lifted, pointing the open road to Appomattox."[104]

As the western Confederacy crumbled, Lee's Army of Northern Virginia barely held on in Virginia. For ten months, in the wake of the Overland Campaign, Grant carried out siege operations against Petersburg, an important railroad hub and key supply center for the Confederate capital at Richmond. Despite numerous setbacks, Grant used his 100,000-man army to tighten the noose slowly and methodically around just forty-five thousand Confederates. Lee attempted to move his skeleton army south to join up with Joseph E. Johnston in North Carolina but the retreating Confederates were cut off at Appomattox Court House.[105]

By this point of the war, most Alabamians understood that the end of the conflict and demise of the Confederacy was all but assured. Governor Watts issued one last desperate appeal to the state's male population, especially the young men:

> I make one more appeal to your manhood and your love of country. Do you love your state? You will not hesitate to rally to her defense. Would you keep and enjoy your property? You must now defend it. Do you love your wives and children? You must prepare, at once, to defend them. . . . Do you love your mother and sisters? Then, young men! put on the amour of war and strike for them "for God and your native land." Do you love liberty? You must draw your swords – shoulder your guns – and show, by your acts, that you will be freemen.

Yet there was little that could be done to halt the Union advance or alter the outcome of the war. Federal cavalry rode more or less unopposed throughout south Alabama while deserters from both armies continued to pillage local citizens and raid towns and neighborhoods along the Florida border. In late March, Joseph Sanders, a former Confederate captain who had deserted and joined the 1st Florida Cavalry (United States), led a small detachment into Newton. Fortunately for the townspeople, word of the raid leaked out and a contingent of angry citizens led by a partially disabled veteran of the 15th Alabama Infantry surprised the raiders and ran them out of town.[106] Two weeks later, Maj. Gen. Benjamin H. Grierson's Federal cavalry raided an area from Conecuh County through Butler, Pike, and Barbour all the way to Eufaula on the Chattahoochee River. For the citizens of the piney woods, the war was finally over.

The final two years of the war brought increasing hardship, poverty, deprivation, and occasional violence to many of the neighborhoods and communities in southeastern Alabama. Violence became all too common for some piney woods communities, especially those in the southernmost counties, where bands of outlaws terrorized local citizens, Confederate forces hunted down deserters, and home guard units harassed and arrested suspected unionists. Although women suffered through deprivations unimaginable four years earlier, they did their best to keep their homes, farms, and families intact.

As for the combatants themselves, the piney woods soldiers who remained faithful to the war effort until the fighting ended in the spring of 1865 did so despite overwhelming odds. From the surviving letters, diaries, and memoirs, it appears that many of the region's soldiers were willing to continue the fight and encouraged their families back home to do the same. To be sure, some men deserted or slipped home for extended unauthorized leaves of absence, but many if not most of these men returned to their units or joined other commands. In the aftermath of the carnage at Cold Harbor, Joseph Green Terry wrote to his wife in Henry County what may have been the motivating factor for every piney woods soldier late in the war: "But we came to fight and we would do it cheerfully if it would end the war. . . . Lord end it for I want to be at home with my lovely little family for they are all that I have and I feel that they are very dear to me. What an awful war this is."[107]

Epilogue

On June 23, 1865, Capt. E. D. Johnson arrived in Elba, Alabama, with thirty of his troopers from the 2nd Maine Cavalry. Their mission was to find out whether the reports of attacks against the citizens of Coffee County were true. "From the best information I could gather," he reported, "more than fifty men, mostly deserters from the First Florida Cavalry, US Army, are engaged in robbing, plundering, and committing acts of violence."[1] By the fall, most of these renegade bands had been cleared out by the Federal army, but the onset of Reconstruction created a whole new dynamic for communities in the piney woods.

Four years of war had practically destroyed the region's economy and left many of its citizens destitute. Johnson witnessed widespread poverty as his cavalry rode through counties in the southeastern corner of the region. "The country is very poor in Coffee County," he observed, "and the whole country in that section of the State of Alabama and those parts of Florida contiguous to it."[2] In Sparta, Judge John Henderson counted more than seven hundred indigent women and children, most without any visible means of support. "It is impossible almost to enumerate the different Reasons or Causes of the indigence of these families," he noted, "the greater number of them have been rendered indigent by the death or disability of their husbands or protectors in the war."[3] Union Gen. Wager Swayne served as Alabama's assistant commissioner for the Bureau of Refugees, Freedmen, and Abandoned Lands, also known as the Freedmen's Bureau. "It is my desire," he wrote to Young M. Rabb of Conecuh County, "being charged with certain [responsibilities] for the general welfare of the destitute white and of all black persons, to employ the assistance of every right minded man who can be got to work with me, and to render what help I can in turn."[4] Rabb became the bureau's assistant superintendent for Conecuh County and immediately began distributing rations, clothing, and medical care to the poor. Superintendents from other piney woods counties also contributed to the relief efforts.[5]

The bureau worked closely with northern aid societies to raise money and provide foodstuffs for the needy. Between April and August 1867, for instance, relief organizations from New York, Philadelphia, Boston, St. Louis, Cincinnati, and Louisville contributed 9,083 bushels of corn and 3,958 pounds of bacon to the counties in the piney woods. Some of these supplies went to impoverished African Americans, but a goodly amount provided sustenance to struggling white families. In his annual report in October 1867, Swayne noted that "the condition of those persons left in destitution by the war, of whom a great majority were white . . . was very far from promising." Yet despite the summer drought and poor crops, "it is not too much to say that by [the aid societies'] timely exercise not only have the poorer counties been relieved from numerous individual cases of starvation, they have been rescued from disorder and disease as results from famine."[6]

The soldiers returning home from war faced a whole new set of challenges. Many were maimed or disfigured. Others suffered long-term or permanent mental, emotional, and physical disabilities. Despite the best efforts of the family members left behind, men often returned to find farms in disrepair, fields overrun with weeds, sickly livestock, fences damaged, broken or worn-out equipment, and barns and outbuildings falling apart. Crop failures in 1865 and 1866 exacerbated the problem. By 1870, the annual income for many veterans had declined dramatically from where they were just a decade earlier. Economic challenges hit poor and landless farmers the hardest, but even wealthy men struggled to recover their former status. In Pike County, Sgt. John Breedlove's annual income dwindled from $5,000 as an engineer before the war to just $1,300 as a farmer in 1870, still a comfortable living by the standards of the day. Private Edward Blacklidge's carriage-making business in Abbeville shrank from nearly $6,000 in 1860 to $2,500 in 1870. On the other hand, there were signs that some veterans were making the best of a difficult situation. Private Crawford Dillard's bottom line as a Dale County farmer actually improved from $900 in 1860 to almost $1,400 a decade later. Similarly, Pvt. William Neal's farm in Coffee County saw a slight increase in his bottom line from $800 to $1,000.[7] Although economic conditions varied widely, evidence suggests that it took years for the average veteran to regain his former socioeconomic status.

In addition to economic difficulties, returning veterans and piney woods residents in general faced new political realities. In the immediate aftermath of the war, political change came slowly. For nearly two years, a period after the war that historians refer to as Presidential Reconstruction, former Confederates held nearly all of the local and statewide political offices. That changed in 1867 when the Republican-controlled Congress asserted its authority over the reconstruction process. Many so-called Radical Republicans believed that President Andrew Johnson's administration had been far too lenient with the former Rebels and dismissive of the plight of the freedmen. Congressional Reconstruction therefore led to major changes to the state's political system. For the first time, African American men exercised the right to vote, black legislators took their seats in the General Assembly, and the state sent its first black congressman, Benjamin S. Turner, to Washington in 1871.

The convention to rewrite the state's constitution met in Montgomery in November 1867. Since many former Confederates could not vote, and others were disqualified from running for office—along with a large number of whites who boycotted the election in protest—most representatives elected from piney woods counties were likely carpetbaggers or scalawags, disparaging terms aimed at Northerners who supported Reconstruction and their Southern allies. Massachusetts native Samuel S. Gardner, for instance, was one of two elected representatives from the fourth district, encompassing Butler and Covington counties. Gardner had been a chaplain in the Union army during the war, took the job of subassistant commissioner for the Freedman's Bureau in Greenville in 1865, and worked tirelessly to educate the region's freedmen concerning their political rights. With help from the large African American vote in Butler County, both Gardner and the district's second representative, Covington's William R. Jones, easily defeated their conservative opponents.[8]

With the exception of Samuel Gardner little is known about the remainder of the region's delegates—other than their names and the likelihood that few, if any, were conservatives. Ransom Deal from Dale County was a young Baptist minister who represented the Fifth District. Richard M. Johnson was an Illinois native who resided in Montgomery but represented Henry County. Dale County's John C. Jolly had served with distinction as a second lieutenant in the 33rd Alabama Infantry during the war. Barbour County sent David Lore, Henry C. Russell, and the region's only African American representative, Thomas Deggs.

Despite charges that Alabama's new constitution was too radical, the document struck a moderate tone by contemporary standards. While the law protected the political rights of the freedmen, guaranteed basic freedoms and legal rights to every Alabamian, and required former Confederates to take a simple loyalty oath in order to vote, it did not address social equality between the races. Michael Fitzgerald argues that many whites believed the constitution went too far, while African Americans and an outspoken minority of carpetbaggers were disappointed that the document did not go far enough. The state's leading Democratic newspapers urged white voters to boycott the ratification vote. Nearly twenty thousand whites voted statewide to call the convention; only 7,500 showed up for the ratification vote. In Eufaula, for instance, just 34 of 2,727 votes in favor of the constitution came from white voters.[9] Democrats were not above using intimidation tactics to keep people away from the polls. "Union men were cursed at the polls by rebels, better known in democratic ranks as 'conservatives,'" reported Jacob Black, chairman of the Barbour County Board of Registration. "They were slandered in every way imaginable, and their names are now published under the captions of 'the roll of infamy.'" Black also pointed to the intimidation of black voters, possibly at the hands of the Ku Klux Klan. "Freedmen were kept from the polls by various contrivances," he noted, "such as threatening them with discharges from their homes, stopping them en route to the polls, [and] stealing their tickets."[10] Threats of violence forced Republicans in Dale County to close down the voting in at least one precinct. Democrats either destroyed the county's registration books or purposely "misplaced" them, leaving election officials scrambling. "The election has just passed over with many difficulties to encounter," one report explained, "with all the threats of mobs and violence we . . . have had to encounter."[11]

The antiratification approach was effective. Out of 5,123 registered voters in Barbour County, fewer than three thousand voted in favor of the new constitution, with the overwhelming majority of pro-ratification votes coming from black voters. Only 42 percent of eligible voters cast a yes vote in Butler County, along with 22 percent in Conecuh and 19 percent in Coffee. Pike, Henry, Dale, and Covington posted no returns—perhaps the result of Democratic intimidation tactics or outright violence against the carpetbaggers, scalawags, and black voters. Statewide, the ratification vote fell short of the required majority of eligible voters in order for the new constitution to become law. Nevertheless, during the summer of 1868, Congress repealed the majority-vote provision, thus activating the new constitution retroactively.

It is impossible to determine from existing evidence the political affiliations of all of the region's representatives during the era of Congressional Reconstruction. While most of the men were residents of the counties in which they lived, few had ever held political office before. Because many former Confederates could neither vote nor hold political office, it is reasonable to suggest that some, if not most, piney woods representatives were Republicans. In 1868, Republican William Miller Jr. narrowly defeated his Democratic rival for the Senate seat that encompassed Butler and Covington counties. The heavy African American vote assured Miller's victory. That same year, representatives J. R. Yates of Conecuh County, James Ard from Coffee, and Henry County's E. E. Tiller were elected to the General Assembly. These men were almost certainly Republicans. Nevertheless, by 1870, former Confederate soldiers such as Jesse M. Carmichael from Dale County, John P. Hubbard from Pike, and William C. Oates from Henry, all Democrats, began to defeat their Republican opponents. As more and more former Confederates regained the right to vote, Democrats launched an all-out effort to stamp out Republican influence. In majority-white counties, such as those in piney woods, their endeavors proved widely successful. As Mark Wetherington remarks, "Reconstruction violated the plain folk's democratic ideal because it 'is not of the people,' meaning that the governed—white male voters—had not consented to Reconstruction. Moreover, its goals violated plain folk notions of race, white supremacy, and polity."[12]

Between 1870 and 1876, the Democratic Party made substantial inroads throughout the region. Butler, Covington, Pike, Coffee, Dale, Henry, and the newly created counties of Crenshaw and Escambia voted solidly Democratic in each of the four gubernatorial races that took place during that time period. In Conecuh County, the votes were almost evenly divided until 1876 when the Democratic Party took firm control. Thanks to the large contingent of black voters, Barbour County remained largely Republican, until 1874 when Democrats finally swept the county's elections.

That year, Eufaula was at the center of the deadliest episode in Alabama's Reconstruction history—an event that cleared the way for Democratic dominance of the county's politics. In the months leading up to the election, Eufaula Democrats organized the White Man's Club, a secret society with the goal of pressuring black voters into voting the Democratic ticket in that year's elections. The organization promised good jobs to those who pledged their support and threatened the jobs of those who would not. As the election approached, rumors of violence circulated widely. Elias M. Keils, Eufaula's Republican city court judge, warned US officials that some of the citizens were stockpiling firearms in anticipation of a fight. He requested troops, but the twenty or so soldiers that responded were specifically instructed to stay away from the polls. On election day, hundreds of black voters showed up in large groups to cast their ballots. An argument concerning the eligibility of one of the young black voters quickly turned to violence when a white man named William Dowdy stabbed Republican Milas Lawrence. Shots rang out as people scattered in all directions. Within minutes, at least six black men lay dead or mortally wounded with dozens more injured, including twelve whites. A few miles away in the heavily black Spring Hill district, Democratic operatives burned more than seven hundred ballots. In the end, the violence in Eufaula and the destruction of ballots in Spring Hill guaranteed a Democratic sweep of the county.[13]

In the piney woods, the elections of 1874 and 1876 sealed the fate of the Republican Party. The Democratic Party successfully united white voters in the region against African Americans, thus helping to usher in the period known historically as Redemption, a time in which Democrats statewide regained complete control of Alabama's political system. Revengeful Democrats then disfranchised black voters, dismantled the state's Reconstruction government, and instituted a repressive socioeconomic system known as Jim Crow.

Notes

Introduction

1. Glenn W. LaFantasie, *Twilight at Little Round Top: July 2, 1863—The Tide Turns at Gettysburg* (New York: Random House, 2007), 183.

2. Kenneth W. Noe, *Reluctant Rebels: The Confederates Who Joined the Army after 1861* (Chapel Hill: University of North Carolina Press, 2010).

3. United States of America, Bureau of the Census, Eighth Census, Population, Dale, Alabama, 225 (microfilm), and Slave Schedule, 7–8 (microfilm). Alabama Department of Archives and History, "Alabama Civil War Service Database," accessed February 3, 2011, http://www.archives.alabama.gov/civilwar/soldier.cfm?id=51059, and accessed February 3, 2011, http://www.archives.alabama.gov/civilwar/soldier.cfm?id=106944. See also Record of Dale County Beauregards Company "E" Fifteenth Regiment of Alabama Volunteer Infantry, Muster Rolls of Alabama Civil War Units, Alabama Department of Archives and History, Montgomery, AL.

4. For the sake of clarity, this study incorporates the present-day counties of Butler, Crenshaw, Pike, Barbour, Henry, Dale, Houston, Geneva, Coffee, Covington, Escambia, and Conecuh. It is also important to note that Crenshaw, Houston, Geneva, and Escambia counties were created after the Civil War. In addition, the term "Wiregrass" was not widely used as a regional identifier for modern Coffee, Dale, Henry, and Houston counties until well after the Civil War. For this reason, I have chosen to refrain from employing this terminology except when referencing the grass itself.

5. Walter Lynwood Fleming, *Civil War and Reconstruction in Alabama*

(New York: Columbia University Press, 1905); Albert B. Moore, *History of Alabama* (Nashville, TN: Benson Printing Company, 1934); Lewy Dorman, *Party Politics in Alabama from 1850 Through 1860* (Tuscaloosa: University of Alabama Press, 1935); Willis Brewer, *Alabama, Her History, Resources, War Record, and Public Men: From 1540 to 1872* (Montgomery, AL: Barrett and Brown, 1872); Thomas M. Owen, *History of Alabama and Dictionary of Alabama Biography*, 4 vols. (Chicago: S. J. Clarke Publishing Company, 1921).

6. Malcolm Cook McMillan, *The Disintegration of a Confederate State: Three Governors and Alabama's Wartime Home Front, 1861–1865* (Macon, GA: Mercer, 1986); J. Mills Thornton, *Politics and Power in a Slave Society: Alabama, 1800–1860* (Baton Rouge: Louisiana State University Press, 1978); Bessie Martin, *Desertion of Alabama Troops from the Confederate Army: A Study in Sectionalism* (New York: Columbia University Press, 1932); Margaret M. Storey, *Loyalty and Loss: Alabama's Unionists in the Civil War and Reconstruction* (Baton Rouge: Louisiana State University Press, 2004); David Williams, *Rich Man's War: Class, Caste, and Confederate Defeat in the Lower Chattahoochee Valley* (Athens: University of Georgia Press, 1998); Christopher Lyle McIlwain, *Civil War Alabama* (Tuscaloosa: University of Alabama Press, 2016).

7. For a sampling of political histories of Alabama, see Lewy Dorman, *Party Politics*; Austin Venable, "Alabama's 'War of the Roses,'" *Alabama Review* 8 (October 1955): 243–59; Grady McWhiney, "Were the Whigs a Class Party in Alabama?" *Journal of Southern History* 23 (November 1957): 510–22; Thomas B. Alexander, "Persistent Whiggery in Alabama and the Lower Class, 1860–1867," *Alabama Review* 12 (January 1959): 35–52; Thomas B. Alexander et al., "Who Were the Alabama Whigs?" *Alabama Review* 16 (January 1963): 5–19; Allen W. Jones, "Unionism and Disaffection in South Alabama: The Case of Alfred Holley," *Alabama Review* 24 (April 1971): 114–42; J. Mills Thornton, *Politics and Power in a Slave Society: Alabama, 1800–1860* (Baton Rouge: Louisiana State University Press, 1978).

Chapter 1

1. United States Census, Conecuh County, Alabama, 1860, Schedules 1 and 2.

2. In March 1865, Union raiders burned Sparta's courthouse, railroad depot, and a number of other structures. A year later, construction began on a new courthouse in the more populous and more centrally located town of Greenville. By the turn of the twentieth century, Sparta was all but abandoned. Marilyn Davis Hahn, *Old Sparta and Elba Land Office Records and Military Warrants, 1822–1860* (Easley, SC: Southern Historical Press, 1983), iii–x.

3. *Acts Passed at the First Session of the First General Assembly of the Alabama Territory* (St. Stephens, AL: Thomas East, 1818), 96.

4. Clarence Edwin Carter, ed., *The Territorial Papers of the United States: The Territory of Alabama, 1817–1819* (Washington, DC: Government Printing Office, 1952), 18:462.

5. Basil Hall, *Travels in North America in the Years 1827 and 1828* (London: Simpkin and Marshall, 1829), 3:256.

6. William S. Campbell, *Report on the Alabama, Florida and Georgia Railroad* (E. G. Dorsey, 1838), 13–14.

7. Nollie W. Hickman, *Mississippi Harvest: Lumbering in the Longleaf Pine Belt, 1840–1915* (Jackson: University Press of Mississippi, 1962), 2; William Byrd, "Wiregrass: The Transformation of Southeast Alabama, 1880–1930" (PhD diss., Auburn University, 2009), 13.

8. Ronald Uchytil, "Aristida Stricta" (US Department of Agriculture, Forest Service, 1992), http://www.fs.fed.us/database/feis/plants/graminoid/aristr/all.html; Joseph Hodgson, ed., *The Alabama Manual and Statistical Register for 1869 Showing the Geographical Position, Commercial Advantages, Agricultural and Manfactural Resources, and National Importance of the State of Alabama—A Statistical Guide for the Immigrant and Hand Book for the Citizen* (Montgomery, AL: Mail Building, 1869), 18.

9. Thomas McAdory Owen, *History of Alabama and Dictionary of Alabama Biography* (Spartanburg, SC: Reprint Company, 1978), 1:232–33.

10. James D. Graham, "Report, Pensacola, Florida, February 6, 1836," *American Railroad Journal and Advocate of Internal Improvements* 5 (1836): 453; Owen, *History of Alabama*, 1:255; Joseph Burney to J. H. Simpson, Mobile, Alabama, April 6, 1872, in *Annual Report of the Chief of Engineers to the Secretary of War for the Year 1872* by United States Army, Corps of Engineers (Washington, DC: Government Printing Office, 1872), 643.

11. Thomas Baldwin and Joseph Thomas, *A New and Complete Gazetteer of the United States: Giving a Full and Comprehensive Review of the Present Condition, Industry, and Resources of the American Confederacy* (Philidelphia, PA: Lippincott, Grambo and Co., 1854), 270.

12. Paul Starrett, *Appraisal Report: Lands in Southern Georgia and Southeastern Alabama Ceded by the Creek Nation, Before the Indian Claims Commission, Docket Number 21, Valued as of August 9, 1814* (1957), 80.

13. Robbie F. Ethridge, *Creek Country: The Creek Indians and Their World* (Chapel Hill: University of North Carolina Press, 2003), 38–46.

14. Ibid., 147.

15. Jeffrey C. Benton, *The Very Worst Road: Travellers' Accounts of Crossing Alabama's Old Creek Indian Territory, 1820–1847* (Eufaula, AL: Historic Chattahoochee Commission of Alabama and Georgia, 1998), 11.

16. Andrew K. Frank, "Creek War," *Encyclopedia of American Indian History* (Santa Barbara, CA: ABC-CLIO, 2007), 246.

17. Kathryn E. Holland Braund, *Deerskins and Duffels: The Creek Indian Trade with Anglo-America, 1685–1815* (Lincoln: University of Nebraska Press, 1993).

18. Henry deLeon Southerland and Jerry Elijah Brown, *The Federal Road Through Georgia, the Creek Nation, and Alabama, 1806–1836* (Tuscaloosa: University of Alabama Press, 1989).

19. Mike Bunn, *Battle for the Southern Frontier: The Creek War and the War of 1812* (Charleston, SC: History Press, 2008); Robert V. Remini, *Andrew Jackson and His Indian Wars* (New York: Viking, 2001); Gregory A. Waselkov, *A Conquering Spirit: Fort Mims and the Redstick War of 1813–1814* (Tuscaloosa: University of Alabama Press, 2006).

20. James David Miller, *South by Southwest: Planter Emigration and Identity in the Slave South* (Charlottesville: University of Virginia Press, 2002), 2.

21. William Warren Rogers et al., *Alabama: The History of a Deep South State* (Tuscaloosa: University of Alabama Press, 1994), 54.

22. Ibid.

23. Lacy K. Ford, *Origins of Southern Radicalism: The South Carolina Upcountry, 1800–1860* (New York: Oxford University Press, 1988), 38–39.

24. Charles C. Bolton, *Poor Whites of the Antebellum South: Tenants and Laborers in Central North Carolina and Northeast Mississippi* (Durham: Duke University Press, 1994), 67.

25. Campbell, *Report on the Alabama*, 13.

26. James Oakes, *The Ruling Race: A History of American Slaveholders* (New York: Vintage, 1983), 76.

27. J. M. Feagin et al., "Alabama Governors, Administrative Files 1819–1899, Miscellaneous Folders" January 10, 1837, Alabama Department of Archives and History; John T. Ellisor, *The Second Creek War: Interethnic Conflict and Collusion on a Collapsing Frontier* (Lincoln: University of Nebraska Press, 2010).

28. Gerald Ray Mathis, *John Horry Dent, South Carolina Aristocrat on the Alabama Frontier* (Tuscaloosa: University of Alabama Press, 1979), 25–40.

29. Ibid.

30. Ray Mathis and Mary Mathis, *Introduction and Index to the John Horry Dent Farm Journals and Account Books, 1840–1892* (Tuscaloosa: University of Alabama Press, 1977), ix–xxviii; John Horry Dent, Farm Journal, 1855–1857, 3:79, John Horry Dent Papers, Auburn University Special Collection and Archives, Auburn, Alabama (microfilm).

31. "Some Old People. Short Sketches That Will Be of Interest to the Public. Men and Women That We Know. Pioneers Who Came to Pike in the Early Days and Have Seen the Changes of Many Years," *Troy Messenger* (Troy, Alabama, June 27, 1889); Gregory A. Boyd, *Family Maps of Pike County, Alabama: With Homesteads, Roads, Waterways, Towns, Cemeteries, Railroads, and More* (Norman, OK: Arphax, 2007), 122, 244.

32. United States Census, Pike County, Henry County, Covington County, Alabama, 1850, 1860, Schedules 1, 2, and 4.

33. Joan E. Cashin, *A Family Venture: Men and Women on the Southern Frontier* (New York: Oxford University Press, 1991), 26.

34. "Alford Alley Land Patent," Military Warrant (Sparta, Alabama, July 10, 1852), Bureau of Land Management, Eastern States Office, www.glorecords.blm.gov; "Caroline Alley Land Patent," State Volume Patent (Elba, Alabama, No-

vember 1, 1858), Bureau of Land Management, Eastern States Office, www.glorecords.blm.gov.

35. Miller, *South by Southwest*, 65.

36. United States Census, Henry County, Alabama, 1860, Schedules 1 and 2.

37. Cashin, *Family Venture*, 67–70.

38. Anson West, *A History of Methodism in Alabama* (Nashville, TN: Methodist Episcopal Church, South, Barbee & Smith, 1893), 271.

39. Wayne Flynt, *Alabama Baptists: Southern Baptists in the Heart of Dixie* (Tuscaloosa: University of Alabama Press, 1998), 3.

40. Anson West, *History of Methodism*, 272.

41. Ibid.

42. Flynt, *Alabama Baptists*, 23.

43. B. F. Riley and Alabama Baptist Historical Society, *History of the Baptists of Alabama: From the Time of Their First Occupation of Alabama in 1808, Until 1894: Being a Detailed Record of Denominational Events in the State During Eighty-Six Years, and Furnishing Biographical Sketches of Those Who Have Been Conspicuous in the Annals of the Denomination, Besides Much Other Incidental Matter Relative to the Secular History of Alabama* (Birmingham: Roberts and Son, 1895); Owen, *History of Alabama*, 1:317.

44. Flynt, *Alabama Baptists*, 45.

45. West, *History of Methodism*, 269–78.

46. The American Baptist Antislavery Convention was organized at the McDougal Street Baptist Church in New York City in April 1840. Convention attendees were proponents of immediate emancipation and adopted the stance that Southern churches must reject slavery or risk what amounted to excommunication. As president of the convention, Elon Galusha's address to the crowd was decidedly harsh and its subsequent publication became a rallying point for Southern Baptists. For a good study of the general conservative trend of Southern churches, see Christine Heyrman, *Southern Cross: The Beginnings of the Bible Belt* (New York: Knopf, 1997).

47. *Minutes of the Twenty-Fourth Anniversary of the Bethlehem Baptist Association* (Bethlehem Baptist Association, 1840), Auburn University Special Collections and Archives.

48. Wilson Fallin, *Uplifting the People: Three Centuries of Black Baptists in Alabama* (Tuscaloosa: University of Alabama Press, 2007), 15; *Minutes of the Thirty-Third Session of the Bethlehem Baptist Association* (Bethlehem Baptist Association, 1849), 8–10, Auburn University Special Collections and Archives.

49. *Minutes of the Thirty-Third Session*, 10.

50. John C. Inscoe, *Mountain Masters: Slavery Sectional Crisis Western North Carolina* (Knoxville: University of Tennessee Press, 1996), 25.

51. Mary Love Edwards Fleming, "Dale County and Its People During the Civil War: Reminiscences of Mary Love (Edwards) Fleming," *Alabama Historical Quarterly* 19 (Spring 1957): 65.

52. Lewy Dorman, *History of Barbour County, Alabama* (Eufaula, AL: Barbour County Genealogy and Local History Society, 2006), 88; Eugene Allen Smith, *Report on the Cotton Production of the State of Alabama* (n.p., 1884), 142–43; Robert H. Flewellen, *Along Broad Street: A History of Eufaula, Alabama, 1823–1984* (Eufaula, AL: City of Eufaula, 1991), 30.

53. Thomas M. Owen, *History of Alabama and Dictionary of Alabama Biography* (Chicago: S. J. Clarke, 1921), 4:1826–29; United States Census, Barbour County, Alabama, 1860, Schedule 1.

54. *Eufaula Democrat*, December 9, 1846.

55. United States Census, Barbour County, Alabama, 1860, Schedule 1.

56. Frank Anderson Chappell, ed., *Dear Sister: Civil War Letters to a Sister in Alabama* (Huntsville, AL: Branch Springs Publishing, 2002), 18–19.

57. Wyley Donald Ward, *Early History of Covington County, Alabama, 1821–1871* (Ann Arbor: The University of Michigan,1976; Spartanburg, SC: Reprint Company, 1991), 88. United States Census, Butler County, Alabama, 1850, 1860, Schedules 1, 2, and 4.

58. H. E. Sterkx, "Joel Dyer Murphree, Troy Merchant, 1843–1868," *Alabama Review* 11 (April 1958): 118. Even as late as 1880, cotton farmers from the southernmost counties continued to haul their cotton to Troy. Of the nine thousand bales of cotton produced in Coffee County, for example, only about five hundred were sold in Elba. The rest were hauled to Troy, "at present the most accessible market for this section of the state." United States War Department, *Annual Reports of the War Department* (Washington, DC: Government Printing Office, 1880), 1122.

59. John Shephard, *Reports of Cases Argued and Determined in the Supreme Court of Alabama* (Montgomery, AL: Barrett & Wimbish, 1859), 32:569–74. United States Census, Pike County, Alabama, 1850, 1860, Schedule 1.

60. Margaret Pace Farmer, *One Hundred Fifty Years in Pike County, Alabama, 1821–1971* (Anniston, AL: Higginbotham, 1973), 328–30; Brent Holcomb, *Marriage and Death Notices from the Southern Christian Advocate* (Easley, SC: Southern Historical Press, 1979), 1:524. United States Census, Pike County, Alabama, 1840, 1850, Schedules 1 and 2.

61. W. L. Andrews, "Early History of Southeast Alabama," *Alabama Historical Quarterly* 10 (1948): 102. United States Census, Dale County, Alabama, 1850, 1860, Schedules 1, 2, and 4.

62. Thomas McAdory Owen and Marie Bankhead Owen, *History of Alabama and Dictionary of Alabama Biography* (Chicago: S. J. Clarke, 1921), 4:1002. United States Census, Covington County, Henry County, Coffee County, Alabama, 1850, 1860, Schedules 1, 2, and 4.

63. Thomas McAdory Owen and Marie Bankhead Owen *History of Alabama and Dictionary of Alabama Biography* (Chicago: S. J. Clarke, 1921), 3:679; Willis Brewer, *Alabama, Her History, Resources, War Record, and Public Men: From 1540 to 1872* (Montgomery: Barrett & Brown, 1872), 279; Marvin Scott, *History*

of Henry County, Alabama (Pensacola, FL: Frank Parkhurst and Son, 1961), 257–58. United States Census, Henry County, Alabama, 1860, Schedules 1, 2, and 4.

Chapter 2

1. United States Census, Dale County, Alabama, 1860, Schedules 1, 2, and 4.

2. Frank Lawrence Owsley, *Plain Folk of the Old South*, Walter Lynwood Fleming Lectures in Southern History (Baton Rouge: Louisiana State University Press, 1949), vii.

3. Bill Cecil-Fronsman, *Common Whites: Class and Culture in Antebellum North Carolina* (Lexington: University Press of Kentucky, 1992), 18.

4. Wayne Flynt, *Dixie's Forgotten People: The South's Poor Whites* (Bloomington: Indiana University Press, 1979), 12; J. William Harris, *Plain Folk and Gentry in a Slave Society: White Liberty and Black Slavery in Augusta's Hinterlands* (Middletown, CT: Wesleyan University Press, 1985), 90; Samuel C. Hyde, "Plain Folk Reconsidered: Historiographical Ambiguity in Search of Definition," *Journal of Southern History* 71 (November, 2005): 803–30.

5. Ford, *Origins of Southern Radicalism*; Hyde Jr., "Plain Folk Reconsidered"; Steven Hahn, *The Roots of Southern Populism: Yeomen Farmers and the Transformation of the Georgia Upcountry, 1850–1890* (New York: Oxford University Press, 1983); Stephanie McCurry, *Masters of Small Worlds: Yeoman Households, Gender Relations, and the Political Culture of the Antebellum South Carolina Low Country* (New York: Oxford University Press, 1997).

6. Joseph T. Glatthaar, *Soldiering in the Army of Northern Virginia: A Statistical Portrait of the Troops Who Served Under Robert E. Lee* (Chapel Hill: University of North Carolina Press, 2011), 140–53.

7. Frederick Law Olmsted, *Journeys and Explorations in the Cotton Kingdom. A Traveller's Observations on Cotton and Slavery in the American Slave States. Based Upon Three Former Volumes of Journeys and Investigations* (S. Low, 1861), 188.

8. For a brief discussion of Olmsted's writings and biases, see Samuel C. Hyde Jr., "Plain Folk Yeomanry in the Antebellum South," in *A Companion to the American South, ed. J. B. Boles*, 139–41 (Malden, MA.: Blackwell Publishing, 2004).

9. Inscoe, *Mountain Masters*; Martin Crawford, *Ashe County's Civil War: Community and Society in the Appalachian South* (Charlottesville: University Press of Virginia, 2001); Ford, *Origins of Southern Radicalism*; Bradley Bond, "Herders, Farmers, and Markets on the Inner Frontier: The Mississippi Piney Woods, 1850–1860," in *Plain Folk of the South Revisited*, ed. Samuel C. Hyde Jr., 73–99 (Baton Rouge: Louisiana State University Press, 1997).

10. Crawford, *Ashe County's Civil War*, 12.

11. Glatthaar, *Soldiering in the Army*, 140.

12. United States Census, Barbour County, Alabama, 1860, Schedules 1 and 4.

13. Pike County, Alabama, Orphan's Court and Probate Minutes, Inventory Book 1856–1865, Chattahoochee Valley Libraries, Columbus, Georgia (microfilm); United States Census, Pike County, Alabama, 1850 and 1860, Schedule 1.

14. The figures for determining the tenancy rate were calculated using Frederick Bode and Donald Ginter's "short method" in *Farm Tenancy and the Census in Antebellum Georgia* (Athens: University of Georgia Press, 1986), 26–33. All other calculations are entirely my own. United States Census, Covington County, Alabama, 1860, Schedules 1 and 4.

15. Coffee County, Alabama, Judge of Probate, Deed Records 1855–1858, Book C, Chattahoochee Valley Libraries, Columbus, Georgia (microfilm); United States Census, Coffee County, Dale County, Alabama, 1850, 1860, Schedules 1 and 4.

16. Daniel Robinson Hundley, *Social Relations in Our Southern States* (New York: Henry B. Price, 1860), 192. In this chapter, the terms "middle class" and "yeomanry" will be used interchangeably.

17. United States Census, Dale County, Alabama, 1860, Schedules 1 and 4.

18. Grady McWhiney, "The Revolution in Nineteenth-Century Alabama Agriculture," in *From Civil War to Civil Rights, Alabama, 1860–1960: An Anthology from the Alabama Review*, ed. Sarah Woolfolk Wiggins (Tuscaloosa: University of Alabama Press, 1987), 112.

19. Joseph Camp Griffith Kennedy, *Agriculture of the United States in 1860; Compiled from the Original Returns of the Eighth Census, Under the Direction of the Secretary of the Interior* (Washington, DC: Government Printing Office, 1864), 2–6.

20. United States Census, Coffee County, Covington County, Alabama, 1860, Schedules 1 and 4. It is worth noting that Eliza Jackson's net worth climbed from just one hundred dollars in 1850, when her husband, William, was still alive, to over eight hundred dollars ten years later. This was impressive for a single mother trying to run a farm in the one of the poorest counties in the state.

21. Robert Russell, *North America, Its Agriculture and Climate: Containing Observations on the Agriculture and Climate of Canada, the United States, and the Island of Cuba* (A. and C. Black, 1857), 285.

22. McCurry, *Masters of Small Worlds*, 104.

23. Ford, *Origins of Southern Radicalism*, 72.

24. Mark V. Wetherington, *Plain Folk's Fight: The Civil War and Reconstruction in Piney Woods Georgia* (Chapel Hill: University of North Carolina Press, 2005), 21.

25. Gavin Wright, *Old South, New South: Revolutions in the Southern Economy Since the Civil War* (New York: Basic Books, 1986), 3–16.

26. Frederick Law Olmsted, *A Journey in the Seaboard Slave States* (New York: Dix and Edwards, 1856), 433.

27. McCurry, *Masters of Small Worlds*, 50.

28. United States Census, Dale County, Alabama, 1860, Schedules 1, 2, and 4.

29. Oakes, *Ruling Race*, 40.

30. United States Census, Macon County, Alabama, 1840, Schedule 1, Coffee County, Alabama, 1850, Schedules 1 and 2, Dale County, Alabama, Schedules 1 and 2; Census of Alabama, 1855, Coffee County; Coffee County, Alabama, Judge of Probate, Deed Records 1855–1858, Book C, Chattahoochee Valley Libraries, Columbus, Georgia (microfilm).

31. United States Census, Pike County, Alabama, 1860, Schedules 1, 2, and 4.

32. Because few middle-class/yeoman slaveholders, as defined by Glatthaar, owned more than three slaves, I have chosen to group "middling" slaveholders as those who owned between four and nineteen slaves. See Joseph T. Glatthaar, *Soldiering in the Army of Northern Virginia*, 140. Also see Mark M. Smith, *Debating Slavery: Economy and Society in the Antebellum American South* (New York: Cambridge University Press, 1998), 15. Smith uses similar categories, but his classification scheme lists middling slaveholders as owning between five and twenty slaves with the yeomanry limited to fewer than five.

33. Joseph Camp Griffin Kennedy, *Agriculture of the United States in 1860: Compiled from the Original Returns of the Eighth Census* (Washington, DC: Government Printing Office, 1864), 223.

34. United States Census, Butler County, Henry County, Alabama, 1860, Schedules 1, 2, and 4.

35. United States Census, Covington County, Pike County, Alabama, 1860, Schedules 1, 2, and 4; Pike County, Alabama, Orphans Court and Probate Minutes, 1844–1929, Chattahoochee Valley Libraries, Columbus, Georgia (microfilm).

36. William J. Cooper and Thomas E. Terrill, *The American South: A History* (Lanham, MD: Rowman & Littlefield, 2009), 1:218.

37. United States Census, Barbour County, Pike County, Butler County, Henry County, Dale County, Coffee County, Covington County, Alabama, 1860, Schedule 2.

38. John Horry Dent, Plantation Journal, 1855–1857, 3:145, John Horry Dent Papers, Auburn University, Auburn, Alabama (microfilm).

39. *Eufaula Democrat*, January 23, 1849.

40. *Eufaula Democrat*, August 19, 1846.

41. David Roediger and Elizabeth Esch accurately and descriptively label Southern agricultural journals as "master-class management journals." While these publications included articles on general farming techniques and agricultural practices, their primary purpose was to support the institution of slavery as well as the slave owners who constituted the bulk of their correspondents and subscribers. David Roediger and Elizabeth Esch, *The Production of Difference: Race and the Management of Labor in US History* (New York: Oxford University Press, 2012), 23.

42. John Kvach, *De Bow's Review: The Antebellum Vision of a New South* (Lexington: University Press of Kentucky, 2013), 181–83.

43. A. B. Allen, ed., *American Agriculturist* (New York: Saxton and Miles, 1844), 3:221.

44. N. B. Cloud, ed., *The American Cotton Planter* (Underwood & Cloud, 1860), 4:101.

45. *Eufaula Democrat*, September 20, 1846.

46. John Horry Dent, Plantation Journal, 1855–1857, 3:49, Dent Papers.

47. Ford, *Origins of Southern Radicalism*, 66.

48. John Horry Dent, Plantation Journal, 1840–1842, 1:11–12, Dent Papers; John Horry Dent, Plantation Journal, 1855–1857, 3:7–12, Dent Papers.

49. Coffee County, Alabama, Judge of Probate, Deed Records 1855–1858, Book C, Chattahoochee Valley Libraries, Columbus, Georgia (microfilm); United States Census, Dale County, Alabama, Coffee County, Alabama, 1850, 1860, Schedule 1.

50. Joseph Camp Griffith Kennedy, *Population of the United States in 1860: Compiled from the Original Returns of the Eighth Census* (Washington, DC: Government Printing Office, 1864).

51. J. D. B. De Bow, *The Seventh Census of the United States, 1850: Embracing a Statistical View of Each of the States and Territories . . .* (Washington, DC: Robert Armstrong, 1853), 414–23; Kennedy, *Population of the United States*, 2–8.

52. De Bow, *Seventh Census*, 419–21; Kennedy, *Population of the United States*, 4–8.

53. John Horry Dent, Plantation Journal, 1855–1857, 3:185, Dent Papers.

54. Juliet E. K. Walker, "Drivers, Slave," in *Dictionary of Afro-American Slavery*, ed. Randall M. Miller and John David Smith (Westport, CT: Praeger, 1997), 197.

55. John Horry Dent, Plantation Journal, 1855–1857, 3:66, Dent Papers.

56. Ibid., 188.

57. For a more detailed look at the impact of sex, race, and gender, see Paula Giddings, *When and Where I Enter: The Impact of Black Women on Race and Sex in America* (New York: W. Morrow, 1984); Catherine Clinton, *The Devil's Lane: Sex and Race in the Early South* (New York: Oxford University Press, 1997); Peter Bardaglio, *Reconstructing the Household: Families, Sex, and the Law in the Nineteenth-Century South* (Chapel Hill: University of North Carolina Press, 1995); Winthrop D. Jordan, *White over Black: American Attitudes toward the Negro, 1550–1812* (Chapel Hill: University of North Carolina Press, 1968); Joel Williamson, *New People: Miscegenation and Mulattoes in the United States* (New York: Free Press, 1980).

58. *Mosser v. Mosser*, 29 John Shephard (Supreme Court of Alabama 1857).

59. Ibid.

60. *Oxford v. The State*, 33 John W. Shephard (Supreme Court of Alabama 1859). For additional reading on the legal history of slavery, see Ariela Julie Gross, *Double Character: Slavery and Mastery in the Antebellum Southern Courtroom* (Princeton, NJ: Princeton University Press, 2000) and Thomas D. Morris, *Southern Slavery and the Law, 1619–1860* (Chapel Hill: University of North Carolina Press, 1996).

61. *Bob (A Slave) v. The State*, 29 John Shephard (Supreme Court of Alabama 1856).

62. Anthony Gene Carey, *Sold Down the River: Slavery in the Lower Chattahoochee Valley of Alabama and Georgia* (Tuscaloosa: University of Alabama Press, 2011), 71–72.

63. Joseph Park to Jeremiah Henderson, Park Family Papers, Manuscript, Archives, and Rare Book Library, Emory University (microfilm).

Chapter 3

1. *New York Herald*, September 17, 1860.

2. Henry W. Hilliard, *Politics and Pen Pictures at Home and Abroad* (New York: G. P. Putnam's Sons, 1892), 293, 302.

3. Unless otherwise noted, the word "Southerner" or "Southerners" in this chapter specifically refers to white Southerners.

4. Malcolm Cook McMillan, *Constitutional Development in Alabama, 1798–1901: A Study in Politics, the Negro, and Sectionalism* (Chapel Hill: University of North Carolina Press, 1955), 31–32.

5. *Pensacola Gazette and West Florida Advertiser*, October 22, 1825; Clarence Edwin Carter, ed., *The Territorial Papers of the United States: The Territory of Alabama, 1817–1819* (Washington, DC: Government Printing Office, 1952), 18:395, 408, 409; Marie Bankhead Owen and Emmett Kilpatrick, eds., "Alabama Census Returns 1820 and An Abstract of Federal Census of Alabama 1830," *Alabama Historical Quarterly* 6 (Fall 1944): 358.

6. *Constitution of the State of Alabama* (Washington, DC: Gales and Seaton, 1819); McMillan, *Constitutional Development in Alabama*, 44–45.

7. James Monroe won the 1820 election without any formidable opposition.

8. Albert B. Moore, *History of Alabama* (Nashville, TN: Benson, 1934), 122.

9. Clanton W. Williams, "Notes and Documents: Presidential Election Returns and Related Data for Antebellum Alabama," *Alabama Review* 1 (October 1948): 284–85.

10. Adams biographer Robert Remini argues that the president's policies toward the Indians were by no means benevolent. Yet Adams believed firmly that the Treaty of Indian Springs, negotiated with the Creeks in Georgia, and adopted one day before to his taking office, and the subsequent negotiations with the Cherokees were downright fraudulent. Adams's "efforts to protect the Indians under the legal authority of the federal government," Remini suggests, "gained him nothing but the hatred of all those southerners who lusted after Indian territory." Robert Vincent Remini, *John Quincy Adams* (New York: Times Books, 2002), 91–102.

11. William W. Freehling, *The Road to Disunion: Secessionists at Bay, 1776–1854* (New York: Oxford University Press, 1990).

12. *Acts Passed at the Eighth Annual Session of the General Assembly of the State of Alabama, Begun and Held in the Town of Tuscaloosa, on the Third Monday in November, 1826* (Tuscaloosa, AL: Grantland and Robinson, 1827), 121, Alabama Department of Archives and History.

13. Daniel Walker Howe argues that between the election of 1824 and 1828, supporters of John Q. Adams began calling themselves National Republicans while the supporters of Jackson were known as Democratic Republicans, later just Democrats. "The terms came into use very slowly," Howe contends. "Accustomed as we are to a two-party system, we seize upon labels that contemporaries hesitated to employ. By the time the new party names gained acceptance, the election was over." Daniel Walker Howe, *What Hath God Wrought: The Transformation of America, 1845–1848* (New York: Oxford University Press, 2007), 275.

14. Donald B. Cole, *Vindicating Andrew Jackson: The 1828 Election and the Rise of the Two-Party System* (Lawrence: University Press of Kansas, 2009); Lynn H. Parsons, *The Birth of Modern Politics: Andrew Jackson, John Quincy Adams, and the Election of 1828* (New York: Oxford University Press, 2009); Clanton W. Williams, "Notes and Documents: Presidential Election Returns and Related Data for Antebellum Alabama," *The Alabama Review* 2 (January 1949): 64–65; 286–87. Williams notes that there are no available returns for Pike, Conecuh, and Dale counties nor are there returns for the counties of Blount, Marengo, and Lowndes. Newspapers from Montgomery and Mobile counties likewise indicate no returns for these counties.

15. Freehling, *Road to Disunion*, 298.

16. *Constitution of the State of Alabama*, December 6, 1819, Article 2, Sections 3 and 12; Thornton, *Politics and Power*, 59–60, 75.

17. Manuscript Census, Conecuh County, Henry County, Butler County, Pike County, 1830, Schedule of Population; Thomas McAdory Owen and Marie Bankhead Owen, *History of Alabama and Dictionary of Alabama Biography* (Chicago: S. J. Clarke Publishing Company, 1921), 3:392, 479, 4:1299, 1725; Thornton, *Politics and Power*, 73.

18. *Journal of the House of Representatives, of the State of Alabama, Begun and Held at the Town of Cahawba, on the Third Monday in November, 1825, Being the Seventh Annual Session of the General Assembly of Said State* (Cahaba, AL: William B. Allen, 1826), 29; *Journal of the House of Representatives of the State of Alabama, Begun and Held At the Town of Tuskaloosa, on the Third Monday in November, 1826, Being the Eighth Annual Session of the General Assembly of Said State* (Tuskaloosa: Grantland and Robinson, 1827), 14; *Journal of the House of Representatives of the State of Alabama, Begun and Held at the Town of Cahawba, on the Third Monday in November 1823. Being the Fifth Annual Session of the General Assembly of Said State* (Cahawba, AL: William B. Allen, 1824), 7.

19. *Acts Passed at the Fourth Annual Session of the General Assembly of the State of Alabama, Begun and Held at the Town of Cahawba, on the Third Monday of November, One Thousand Eight Hundred and Twenty Two* (Cahawba, AL: William B. Allen, 1823), 61; *Journal of the House of Representatives of the State of Alabama, Begun and Held at the Town of Cahawba, on the Third Monday in November 1822, Being the Fourth Session of the General Assembly of Said State* (Cahawba, AL: William B. Allen, 1823), 70; *Acts Passed at the Sixth Annual Session*

of the General Assembly of the State of Alabama; Begun and Held in the Town of Cahawba on the Third Monday in November, One Thousand Eight Hundred and Twenty Four (Cahawba, AL: William B. Allen, 1825), 41–42; *Journal of the House of Representatives of the State of Alabama, Begun and Held at the Town of Cahawba, on the Third Monday in November, 1824, Being the Sixth Annual Session of the General Assembly of Said State* (Cahawba, AL: William B. Allen, 1825), 93.

20. Freehling, *Road to Disunion*, 295.

21. Jackson's propensity for rejecting some projects while embracing others did not seem to bother most of his supporters. Daniel Walker Howe notes that "the Jackson-Van Buren practice of generous ad hoc appropriations coupled with professions of Old Republican strict construction pleased the friends of particular projects while reassuring slaveholders and staple exporters that the federal government was not being strengthened in principle or undertaking long-term, expensive commitments." See Daniel Walker Howe, *What Hath God Wrought: The Transformation of America, 1815–1848* (New York: Oxford University Press, 2007), 365.

22. Theodore H. Jack, "Alabama and the Federal Government," *Mississippi Valley Historical Review* 3 (December 1916): 302.

23. The majority of the representatives from Tennessee and Kentucky voted in favor of the bill.

24. Howe, *What Hath God Wrought*, 273.

25. *A Remonstrance of the General Assembly of Alabama, on the Subject of Protecting Duties*, February 4, 1828, US Congressional Serial Set, vol. 171, session 3, doc. 113 (Washington, DC: Gales and Seaton, 1828), accessed October 19, 2013, http://infoweb.newsbank.com.

26. *Journal of the House of Representatives of the State of Alabama, Begun and Held at the Town of Tuscaloosa, on the First Monday in November, 1832, Being a Called Session of the General Assembly of Said State* (Tuscaloosa, AL: E. Walker, 1832), 16.

27. *Acts Passed at the Extra and Annual Sessions of the General Assembly of the State of Alabama, Begun and Held in the Town of Tuscaloosa, on the First Monday in November, One Thousand Eight Hundred and Thirty-Two* (Tuscaloosa, AL: E. Walker, 1833), 140.

28. Howe, *What Hath God Wrought*, 400–01; Richard E. Ellis, *The Union at Risk: Jacksonian Democracy, States' Rights, and the Nullification Crisis* (New York: Oxford University Press, 1989), 68.

29. *Acts of the General Assembly, 1832*, 139–41; *Journal of the House of Representatives of the State of Alabama, Begun and Held at the Town of Tuscaloosa, on the Third Monday in November, 1832, Being the Fourteenth Annual Session of the General Assembly of Said State* (Tuscaloosa: E. Walker, 1833), 217–19.

30. Thornton, *Politics and Power*, 27.

31. *Journal of the House, Called Session, 1832*, 18. Ironically, Gayle's support for Andrew Jackson and opposition to nullification changed dramatically when his administration clashed with Jackson and federal government over Alabama's

jurisdictional claims to administer former Indian lands free from federal control. See Samuel L. Webb and Margaret E. Armbrester, eds., *Alabama Governors: A Political History of the State* (Tuscaloosa: University of Alabama Press, 2001), 31–34.

32. *Acts of the General Assembly, 1832*, 144.

33. *Acts Passed at the Annual Session of the General Assembly of the State of Alabama, Begun and Held in the City of Tuscaloosa, on the Third Monday in November, One Thousand Eight Hundred and Thirty-Four* (Tuscaloosa, AL: David Ferguson, 1835), 152; William Warren Rogers et al., *Alabama*,139; Thornton, *Politics and Power*, 18–19.

34. Howe, *What Hath God Wrought*, 409.

35. Stanley Harold, *Border War: Fighting Over Slavery Before the Civil War* (Chapel Hill: University of North Carolina Press, 2010), 38.

36. John W. Womack to Lewis Womack, "Marcus Joseph Wright Papers," August 30, 1835, Southern Historical Collection, University of North Carolina, Chapel Hill, North Carolina.

37. Howe, *What Hath God Wrought*, 429. Howe argues that the "refusal of the Post Office to deliver abolitionist mail to the South may well represent the largest peacetime violation of civil liberty in US history."

38. *Acts Passed at the Thirteenth Annual Session of the General Assembly of the State of Alabama, Begun and Held in the Town of Tuscaloosa, on the Third Monday in November, One Thousand Eight Hundred and Thirty-One* (Tuscaloosa, AL: E. Walker, 1832), 116–17.

39. William Lloyd Garrison, *The Letters of William Lloyd Garrison: A House Dividing Against Itself, 1836–1840*, ed. Louis Ruchames (Cambridge, MA: Harvard University Press, 1971), 11–12; Michael Kent Curtis, *Free Speech, "The People's Darling Privilege": Struggles for Freedom of Expression in American History* (Durham, NC: Duke University Press, 2000), 11–12; Jeannine Marie DeLombard, *Slavery on Trial: Law, Abolitionism, and Print Culture* (Chapel Hill: University of North Carolina Press, 2007), 51–53; Tara Mitchell Mielnik, "The Emancipator," *Tennessee Encyclopedia of History and Culture*, accessed on March 20, 2014, http://tennesseeencyclopedia.net/entry.php?rec=432 .

40. John W. Womack to Lewis Womack, "Marcus Joseph Wright Papers," August 30, 1835, Southern Historical Collection, University of North Carolina, Chapel Hill, North Carolina.

41. William Garrett, *Reminiscences of Public Men in Alabama: For Thirty Years* (Atlanta, GA: Plantation Publishing Company, 1872), 57–59.

42. On March 28, 1834, in response to Andrew Jackson's veto of the recharter of the Bank of the United States as well as his directive to remove deposits from the bank, the United States Senate passed resolutions of censure against the president. Jackson penned a protest statement that the Senate refused to place in that body's official journal. The president then launched an all-out public relations campaign to drum up support from the people. He also corresponded and petitioned state legislators directly in an attempt to affect future senate elec-

tions in his favor. Many Whigs naturally saw this as an unconstitutional abuse of executive power.

43. *Nile's Weekly Register*, November 18, 1835.

44. William J. Cooper, *Liberty and Slavery: Southern Politics to 1860* (New York: Alfred A. Knopf, 1983), 176. Michael Holt contends that Whigs were not just bound together by their opposition to Jackson. Rather, by opposing what they saw as a tyrannical chief executive, the party stood on the principle of individual rights and republican governance. According to Holt, "Whigs saw themselves acting from the necessity, as Clay had put it, 'to rescue the Government and public liberty, from the impending dangers, which Jackson has created.' . . . Rank-and-file Whigs repeatedly echoed their leaders' fears about the threat that executive tyranny posed to republican self-government." See Michael Holt, *The Rise and Fall of the American Whig Party* (New York: Oxford University Press, 1999), 28–32.

45. Clement Eaton, *History of the Old South*, 2nd ed. (New York: Macmillan Company, 1966), 284; Thomas B. Alexander et al., "Who Were the Alabama Whigs?" 5–6. Other such class-based histories include Theodore H. Jack, *Sectionalism and Party Politics in Alabama* (Menasha, WI: George Banta, 1919); Albert B. Moore, *History of Alabama and Her People* (Chicago: American Historical Society, 1927); Charles G. Sellers Jr., "Who Were the Southern Whigs?" *American Historical Review* (January 1954), 335–46.

46. Paul Murray, *The Whig Party in Georgia, 1825–1853* (Chapel Hill: University of North Carolina Press, 1948); Grady McWhiney, "Were the Whigs a Class Party in Alabama?"; Alexander et al., "Who Were the Alabama Whigs?"; Thomas B. Alexander and Peggy J. Duckworth, "Alabama Black Belt Whigs During Secession: A New Viewpoint," *Alabama Review* 17 (July 1964); Holt, *Rise and Fall.*

47. Thornton, *Politics and Power*, 117.

48. Anthony Gene Carey, *Parties, Slavery, and the Union in Antebellum Georgia* (Athens, GA: University of Georgia Press, 1997), 113.

49. Thornton, *Politics and Power*, 51–52, 326.

50. Cooper and Terrill, *American South*, 1:161–65.

51. Garrett, *Reminiscences of Public Men*, 111.

52. Hilliard, *Politics and Pen Pictures*, 19.

53. Williams, "Notes and Documents, 1948," 290–93. Oliver also benefitted from the economic downturn that began in 1837.

54. *The Whig Almanac, and Politicians Register, for 1838* (New York: George Dearborn, 1838), 31.

55. Owen, *History of Alabama*, 3:423–24; Garrett, *Reminiscences of Public Men*, 179; Manuscript Census, Butler County, Alabama, 1850, Schedules 1 and 2.

56. Owen, *History of Alabama*, 4:1732; John Buckner Little, *The History of Butler County, Alabama, 1815 to 1885: With Sketches of Some of Her Most Distinguished Citizens and Glances at Her Rich and Varied Resources* (Cincinnati, OH: Elm Street Printing, 1885), 47–53.

57. In addition to Montgomery, the district included Macon, Russell, Pike,

Barbour, Coffee, Henry, Dale, and Covington counties. Hilliard was first elected to Congress in 1845.

58. David I. Durham, *A Southern Moderate in Radical Times: Henry Washington Hilliard, 1808–1892* (Baton Rouge: Louisiana State University Press, 2008), 21.

59. Garrett, *Reminiscences of Public Men*, 96.

60. Thornton, *Politics and Power*, 181.

61. Henry W. Hilliard, "Charles Carroll, of Carrollton. An Oration Delivered in the Representatives' Hall, Before the Legislature of Alabama and the Citizens of Tuscaloosa, December 7th, 1832," *Speeches and Addresses* (New York: Harper and Brothers Publishers, 1855), 396.

62. Garrett, *Reminiscences of Public Men*, 96.

63. At the time, Lewis represented Alabama's Fourth Congressional District, a fifteen-county district that included several piney woods counties but was weighted heavily in favor of the Black Belt counties of Autauga, Coosa, Montgomery, Lowndes, Tallapoosa, Chambers, Macon, and Russell. See Durham, *Southern Moderate*, 64–65.

64. *Journal of the House of Representatives, at the Annual Session of the General Assembly of the State of Alabama; Begun and Held in the City of Tuskaloosa, on the First Monday in November, 1840* (Tuscaloosa, AL: Hale and Phelan, 1841), 20.

65. Ibid., 292.

66. Garrett, *Reminiscences of Public Men*, 142.

67. In this case, party identity was determined through the following legislative action. During the 1840 session, along a strict party-line vote, Democrats in the House chose William Rufus King over Whig candidate John Gayle to represent Alabama in the US Senate. Barbour's J. W. Mann and William T. Shanks, Butler's W. H. Crenshaw and Edward Bowen, Conecuh's W. A. Bell, Covington's Laird B. Flemming, and Pike's L. R. Simmons supported John Gayle, while Henry County's Alexander Blackshear and James Pynes, and Pike's Samuel Dixon voted for King. Based upon this vote and other such party-line votes, it is entirely reasonable to suggest that all seven Whigs and three Democrats supported their party's stance regarding the General Ticket System. Also, there is no indication that Dale County's J. G. Blair attended the 1840 session. See *House Journal, 1840*, 69–70.

68. Ibid., 295.

69. Proposed by Governor Benjamin Fitzpatrick and introduced in the House by Lawrence County's David Hubbard, the white basis resolution declared: "the Select Committee to whom was referred so much of the Governor's message as relates to laying off the State into Congressional districts, be instructed to report a bill for that purpose, having regard to the white population only, as the basis of such Congressional representation." See *Journal of the House of Representatives of the General Assembly of the State of Alabama, Begun and Held in the City of Tuskaloosa, on the First Monday in December 1842* (Tuscaloosa, AL: Phelan, 1843), 375.

70. Garrett, *Reminiscences of Public Men*, 248.

71. Carlton Jackson, "The White Basis System and the Decline of Alabama Whiggery," *Alabama Historical Quarterly* 25 (Spring–Summer 1963): 249.

72. Calvin Colton and Henry Clay, *The Life, Correspondence, and Speeches of Henry Clay* (A. S. Barnes and Company, 1857), 4:490–91.

73. Freehling, *Road to Disunion*, 437–39.

74. "Letter of Mr. Polk of Tennessee to Committee of Cincinnatti," *Mobile Advertiser*, May 11, 1844. Polk's reference to reannexation stems from his argument that, between 1803 and 1819, Texas belonged to the United States as part of the original Louisiana Purchase.

75. Hilliard, *Politics and Pen Pictures*, 119–20.

76. Clanton W. Williams, "Notes and Documents: Presidential Election Returns and Related Data for Antebellum Alabama," *The Alabama Review* 2 (January 1949): 64–65; "Alabama: Official Returns of Election Counties," *Mobile Advertiser*, December 5, 1844.

77. Hilliard, *Politics and Pen Pictures*, 123–25.

78. Ibid., 124.

Chapter 4

1. William Russell Smith, *The History and Debates of the Convention of the People of Alabama: Begun and Held in the City of Montgomery, on the Seventh Day of January, 1861: In Which Is Preserved the Speeches of the Secret Sessions, and Many Valuable State Papers* (Montgomery, AL: White and Pfister, 1861), 119.

2. *Journal of the House of Representatives of the General Assembly of the State of Alabama, Begun and Held in the City of Tuskaloosa, on the First Monday in December 1844* (Tuscaloosa, AL: John McCormick, 1845), 73.

3. Cooper and Terrill, *American South*, 1:282.

4. Henry W. Hilliard, *Speeches and Addresses* (New York: Harper and Brothers Publishers, 1855), 88.

5. *The Congressional Globe: 29th Congress, 1st Session* (Washington, DC: Blair and Rives, 1846), 77.

6. Cooper and Terrill, *American South*, 1:285.

7. Holt, *Rise and Fall*, 252.

8. Hilliard, *Speeches and Addresses*, 112.

9. *Acts Passed At the First Biennial Session of the General Assembly of the State of Alabama, Begun and Held in the City of Montgomery on the First Monday in December, 1847* (Montgomery, AL: McCormick and Walshe, 1848), 500–501.

10. *Eufaula Democrat*, July 14, 1847.

11. Eric H. Walther, *William Lowndes Yancey and the Coming of the Civil War* (Chapel Hill: University of North Carolina Press, 2006), 97–98; Holt, *Rise and Fall*, 464–65.

12. Freehling, *Road to Disunion*, 476.

13. Cooper and Terrill, *American South*, 1:290.

14. Garrett, *Reminiscences of Public Men*, 617.

15. Joseph Hodgson, *The Cradle of the Confederacy: Or, the Times of Troup, Quitman, and Yancey. A Sketch of Southwestern Political History from the Formation of the Federal Government to A.D. 1861* (Mobile, AL Register Publishing Office, 1876), 306.

16. Glenn W. LaFantasie, *Gettysburg Requiem: The Life and Lost Causes of Confederate Colonel William C. Oates* (New York: Oxford University Press, 2006), 15; Thornton, *Politics and Power*, 251.

17. Thornton, *Politics and Power*, 253.

18. Mike Bunn, "Eufaula Regency," *Encyclopedia of Alabama*, 2010, accessed October 12, 2012, www.encyclopediaofalabama.org; Elbert Watson, "James Pugh," *Encyclopedia of Alabama*, 2010, accessed November 6, 2012, www.encyclopediaofalabama.org; Rogers et al., *Alabama*, 158–59; Durham, *Southern Moderate*, 106–9.

19. Even though Yancey was not on the ballot, the Democrats believed that his debating skills were superior to Pugh's and asked him to join the debate.

20. Hilliard, *Politics and Pen Pictures*, 209.

21. Venable, "Alabama's 'War of the Roses.'"

22. Cooper, *Liberty and Slavery*,290.

23. Hilliard, *Speeches and Addresses*, 252.

24. Albert B. Moore, *History of Alabama* (Nashville, TN: Benson, 1934), 243.

25. William Freehling has argued that Taylor was attempting to avoid the entire sectional controversy by urging politicians in the territories of California and New Mexico to apply for statehood directly, thus bypassing the traditional entanglements and in-fighting that accompanied congressional territorial governance. "Taylor only desired to keep the nation free of slavery controversy. He succeeded in deepening the turmoil in his land and party." Freehling, *Road to Disunion*, 491.

26. Hilliard, *Speeches and Addresses*, 237.

27. Dorman, *Party Politics*, 44.

28. Ibid.

29. *Report of the Debates and Proceedings of the Convention for the Revision of the Constitution of the State of Indiana, 1850* (Indianapolis, IN: A. H. Brown, 1850), 598.

30. *Journal of the Third Biennial Session of the Senate of Alabama, Session, 1851–1852, Held in the City of Montgomery* (Montgomery, AL: Brittan and De Wolfe, 1852), 57.

31. Garrett, *Reminiscences of Public Men*, 544.

32. Ibid., 182–85; *Journal of the Third Biennial Session of the House of Representatives of the State of Alabama, Session 1851–1852, Held in the City of Montgomery* (Montgomery, AL: Brittan and De Wolf, 1852), 318–19; Durham, *Southern Moderate*, 120–25; Rogers et al., *Alabama*, 162.

33. Cooper and Terrill, *American South*, 1:296–97.

34. Clanton W. Williams, "Notes and Documents," 66–69; Cooper and Ter-

rill, *American South*, 1:296–97; Thornton, *Politics and Power*, 264–65; Rogers et al., *Alabama*,162–63.

35. Holt, *Rise and Fall*, 844.

36. "Synopsis of the Speech of Honorable H. W. Hilliard," *Weekly Alabama Journal*, July 21, 1855.

37. "To Kansas Emigrants," *Weekly Alabama Journal*, January 12, 1856; "Kansas Emigration," *Weekly Alabama Journal*, February 5, 1836.

38. Walter L. Fleming, "The Buford Expedition to Kansas, 1899–1903," *Transactions of the Alabama Historical Society* 4 (Montgomery: Brown Printing, 1904), 178–79.

39. Ibid., 181.

40. James M. McPherson, *Battle Cry of Freedom: The Civil War Era* (New York: Oxford University Press, 1988), 152.

41. Ibid., 153.

42. Dorman, *Party Politics*, 106–16; Thornton, *Politics and Power*, 324–27.

43. Garrett, *Reminiscences of Public Men*, 618.

44. *The Tribune Almanac and Political Register for 1856* (New York: Greeley and McElrath, 1856), 63.

45. For more information on the formation of the Republican Party, see William E. Gienapp, *The Origins of the Republican Party: 1852–1856* (New York: Oxford University Press, 1987); Eric Foner, *Free Soil, Free Labor, Free Men: The Ideology of the Republican Party before the Civil War* (New York: Oxford University Press, 1995).

46. Tyler G. Anbinder, *Nativism and Slavery: The Northern Know Nothings and the Politics of the 1850s* (New York: Oxford University Press, 1992), 220–21.

47. Freehling, *Road to Disunion*, 98–99.

48. "Presidential Election in Alabama," *Weekly Alabama Journal*, February 5, 1856; Rogers et al., *Alabama*, 170–72; Thornton, *Politics and Power*, 358–61.

49. Freehling, *Road to Disunion*, 117–42; Cooper and Terrill, *American South*, 1:302–4; *Journal of the Sixth Biennial Session of the House of Representatives of the State of Alabama, Session of 1857–1858, Held in the City of Montgomery* (Montgomery, AL: N. B. Cloud, 1858), 77–79, 131–32.

50. McPherson, *Battle Cry*, 205–6.

51. *Journal of the Seventh Biennial Session of the House of Representatives of the State of Alabama, Session of 1859–1860, Held in the City of Montgomery* (Montgomery, AL: Shorter and Reid, 1858), 281. It should be noted that Moore refused to support South Carolina's call for a secession convention in 1860. "To call a convention, with this view, at this time, is in my opinion, premature," he argued. "I fully concur with the legislature of South Carolina, in the principles set forth in [her] resolutions, but deem it inexpedient to call a convention of the slaveholding states 'immediately,' for the purposes contemplated in the resolutions." The resolutions adopted by the Alabama General Assembly and supported by Moore were actually seen as a way to compromise and avert a secession fight with the fire-eaters.

52. Williams, "Notes and Documents, 1949," 72–73.

53. Thornton, *Politics and Power*, 403.

54. Ibid., 403–14.

55. *Montgomery Daily Mail*, December 21, 1860.

56. Hilliard, *Politics and Pen Pictures*, 310.

57. Clarence Phillips Denman, *The Secession Movement in Alabama* (Montgomery: Alabama State Department of Archives and History, 1933), 162–65. Since most of the counties appear to have retained much of their traditional political alliances—Love, Starke, and Henderson were all former Whigs, as was Samuel J. Bolling of Butler—the common thread shared by almost all of the delegates was immediate secession.

58. Robert Leslie Scribner, "A Short History of Brewton, Alabama," *Alabama Historical Quarterly* 11 (1949): 15.

59. Smith, *History and Debates*, 98.

60. Ibid., 446.

61. Hilliard, *Politics and Pen Pictures*, 308–24.

62. Smith, *History and Debates*, 66.

63. Ibid.

64. Ibid., 51.

65. Ibid., 100.

Chapter 5

1. Lewy Dorman, *History of Barbour County, Alabama* (Eufaula, AL: Barbour County Genealogy and Local History Society, 2006), 207–209; *Clayton Banner*, November 22 and December 6, 1860.

2. *War of the Rebellion: A Compilation of the Official Records of the Union and Confederate Armies, 128 Vols.* (Washington, DC: Government Printing Office, 1880), ser. 1, pt. 1, 328. Hereafter cited as *O.R.*

3. *Acts of the Called Session of the General Assembly of Alabama, Held in the City of Montgomery, Commencing on the Second Monday in January, 1861* (Montgomery, AL: Shorter and Reid, 1861), 34, 43–46.

4. Ibid., 37–38.

5. *Ordinances and Constitution of the State of Alabama, With the Constitution of the Provisional Government and of the Confederate States of America* (Montgomery, AL: Montgomery Advertiser Book and Job Printing Office, 1861), 9.

6. Hubert Dent to Anna Dent, November 8, 1860, Stouten Hubert Dent Papers, Alabama Department of Archives and History, Montgomery, Alabama.

7. Robert C. Kenzer, *Kinship and Neighborhood in a Southern Community: Orange County, North Carolina, 1849–1881* (Knoxville: University of Tennessee Press, 1987), 71–72.

8. *Acts of the Seventh Biennial Session, of the General Assembly of Alabama, Held in the City of Montgomery, Commencing on the Second Monday in November, 1859* (Montgomery, AL: Shorter and Reid, 1860), 38.

9. *Montgomery Weekly Advertiser*, May 1, 1861.

10. Thomas Crenshaw to Edward Crenshaw, Crenshaw Family Papers, April 15, 1861, Auburn University Special Collections and Archives, Auburn, Alabama. Edward remained in school until the end of the semester but returned home in time to join Company K, 17th Alabama as a 3rd Lieutenant.

11. Hilliard, *Politics and Pen Pictures*, 324.

12. Martin Crawford, *Ashe County's Civil War*, 80.

13. Wetherington, *Plain Folk's Fight*, 93.

14. Wyley Donald Ward, *Early History of Covington County, Alabama, 1821–1871* (Spartanburg, SC: Reprint Co., 1991), 123–78; United States Census, Covington County, Alabama, 1860, Schedules 1, 2, and 4.

15. Muster Rolls of Alabama Civil War Units, Company B, 18th Alabama, Alabama Department of Archives and History, Montgomery, Alabama.

16. Thomas W. Cutrer, ed., *Oh, What a Lonesome Time I Had: The Civil War Letters of Major William Morel Moxley, Eighteenth Alabama Infantry, and Emily Beck Moxley* (Tuscaloosa: University of Alabama Press, 2002), 4–5, 22, 89.

17. Crawford, *Ashe County's Civil War*, 82.

18. Scott R. Smith, trans., "Memoirs of the War, 1861–1865, Company B, 33rd Alabama: As Written by a Former Member of This Company from Dale County, W. E. Preston," *Pea River Trails* 36 (Spring 2011): 14.

19. James M. Cumbia to Governor Moore, July 1, 1861, Governor Andrew Barry Moore, 1857–1861, Administrative Files, Alabama Department of Archives and History, Montgomery, Alabama (microfilm).

20. Cutrer, *Oh, What A Lonesome Time*, 20, 45.

21. W. V. Fleming to Margaret Fleming, W. V. Fleming Civil War Letters, May 12, 1862, Alabama Department of Archives and History, Montgomery, Alabama; ibid., May 29, 1862.

22. McPherson, *Battle Cry of Freedom*,487.

23. Cutrer, *Oh, What A Lonesome Time*, 41, 26.

24. Ibid., 42.

25. McMillan, *Disintegration*,36.

26. "Diary of Captain Edward Crenshaw," *Alabama Historical Quarterly* 1 (Fall 1930): 265.

27. Harold Eugene Sterkx, *Partners in Rebellion: Alabama Women in the Civil War* (Rutherford, NJ: Associated University Presses, 1970), 95–96.

28. "Diary of Mrs. Elizabeth Rhodes, 1861, Book 3," Auburn University, Special Collections and Archives, Auburn, Alabama.

29. Ibid.

30. *Montgomery Weekly Advertiser*, August 7, 1861

31. W. H. Crenshaw to A. B. Moore, September 11, 1861, Governor Andrew Barry Moore, 1857–1861, Administrative Files, Alabama Department of Archives and History, Montgomery, Alabama (microfilm).

32. C. Cunningham to A. B. Moore, September 9, 1861, Governor Andrew Barry Moore, 1857–1861, Administrative Files, Alabama Department of Archives

and History, Montgomery, Alabama (microfilm); Sterkx, *Partners in Rebellion*, 106.

33. Mary Love Edwards Fleming, "Dale County and Its People During the Civil War: Reminiscences of Mary Love (Edwards) Fleming," *Alabama Historical Quarterly* 19 (Spring 1957): 90.

34. Thomas T. Bigbie to Mary Bigbie, August 28, 1862, Thomas T. Bigbie Papers, Auburn University Special Collections and Archives, Auburn, Alabama. Bigbie's reference to the cold weather was most likely in anticipation of the fall, especially since he is writing in late August.

35. Thomas T. Bigbie to Mary Bigbie, July 15, 1863, Thomas T. Bigbie Papers, Auburn University Special Collections and Archives, Auburn, Alabama.

36. Pierre D. Costello to Cordilia Costello, July 17, 1862, Pierre D. Costello Civil War Letters, Alabama Department of Archives and History, Montgomery, Alabama.

37. LeeAnn Whites, *The Civil War as A Crisis in Gender: Augusta, Georgia, 1860–1890* (Athens: University of Georgia Press, 1995), 54.

38. For a good narrative history of the battle, see David Detzer, *Donnybrook: The Battle of Bull Run, 1861* (New York: Harcourt, 2005).

39. *O.R.*, ser. 1, 2:490.

40. McMillan, *Disintegration*, 30–31.

41. *Montgomery Weekly Post*, November 14, 1860.

42. *Montgomery Weekly Advertiser*, June 5, 1861.

43. *Montgomery Weekly Advertiser*, June 12, 1861; McMillan, *Disintegration*, 31–33.

44. McMillan, *Disintegration*, 32.

45. W. H. Crenshaw to Edward Crenshaw, December 4, 1861, Edward Crenshaw Family Letters, Auburn University Special Collections and Archives, Auburn, Alabama.

46. McMillan, *Disintegration*, 36.

47. Abstract from Field Return of the Department of Alabama and West Florida, Commanded by Major General Braxton Bragg, February 1, 1862, *O.R.*, ser. 1, 6:819; Hubert Dent to Anna Dent, December 7, 1861, S. H. Dent Papers, Auburn University Special Collections and Archives, Auburn, Alabama.

48. Joseph Allan Frank and George A. Reaves, *"Seeing the Elephant" Raw Recruits at the Battle of Shiloh* (Westport, CT: Greenwood Press, 1989), 72–75.

49. Cutrer, *Oh, What A Lonesome Time*, 51.

50. Stouten Dent to Anna Dent, June 26, 1861, S. H. Dent Papers, Auburn University Special Collections and Archives, Auburn, Alabama.

51. *O.R.*, ser. 1, pt. 2, 52:169.

52. *O.R.*, ser. 1, 6:777.

53. *O.R.*, ser. 1, 6:807

54. Hubert Dent to Anna Dent, December 19, 1861, S. H. Dent Papers, Auburn University Special Collections and Archives, Auburn, Alabama.

55. Two traditional narratives of the battle include Wiley Sword, *Shiloh:*

Bloody April (New York: Morrow, 1974) and Larry J. Daniel, *Shiloh: The Battle That Changed the Civil War* (New York: Simon and Schuster, 2008). For a revisionist history that challenges many of the traditional interpretations of the battle, see Timothy B. Smith, *The Untold Story of Shiloh: The Battle and the Battlefield* (Knoxville: University of Tennessee Press, 2008).

56. Illene D. Thompson and Wilbur E. Thompson, *The Seventeenth Alabama Infantry: A Regimental History and Roster* (Bowie, MD: Heritage Books, 2001), 43; see also, Kenneth W. Noe, "'The Fighting Chaplain of Shiloh': Isaac Tichenor's Civil War and the Roles of Confederate Ministers," in *Politics and Culture of the Civil War Era: Essays in Honor of Robert W. Johannsen, ed. Daniel McDonough and Kenneth W. Noe* (Selinsgrove, PA: Susquehanna University Press, 2006), 245–46.

57. "Diary of Captain Edward Crenshaw," *Alabama Historical Quarterly* 1 (Fall 1930): 266.

58. As it turned out, Gladden's and Jackson's brigades played a key role in decimating Brig. Gen. Benjamin Printiss's division during the first day of battle, forcing the surrender of much of his command.

59. Felix Robertson to Hubert Dent, April 25, 1909, S. H. Dent Papers, Alabama Department of Archives and History, Montgomery, Alabama; Sword, *Shiloh*, 161.

60. "The Battle of Shiloh, Part 1," in *Sketches of War History, 1861–1865: Papers Prepared for the Commandery of the State of Ohio Military Order of the Loyal Legion of the United States* (Cincinnati, OH: Robert Clarke and Company, 1903), 5:415.

61. Ibid.

62. *O.R.*, Ser. 1, pt. 1, 10:537.

63. Noe, "Isaac Tichenor's Civil War," 252.

64. *O.R.*, Ser. 1, pt. 1, 10:557.

65. Noe, "'Fighting Chaplain,'" 249–54.

66. *O.R.*, ser. 1, pt. 1, 10:539.

67. Ibid.

68. Ibid.

69. Sword, *Shiloh*, 422.

70. John Wesley Brinsfield, *The Spirit Divided: Memoirs of Civil War Chaplains: The Confederacy* (Macon, GA: Mercer University Press, 2006), 104.

71. Frank and Reaves, *Seeing the Elephant*, 78.

Chapter 6

1. Sarah A. Driggers to John Gill Shorter, June 18, 1862, John Gill Shorter Administrative Files, Alabama Department of Archives and History, Montgomery, Alabama (microfilm); Benjamin D. Simmons, Compiled Service Records of Confederate Soldiers Who Served in Organizations from the State of Alabama, National Archives and Records Administration, Washington, DC (microfilm);

Census or Enumeration of Confederate Soldiers Residing in Alabama, 1907, Coffee County, Alabama Department of Archives and History, Montgomery, Alabama (microfilm).

2. United States Census, Coffee County, Alabama, 1860, Schedules 1 and 4; Zachariah Blackman, Compiled Service Records of Confederate Soldiers Who Served in Organizations from the State of Alabama, National Archives and Records Administration, Washington, DC (microfilm).

3. Edward S. Cooper, *Louis Trezevant Wigfall: The Disintegration of the Union and Collapse of the Confederacy* (Madison, NJ: Fairleigh Dickinson University Press, 2012), 98; McPherson, *Battle Cry of Freedom,* 430.

4. Albert Burton Moore, *Conscription and Conflict in the Confederacy* (New York: Macmillan, 1924), 14.

5. Jefferson Davis to George W. Randolph, March 28, 1862, *War of the Rebellion: A Compilation of the Official Records of the Union and Confederate Armies,* ser. 4 (Washington, DC: Government Printing Office, 1880), 1:1031.

6. James Matthews, ed., *Statutes at Large of the Confederate States of America* (Richmond, VA: R. M. Smith, 1862), 29–32, 52; McPherson, *Battle Cry of Freedom,* 429–31; Moore, *Conscription and Conflict,* 15–16.

7. Malcolm Cook McMillan, *The Disintegration of a Confederate State: Three Governors and Alabama's Wartime Home Front, 1861–1865* (Macon GA: Mercer University Press, 1986), 40.

8. Stephanie McCurry, *Confederate Reckoning: Power and Politics in the Civil War South* (Cambridge, MA: Harvard University Press, 2010), 195. For more information on the divisiveness of conscription on the home front, see Jonathan D. Sarris, "An Execution in Lumpkin County: Localized Loyalties in North Georgia's Civil War," in *The Civil War in Appalachia: Collected Essays, ed. Kenneth W. Noe and Shannon H. Wilson* (Knoxville: University of Tennessee Press, 1997), 131–57 and John C. Inscoe and Gordon B. McKinney, *The Heart of Confederate Appalachia: Western North Carolina in the Civil War* (Chapel Hill: University of North Carolina Press, 2000), 139–86.

9. *O.R.,* ser. 4, 2:87.

10. Crawford, *Ashe County's Civil War,* 92.

11. Muster Rolls of Alabama Civil War Units, Company K, 37th Alabama, Alabama Department of Archives and History, Montgomery, Alabama; United States Census, Pike County, Alabama, 1860, Schedules 1 and 4.

12. Muster Rolls of Alabama Civil War Units, Company G, 15th Alabama, and Company B, 33rd Alabama, Department of Archives and History, Montgomery, Alabama; United States Census, Dale County, Alabama, 1860, Schedule 1.

13. McCurry, *Confederate Reckoning,* 137.

14. Nancy Boswell to John Gill Shorter, April 28, 1862, Letters Received by the Confederate Secretary of War, 1861–1865, National Archives and Records Administration, Washington, DC (microfilm).

15. William DuBose to John Gill Shorter, August 24, 1862, John Gill Shorter Administrative Files, Alabama Department of Archives and History, Montgomery, Alabama (microfilm).

16. G. H. McClure to George Randolph, June 13, 1862, Letters Received by the Confederate Secretary of War, 1861–1865, National Archives and Records Administration, Washington, DC (microfilm).

17. J. C. Moody to John Gill Shorter, August 6, 1862, John Gill Shorter Administrative Files, Alabama Department of Archives and History, Montgomery, Alabama (microfilm).

18. Citizens of Henry to John Gill Shorter, September 12, 1862, John Gill Shorter Administrative Files, Alabama Department of Archives and History, Montgomery, Alabama (microfilm); W. C. Capps, Compiled Service Records of Confederate Soldiers Who Served in Organizations from the State of Alabama, National Archives and Records Administration, Washington, DC (microfilm). Unfortunately for the community, Capps remained in the army, was captured at the Battle of Spotsylvania Court House in May 1864, and died at Elmira Prison just three months before the end of the war.

19. Sally McLean et al. to John Gill Shorter, November 1862, John Gill Shorter Administrative Files, Alabama Department of Archives and History, Montgomery, Alabama (microfilm); McCurry, *Confederate Reckoning*, 135.

20. United States Census, Coffee County, Alabama, 1860, Schedule 1; W. R. Roberts to John Gill Shorter, September 12, 1862, John Gill Shorter Administrative Files, Alabama Department of Archives and History, Montgomery, Alabama (microfilm).

21. Joel D. Holt to John Gill Shorter, July 29, 1862, John Gill Shorter Administrative Files, Alabama Department of Archives and History, Montgomery, Alabama (microfilm); United States Census, Henry County, Alabama, 1860, Schedule 1.

22. John Munn to John Gill Shorter, July 8, 1862, Shorter Administrative Files, Alabama Department of Archives and History, Montgomery, Alabama (microfilm); Muster Roll Company E, 15th Alabama, Muster Rolls of Alabama Civil War Units, Alabama Department of Archives and History, Montgomery, Alabama.

23. Angus A. Stewart to John Gill Shorter, August 30, 1862, John Gill Shorter Administrative Papers, Alabama Department of Archives and History, Montgomery, Alabama; A. A. Stewart, Compiled Service Records of Confederate Soldiers Who Served in Organizations from the State of Alabama, National Archives and Records Administration, Washington, DC (microfilm). It was common practice for Governors Moore, Shorter, and Watts to make brief notes on incoming letters or envelopes. Clerks would take the notations and formulate formal replies based upon the governor's decision for each case. Some of these notations have been preserved but many have not.

24. Noe, *Reluctant Rebels*, 195.

25. *Journal of the Congress of the Confederate States of America, 1861–1865* (Washington, DC: Government Printing Office, 1905), 5:490.

26. James M. K. Little to John Gill Shorter, September 1, 1862, John Gill Shorter Administrative Files, Alabama Department of Archives and History, Montgomery, Alabama (microfilm).

27. Lewis Cato to John Gill Shorter, June 10, 1862, John Gill Shorter Administrative Files, Alabama Department of Archives and History, Montgomery, Alabama (microfilm).

28. Zechariah Bush to John Gill Shorter, November 21, 1862, John Gill Shorter Administrative Files, Alabama Department of Archives and History, Montgomery, Alabama (microfilm).

29. Thomas Richards to John Gill Shorter, May 8, 1862, John Gill Shorter Administrative Files, Alabama Department of Archives and History, Montgomery, Alabama (microfilm); Benjamin Franklin Richards, Compiled Service Records of Confederate Soldiers Who Served in Organizations from the State of Alabama, National Archives and Records Administration, Washington, DC (microfilm).

30. John Blair to John Gill Shorter, November 12, 1862, John Gill Shorter Administrative Files, Alabama Department of Archives and History, Montgomery, Alabama (microfilm); Levi Blair, Compiled Service Records of Confederate Soldiers Who Served in Organizations from the State of Alabama, National Archives and Records Administration, Washington, DC (microfilm).

31. *O.R.*, ser.1, pt. 1, 12:713. See also Peter Cozzens, *Shenandoah 1862: Stonewall Jackson's Valley Campaign* (Chapel Hill: University of North Carolina Press, 2008).

32. Two good studies of the Peninsula Campaign are Gary W. Gallagher, *The Richmond Campaign of 1862: The Peninsula and the Seven Days* (Chapel Hill: University of North Carolina Press, 2000) and Stephen W. Sears, *To the Gates of Richmond: The Peninsula Campaign* (New York: Ticknor and Fields, 1992).

33. *O.R.*, ser. 1, no. 1, 11:980.

34. G. Ward Hubbs, ed., *Voices from Company D: Diaries by the Greensboro Guards, Fifth Alabama Infantry Regiment, Army of Northern Virginia* (Athens: University of Georgia Press, 2003), 89.

35. O.R., ser. 1, pt. 1, 11:981.

36. Robert E. Park, "The Twelfth Alabama Infantry, Confederate States Army," *Southern Historical Society Papers* 33 (1905): 202.

37. *O.R.*, ser. 1, pt. 2, 10:632–33.

38. "Short History of the 8th Alabama Regiment, 1864: Written by Lieutenant Colonel Hilary A. Herbert at Orange Court House, Virginia," Manuscript Copy, Hilary A. Herbert Papers, Southern Historical Collection, Louis Round Wilson Special Collections Library, Chapel Hill, North Carolina.

39. *O.R.*, ser. 1, pt. 2, 11:774.

40. William Calvin Oates, *The War Between the Union and the Confederacy, and Its Lost Opportunities* (New York: Neale Publishing Company, 1905), 114–23; Ben H. Severance, *Portraits of Conflict: A Photographic History of Alabama During the Civil War* (Fayetteville: University of Arkansas Press, 2012), 50–51.

41. Oates, *War Between the Union*, 140.

42. Ibid.

43. John J. Hennessy, *Return to Bull Run: The Campaign and Battle of Second Manassas* (New York: Simon and Schuster, 1994).

44. Jeffrey D. Stocker, ed., *From Huntsville to Appomattox: R. T. Coles History of 4th Regiment, Alabama Volunteer Infantry, C. S. A., Army of Northern Virginia* (Knoxville: University of Tennessee Press, 1996), 70.

45. *O.R.*, ser. 1, pt. 1, 19:1036–39; Stephen W. Sears, *Landscape Turned Red: The Battle of Antietam*, First Mariner Edition (Boston: Houghton Mifflin Harcourt, 2003), 246. See also Joseph L. Harsh, *Taken at the Flood: Robert E. Lee and Confederate Strategy in the Maryland Campaign of 1862* (Kent, OH: Kent State University Press, 1999).

46. G. D. Bush to Dear Father, October 22, 1862, Thomas T. Bigbie Papers, Auburn University Special Collections and Archives, Auburn, Alabama.

47. Severance, *Portraits of Conflict*, 120; Noe, *Perryville*, 292–305, 372; W. E. Preston, "The 33rd Alabama Regiment in the Civil War," ed. L. B. Williams, Auburn University Special Collections and Archives, Auburn, Alabama (typescript), 27–29.

48. Pierre Costello to Cordelia Costello, October 26, 1862, Pierre D. Costello Civil War Letters, Alabama Department of Archives and History, Montgomery, Alabama.

49. Noe, *Perryville*, 334–36.

50. Martin, *Desertion of Alabama Troops*, 128–30.

51. *Acts of the Second Called Session, 1861 and of the First Regular Annual Session of the General Assembly of Alabama, Held in the City of Montgomery, Commencing on the 28th Day of October and Second Monday in November, 1861* (Montgomery, AL: Montgomery Advertiser and Job Office, 1862), 4.

52. List of Families from Henry County, Alabama, Eligible to Receive Relief from the State Government During the Civil War, June 12, 1862, Military Volunteer Family Assistance Records, Alabama Department of Archives and History, Montgomery, Alabama.

53. H. J. Marley to John Gill Shorter, July 20, 1862, John Gill Shorter Administrative Files, Alabama Department of Archives and History, Montgomery, Alabama (microfilm).

54. Lucreesy Simmons to John Gill Shorter, July 17, 1862, John Gill Shorter Administrative Files, Alabama Department of Archives and History, Montgomery, Alabama (microfilm).

55. Phyllis LaRue LeGrand, "Destitution and Relief of the Indigent Soldiers' Families of Alabama During the Civil War" (PhD diss., Auburn University, 1964), 116–25.

56. Severance, *Portraits of Conflict*, 234–35.

57. Ralph Brannen, "John Gill Shorter: War Governor of Alabama, 1861–1863" (PhD., diss., Alabama Polytechnic Institute, 1956), 53–54.

58. *Journal of the Called Session, 1862, and the Second Regular Annual Session of the House of Representatives of the State of Alabama, Held in the City of Montgomery, Commencing on the 27th October, and the Second Monday in November, 1862* (Montgomery, AL: Montgomery Advertiser Book and Job Printing Office, 1863), 92–93.

59. *Journal of the Called Session, 1862, and the Second Regular Session of the*

Senate of the State of Alabama Held in the City of Montgomery, Commencing on the 27th October, and the Second Monday in November, 1862 (Montgomery, AL: Montgomery Advertiser Book and Job Printing Office, 1863), 16.

60. T. Bement to John Gill Shorter, July 30, 1862, John Gill Shorter Administrative Files, Alabama Department of Archives and History, Montgomery, Alabama (microfilm).

61. Charles Pickett and W. A. Andrews to John Gill Shorter, July 18, 1862, John Gill Shorter Administrative Files, Alabama Department of Archives and History, Montgomery, Alabama (microfilm). The "H. Baily" mentioned here is almost certainly the Hosea Bailey in the letter above. It is obvious that at this stage the governor trusted physicians more than ordinary citizens, even if citizen requests included endorsements from judges or other county officials.

62. *House Journal, 1862*, 151–52.

63. *Senate Journal 1862*, 159.

64. United States Census, Barbour County, Alabama, 1860, Schedules 1 and 2; United States Census, Covington County, Alabama, 1860, Schedules 1, 2, and 4.

65. W. H. Crenshaw to John Gill Shorter, December 15, 1862, John Gill Shorter Administrative Files, Alabama Department of Archives and History, Montgomery, Alabama (microfilm).

66. B. W. Starke to John Gill Shorter, October 24, 1862, John Gill Shorter Administrative Files, Alabama Department of Archives and History, Montgomery, Alabama (microfilm).

67. Augustus Benners, *Disunion, War, Defeat, and Recovery in Alabama: The Journal of Augustus Benners, 1850–1885* (Macon, GA: Mercer University Press, 2007), 90; *House Journal, 1862*, 9–14.

68. Ship captains often used bags of salt as ballast on long voyages.

69. McMillan, *Disintegration*, 48–50; William C. Davis, *Look Away!: A History of the Confederate States of America* (New York: Simon and Schuster, 2003), 287–88.

70. Affidavit of Eliza Coleman, April 28, 1862, Alabama Salt Commission: Affidavits to Obtain Salt, Butler County, Alabama Department of Archives and History, Montgomery, Alabama (microfilm); Brewer, *Alabama, Her History*, 616–17; United States Census, Butler County, Alabama, 1860, Schedules 1 and 4.

71. Ella Lonn, *Salt as a Factor in the Confederacy* (Tuscaloosa: University Alabama Press, 1965), 38.

72. Ibid., 17; Jeff Darby to John Gill Shorter, June 8, 1862, John Gill Shorter Administrative Files, Alabama Department of Archives and History, Montgomery, Alabama (microfilm).

73. *O.R.*, ser. 1, pt. 2, 52:372–73.

Chapter 7

1. Fred Shelton Watson, *Coffee Grounds; A History of Coffee County, Alabama, 1841–1970* (Anniston, AL: Higginbotham, 1970), 234–35.

2. Pierre Costello to Cordelia Costello, December 30, 1863, Pierre D. Costello Civil War Letters, Alabama Department of Archives and History, Montgomery, Alabama.

3. Elisha K. Flournoy to Martha Flournoy, April 15, 1863, Elisha K. Flournoy Civil War Letters, 1862–1864, Alabama Department of Archives and History, Montgomery, Alabama; Ibid., July 15, 1863.

4. Pierre Costello to Cordelia Costello, December 14, 1862, Pierre D. Costello Civil War Letters, Alabama Department of Archives and History, Montgomery, Alabama; Elisabeth Lauterbach Laskin, "Good Old Rebels: Soldiering in the Army of Northern Virginia, 1862–1865" (PhD diss., Harvard University, 2003), 388.

5. Sarah Terry to Joseph Green Terry, April 4, 1863, Terry Family Papers, University of North Carolina, Southern Historical Collection, Chapel Hill, North Carolina.

6. Nimrod Long to My Dear Wife, March 30, 1863, Nimrod William Ezekiel Long papers, 1860–1865, Manuscript, Archives, and Rare Book Library, Emory University, Atlanta, Georgia (microfilm).

7. Sarah Terry to Joseph Green Terry, May 4, 1863, Terry Family Papers, University of North Carolina, Southern Historical Collection, Chapel Hill, North Carolina.

8. LeGrand, "Destitution and Relief," 33–34; Bessie Martin, *Desertion of Alabama Troops from the Confederate Army: A Study in Sectionalism* (New York: Columbia University Press, 1932), 137.

9. Maxine T. Turner, *Navy Gray: A Story of the Confederate Navy on the Chattahoochee and Apalachicola Rivers* (Tuscaloosa: University of Alabama Press, 1987), 130.

10. Allen W. Jones, "A Federal Raid into Southeast Alabama," *Alabama Review* (October 1961): 4–6; *War of the Rebellion: A Compilation of the Official Records of the Union and Confederate Armies*, ser. 1 (Washington, DC: Government Printing Office, 1880), 15:939.

11. *O.R.*, ser. 1, 15:939.

12. E. D. Brunner to D. G. Farragut, *Official Records of the Union and Confederate Navies in the War of the Rebellion*, ser. 1 (Washington, DC: Government Printing Office, 1909), 19:574–75.

13. John Gill Shorter to James A. Seddon, March 5, 1863, *O.R.*, ser. 4:419.

14. *O.R.*, ser. 1, pt. 2, 26:549–53. The 57th fought with distinction at Peachtree Creek, Franklin, and Nashville, and the 61st at the Wilderness (1864), Spotsylvania, Winchester, and Fisher's Hill.

15. John Gill Shorter to Sevard Lee Jr., July 6, 1863, John Gill Shorter Administrative Files, Alabama Department of Archives and History, Montgomery, Alabama (microfilm).

16. John Gill Shorter to Thomas Armstrong, July 7, 1863, John Gill Shorter Administrative Files, Alabama Department of Archives and History, Montgomery, Alabama (microfilm).

17. John Gill Shorter to D. H. Maury, September 4, 1863, John Gill Shorter Administrative Files, Alabama Department of Archives and History, Montgomery, Alabama (microfilm).

18. "Organization of the Confederate Army of Vicksburg, Demopolis, Alabama, August 29," *O.R.*, ser. 1, pt. 3, 24:1060–61.

19. Elisha K. Flournoy to Martha Flournoy, July 15, 1863, Elisha K. Flournoy Civil War Letters, 1862–1864, Alabama Department of Archives and History, Montgomery, Alabama.

20. Elisha K. Flournoy to Martha Flournoy, October 11, 1863, Elisha K. Flournoy Civil War Letters, 1862–1864, Alabama Department of Archives and History, Montgomery, Alabama.

21. Laskin, "Good Old Rebels," 332.

22. Benjamin Gardner to John Gill Shorter, October 23, 1863, John Gill Shorter Administrative Files, Alabama Department of Archives and History, Montgomery, Alabama (microfilm).

23. John Gill Shorter to Gideon Pillow, October 27, 1863, John Gill Shorter Administrative Files, Alabama Department of Archives and History, Montgomery, Alabama (microfilm)

24. Malcolm Cook McMillan, *The Disintegration of a Confederate State: Three Governors and Alabama's Wartime Home Front, 1861–1865* (Macon, GA: Mercer, 1986), 78–79.

25. *Journal Called Session, 1863, and the Third Regular Annual Session, of the Senate, of the State of Alabama, Held in the City of Montgomery, Commencing on the 17th August and the Second Monday in November, 1863* (Montgomery, AL: Saffold and Figures, 1864), 109.

26. McMillan, *Disintegration*, 69–70.

27. Ibid., 55.

28. Ibid., 69.

29. John Gill Shorter to Braxton Bragg, July 24, 1863, John Gill Shorter Administrative Files, Alabama Department of Archives and History, Montgomery, Alabama (microfilm).

30. McMillan, *Disintegration*, 73.

31. For a good narrative history of the Battle of Chancellorsville, see Stephen W. Sears, *Chancellorsville* (New York: Houghton Mifflin, 1998).

32. "Reports of Col. Samuel B. Pickens, Twelfth Alabama Infantry," *O.R.*, ser. 1, pt. 1, 25:960–61.

33. "Report of Lieut. Col. James N. Lightfoot, Sixth Alabama Infantry," *O.R.*, ser. 1, pt. 1, 25:959–60.

34. "Report of Capt. T. M. Riley, Fifth Alabama Infantry," *O.R.*, ser. 1, pt. 1, 25:958–59.

35. Soldiers from the piney woods were only marginally involved in the Battle of Fredericksburg. The evidence suggests that casualties were light and caused mainly by long-range Union artillery fire.

36. Ben Severance, "Confederate Alabama's Finest Hour: The Battle of Salem

Church, May 3, 1863," in *The Yellowhammer War: The Civil War and Reconstruction in Alabama, ed. Kenneth W. Noe* (Tuscaloosa: University of Alabama Press, 2013), 55.

37. "Short History of the 8th Alabama Regiment, 1864: Written by Lieutenant Colonel Hilary A. Herbert at Orange Court House, Virginia," Manuscript Copy, Hilary A. Herbert Papers, Southern Historical Collection, Louis Round Wilson Special Collections Library, Chapel Hill, North Carolina.

38. "Reports of General Robert E. Lee, C. S. Army, Commanding Army of Northern Virginia, With Congratulatory Orders, *O.R.*, ser. 1, pt. 1, 25:803.

39. For a good history of the Vicksburg Campaign, see Michael B. Ballard, *Vicksburg: The Campaign That Opened the Mississippi* (University of North Carolina Press, 2004).

40. Report of Brig. Gen. Stephen D. Lee, C. S. Army, Commanding Second Brigade, July 25, 1863, *O.R.*, ser. 1, pt. 2, 24:101–3.

41. Ibid., 637.

42. "Short History of the 8th Alabama Regiment, 1864: Written by Lieutenant Colonel Hilary A. Herbert at Orange Court House, Virginia," Manuscript Copy, Hilary A. Herbert Papers, Southern Historical Collection, Louis Round Wilson Special Collections Library, Chapel Hill, North Carolina.

43. Reports of Maj. Eugene Blackford, Fifth Alabama Infantry, July 17, 1863, *O.R.*, ser. 1, pt. 2, 27:597–98.

44. Paul M. Pruitt, "William Calvin Oates (1894–96)," accessed February 14, 2014, http://www.encyclopediaofalabama.org/face/Article.jsp?id=h-1410.

45. For a good narrative history of the Battle of Little Round Top, see Harry W. Pfanz, *Gettysburg: The Second Day* (Chapel Hill: University of North Carolina Press, 1987).

46. William Calvin Oates, *The War Between the Union and the Confederacy, and Its Lost Opportunities* (New York: Neale Publishing Company, 1905), 214.

47. Ibid., 220.

48. Ibid., 218.

49. Pfanz, *Gettysburg*, 231–32.

50. Oates, *War Between the Union*, 220. Also see Oates's report of the battle: Report of Col. William C. Oates, Fifteenth Alabama Infantry, August 8, 1863, *O.R.*, ser. 1, pt. 2, 27:392–93.

51. For a comprehensive narrative history of the third day at Gettysburg, see Earl J. Hess, *Pickett's Charge: The Last Attack at Gettysburg* (Chapel Hill: University of North Carolina Press, 2001).

52. Report of Brig. Gen. Cadmus M. Wilcox, C. S. Army, July 17, 1863, *O.R.*, ser. 1, pt. 2, 27:620.

53. McPherson, *Battle Cry of Freedom*, 661.

54. James M. McPherson, *Battle Cry of Freedom*, 163; Jason Phillips, *Diehard Rebels: The Confederate Culture of Invincibility* (Athens: University of Georgia Press, 2007), 119–20; Judith Lee Hallock, ed., *The Civil War Letters of Joshua K. Callaway* (Athens: University of Georgia Press, 1997), 110–11.

55. Report of Maj. P. F. Hunley, Eighteenth Alabama Infantry, September 28, 1863, *O.R.*, ser. 1, pt. 2, 30:404–5.

56. Peter Cozzens, *This Terrible Sound: The Battle of Chickamauga* (Urbana: University of Illinois Press, 1992), 269; Report of Col. Samuel Adams, Thirty-Third Alabama Infantry, Commanding Thirty-Third Alabama and Gibson's Battalion, October 8, 1863, *O.R.*, ser. 1, pt. 2, 30:165–67.

57. William E. Matthews, "The 33rd Alabama Regiment in the Civil War," L.B. Williams, ed., Auburn University Special Collections and Archives, Auburn, Alabama.

58. Cozzens, *This Terrible Sound*, 338–56.

59. Thomas T. Bigbie to Bigbie Mary, Thomas T. Bigbie Papers, September 22, 1863, Auburn University Special Collections and Archives, Auburn, Alabama.

60. Elisha K. Flournoy to Martha Flournoy, February 10, 1864, Elisha K. Flournoy Civil War Letters, 1862–1864, Alabama Department of Archives and History, Montgomery, Alabama.

61. "Col. Holland's Florida Expedition," April 17, 1864, *Mobile Advertiser and Register*.

62. Thomas P. Cottle to Thomas A. Watts, April 21, 1864, Thomas H. Watts Administrative Files, Alabama Department of Archives and History, Montgomery, Alabama (microfilm).

63. *Public Laws of the Confederate States of America: Passed at the Fourth Session of the First Congress, 1863–1864* (Richmond, VA: R. M. Smith, 1864), 211–15.

64. For further discussion of the Confederate congress responding to public pressure, see Stephanie McCurry, *Confederate Reckoning;* William Blair, *Virginia's Private War* (New York: Oxford University Press, 1998).

65. The state legislature actually weakened the militia in 1863 by creating a two-tier system that proved unworkable. The first-class militia was comprised solely of boys and men not subject to conscription who would serve only within the confines of their home counties. The second-class included men within the conscription age that could be used anywhere in the state and were subject to Confederate service. Thus, the governor had no authority to mobilize companies outside of their respective counties. According to historian Walter Fleming, "the stupid conduct of the legislature during the last two years of the war in failing to provide for the defence of the state cannot be too strongly condemned. The final result would have been the same, but a strong force of militia would have enabled Governor Watts to execute the laws in all parts of the state, and to protect the families of loyal citizens from outrage by tories and deserters." Walter L. Fleming, *Civil War and Reconstruction in Alabama* (New York: Columbia University Press, 1905), 88–92.

66. Samuel J. Bolling and S. F. Gafford to Thomas H. Watts, February 20, 1864, Thomas H. Watts Administrative Files, Alabama Department of Archives and History, Montgomery, Alabama (microfilm); S. F. Gafford to Thomas H. Watts, March 1, 1864, Thomas H. Watts Administrative Files, Alabama Department of Archives and History, Montgomery, Alabama (microfilm).

67. Lovard Lee to Thomas H. Watts, February 26, 1864, Thomas H. Watts Administrative Files, February 26, 1864, Alabama Department of Archives and History, Montgomery, Alabama.

68. Gideon Welles and Edgar Thaddeus Welles, *Diary of Gideon Welles in Three Volumes* (New York: Houghton Mifflin, 1911), 2:44.

69. Dabney H. Maury to James A. Seddon, December 28, 1863, *O.R.*, ser. 1, pt. 2, 26:548.

70. Cullen Andrews Battle, *Third Alabama!: The Civil War Memoir of Brigadier General Cullen Andrews Battle, CSA* (Tuscaloosa: University of Alabama Press, 2000), 106–7; Ben H. Severance, *Portraits of Conflict: A Photographic History of Alabama During the Civil War* (Fayetteville: University of Arkansas Press, 2012), 169; Manuscript Census, Coffee County, Alabama, 1860, Schedule 1.

71. Oates, *War Between the Union*, 366–67.

72. Ulysses Simpson Grant, *Personal Memoirs of U. S. Grant* (New York: Charles L. Webster, 1894), 503.

73. For a good study of the Atlanta Campaign, see Albert Castel, *Decision in the West: The Atlanta Campaign of 1864* (Lawrence: University Press of Kansas, 1995).

74. For the most recent treatment of the battle, see Earl J. Hess, *Kennesaw Mountain: Sherman, Johnston, and the Atlanta Campaign* (Chapel Hill: University of North Carolina Press, 2013).

75. Sam R. Watkins, *Co. Aytch: A Confederate Memoir of the Civil War* (Simon and Schuster, 2008), 144.

76. *O.R.*, ser. 1, pt. 3, 38:703; Brewer, *Alabama, Her History*, 642; Manuscript Census, Butler County, Alabama, 1860, Schedule 1.

77. Matthews, "33rd Alabama Regiment."

78. H. E. Sterkx, "Autobiography and Civil War Letters of Joel Murphree of Troy, Alabama," *Alabama Historical Quarterly* 19 (1957): 185.

79. Brewer, *Alabama, Her History*, 669; Manuscript Census, Pike County, Alabama, 1860, Schedule 1.

80. Report of Capt. Augustus L. Milligan, Fifty-Seventh Alabama Infantry, of Operations July 20, July 24, 1864, *O.R.*, ser. 1, pt. 3, 38:897.

81. Sterkx, "Autobiography and Civil War Letters," 194.

82. Reports of Brig. Gen. Mark P. Lowrey, Commanding Brigade, of Operations July 20–September 1, September 20, 1864, *O.R.*, ser. 1, pt. 3, 38:734.

83. Matthews, "33rd Alabama Regiment."

84. McPherson, *Battle Cry of Freedom*, 774.

85. G. T. Yelverton to Col. M.A. Baldwin, *O.R.*, ser. 4, 3:1044.

86. McMillan, *Disintegration*, 128.

87. Andrew Jay to Thomas A. Watts, September 12, 1864, Thomas H. Watts Administrative Files, Alabama Department of Archives and History, Montgomery, Alabama.

88. David Williams, *Rich Man's War: Class, Caste, and Confederate Defeat*

in the Lower Chattahoochee Valley (Athens: University of Georgia Press, 1998), 144–45.

89. B. W. Starke et al. to Thomas H. Watts, September 6, 1864, Thomas H. Watts Administrative Files, Alabama Department of Archives and History, Montgomery, Alabama (microfilm).

90. James N. Lightfoot to Thomas H. Watts, October 18, 1864, Thomas H. Watts Administrative Files, Alabama Department of Archives and History, Montgomery, Alabama.

91. C. H. Reading to Thomas H. Watts, November 19, 1864, Thomas H. Watts Administrative Files, Alabama Department of Archives and History, Montgomery, Alabama.

92. John C. Brown, Compiled Service Records of Confederate Soldiers Who Served in Organizations from the State of Alabama, National Archives and Records Administration, Washington, DC (microfilm).

93. James M. Arrington to J. M. Withers, January 30, 1865, *O.R.*, ser. 4, 3:1043.

94. M. A. Baldwin to Jonas Withers, January 30, 1865, *O.R.*, ser. 4, 3:1043.

95. Wetherington, *Plain Folk's Fight*, 221.

96. *O.R.*, ser. 1, pt. 2, 39:894.

97. Allen W. Jones, "Unionism and Disaffection in South Alabama: The Case of Alfred Holley," *Alabama Review* 24 (1971): 114–32; *Mobile Daily Advertiser and Register*, April 17, 1864; Reports of Brig. Gen. Alexander Asboth, US Army. *O.R.*, ser. 1, pt. 1, 53:386. In March 1865, Alfred Holley accompanied a Federal cavalry force of nine hundred soldiers into Covington County and personally supervised the arrest of a half-dozen county officials, most of whom were old personal and political enemies.

98. James M. McPherson, *Battle Cry of Freedom*, 811.

99. Two excellent studies of the Battle of Franklin include: James L. McDonough and Thomas L Connelly, *Five Tragic Hours: The Battle of Franklin* (Knoxville: University of Tennessee Press, 1983); Wiley Sword, *Embrace an Angry Wind: The Confederacy's Last Hurrah—Spring Hill, Franklin, and Nashville* (New York: Harper Collins, 1992).

100. Matthews, "33rd Alabama Regiment."

101. Report of Lieut. Gen. Stephen D. Lee, C. S. Army, Commanding Army Corps, of Operations November 2–December 17, 1864, January 30, 1865, *O.R.*, ser. 1, pt. 1, 45:688.

102. Reports of Maj. Gen. Edward C. Walthall, C. S. Army, Commanding Division and Rear Guard of Infantry, of Operations November 20, 1864–January 8, 1865, January 14, 1865, *O.R.*, ser. 1, pt. 1, 45:720–21.

103. "Virgil S. Murphree Diary," University of North Carolina, Southern Historical Collection, Chapel Hill, North Carolina (microfilm).

104. Isaac R. Sherwood, *Memories of the War* (New York: H. J. Chittenden, 1923), 141–42.

105. For an extensive treatment of the Union siege at Petersburg, see Noah

Andre Trudeau, *The Last Citadel: Petersburg, Virginia, June 1864–April 1865* (Baton Rouge: Louisiana State University Press, 1993).

106. Williams, *Rich Man's War*, 145–47.

107. Joseph Green Terry, June 10, 1864, Terry Family Papers, University of North Carolina, Southern Historical Collection, Chapel Hill, North Carolina.

Epilogue

1. *O.R.*, ser. 1, pt. 1, 49:1044–45.

2. Ibid.

3. John M. Henderson to W. A. Ashley, November 30, 1865, Military Volunteer Family Assistance Records, Alabama Department of Archives and History, Montgomery, Alabama, accessed May 6, 2014, http://digital.archives.alabama.gov/cdm/ref/collection/voices/id/2131.

4. Wager Swayne to Y. M. Rabb, December 14, 1865, Assistant Commissioner for the State of Alabama, Bureau of Refugees, Freedmen, and Abandoned Lands, 1865–1870, National Archives and Records Administration, Washington, DC (microfilm).

5. John B. Myers, "The Alabama Freedmen and the Economic Adjustments During Presidential Reconstruction, 1865–1867," *Alabama Review* 26 (October 1973), 252–66. For a fresh assessment of the Freedmen's Bureau in Alabama under the administration of Wager Swayne, see Jason J. Battles, "Labor, Law, and the Freedmen's Bureau in Alabama, 1865–1867," in *The Yellowhammer War: The Civil War and Reconstruction in Alabama, ed.* Kenneth W. Noe (Tuscaloosa: University of Alabama Press, 2013), 240–57.

6. Wager Swayne to O. O. Howard, October 10, 1867, Assistant Commissioner for the State of Alabama, Bureau of Refugees, Freedmen, and Abandoned Lands, 1865–1870, National Archives and Records Administration, Washington, DC (microfilm).

7. United States Census, Pike County, Henry County, Dale County, Coffee County, Alabama, 1860 and 1870, Schedule 1.

8. Richard L. Hume, "The Freedman's Bureau and the Freedman's Vote in the Reconstruction of Southern Alabama: An Account by Agent Samuel S. Gardner," *Alabama Review* 37 (Fall 1975): 217–24; Ward, *Early History of Covington County, Alabama, 1821–1871*, 203. Late nineteenth-century historian Walter Fleming defined conservatives generally as whites who opposed Reconstruction efforts in the South after the war. The Democratic Party embodied this philosophy.

9. Michael W. Fitzgerald, *The Union League Movement in the Deep South: Politics and Agricultural Change During Reconstruction* (Baton Rouge: Louisiana State University Press, 2000), 82.

10. *Index to Miscellaneous Documents of the House of Representatives for the Second Session of the Fortieth Congress* (Washington, DC: Government Printing Office, 1868), 34.

11. Ibid., 45.

12. Garrett, *Reminiscences of Public Men*; Thomas Owen, *Alabama Official and Statistical Register* (Brown Printing Company, 1915), 132; Wetherington, *Plain Folks Fight*, 268.

13. Harry P. Owens, "The Eufaula Riot of 1874," *Alabama Review* 16 (July 1963): 224–37; Blake Wilhelm, "Election Riots of 1874," *Encyclopedia of Alabama*, accessed June 24, 2014, http://www.encyclopediaofalabama.org/face/Article.jsp?id=h-2484.

Bibliography

Manuscripts and Primary Source Documents

Alabama Census of Confederate Soldiers, 1907 and 1921. Alabama Department of Archives and History, Montgomery, Alabama.

Alabama Governors, Administrative Files 1819–1899, Miscellaneous Folders. Alabama Department of Archives and History, Montgomery, Alabama.

Alabama Salt Commission, Affidavits to Obtain Salt, Butler County. Alabama Department of Archives and History, Montgomery, Alabama.

Alford Alley Land Patent. Military Warrant. Sparta, Alabama, July 10, 1852. Bureau of Land Management, Eastern States Office. http://www.glorecords.blm.gov/details/patent/default.aspx?accession=0624-450&docClass=MW&sid=jjag5ffr.mxr#patentDetailsTabIndex=1.

Alley, Caroline Land Patent. State Volume Patent. Elba, Alabama, November 1, 1858. Bureau of Land Management, Eastern States Office. http://www.glorecords.blm.gov/details/patent/default.aspx?accession=AL2470__.274&docClass=STA&sid=1cyapw5l.toz#patentDetailsTabIndex=1.

Bigbie, Thomas T. Papers. Auburn University Special Collections and Archives, Auburn, Alabama.

Compiled Service Records of Confederate Soldiers Who Served in Organizations from the State of Alabama. National Archives and Records Administration, Washington, DC.

Costello, Pierre D. Civil War Letters. Alabama Department of Archives and History, Montgomery, Alabama.

Crenshaw Family Papers. Auburn University Special Collections and Archives, Auburn, Alabama.

Dent, John Horry Papers. Plantation Journal, Volume I, 1842. W. S. Hoole Special Collections Library, University of Alabama, Tuscaloosa, Alabama.

Dent, Stouten H. Papers. Auburn University Special Collections and Archives, Auburn, Alabama.

Dent, Stouten Hubert Papers. Alabama Department of Archives and History, Montgomery, Alabama.

Fleming, William V. Civil War Letters. Alabama Department of Archives and History, Montgomery, Alabama.

Flournoy, Elisha K., Civil War Letters, 1862–1864. Alabama Department of Archives and History, Montgomery, Alabama.

Letters Received by the Confederate Secretary of War, 1861–1865. National Archives and Records Administration, Washington, DC.

List of Families from Henry County, Alabama, Eligible to Receive Relief from the State Government During the Civil War. Military Volunteer Family Assistance Records. Alabama Department of Archives and History, Montgomery, Alabama.

Matthews, William E. "The 33rd Alabama Regiment in the Civil War." Edited by L. B. Williams, n.d. Auburn University Special Collections and Archives, Auburn, Alabama.

Minutes of the Thirty-Third Session of the Bethlehem Baptist Association. Auburn University Special Collections and Archives, Auburn, Alabama.

Minutes of the Twenty-Fourth Anniversary of the Bethlehem Baptist Association. Auburn University Special Collections and Archives, Auburn, Alabama.

Moore, Andrew Barry Administrative Files. Alabama Department of Archives and History, Montgomery, Alabama.

Murphree, Virgil S. Diary. Alabama Department of Archives and History, Montgomery, Alabama.

Muster Rolls of Alabama Civil War Units, 1861–1865. Alabama Department of Archives and History, Montgomery, Alabama.

Records of the Assistant Commissioner for the State of Alabama, Bureau of Refugees, Freedmen, and Abandoned Lands, 1865–1870. National Archives and Records Administration, Washington, DC.

Rhodes, Elizabeth, Diary, 1861. Auburn University Special Collections and Archives, Auburn, Alabama.

Short History of the 8th Alabama Regiment, 1864: Written by Lieutenant Colonel Hilary A. Herbert at Orange Court House, Virginia. Manuscript Copy. Southern Historical Collection, University of North Carolina, Chapel Hill, North Carolina.

Shorter, John Gill Administrative Files. Alabama Department of Archives and History, Montgomery, Alabama.

Terry Family Papers. Southern Historical Collection, University of North Carolina, Chapel Hill, North Carolina.

Watts, Thomas H. Administrative Files. Alabama Department of Archives and History, Montgomery, Alabama.

Wright, Marcus Joseph Papers. Southern Historical Collection, University of North Carolina, Chapel Hill, North Carolina.

PUBLISHED PRIMARY SOURCES

Abridgment of the Debates of Congress, From 1789 to 1856. Vol. 7. New York: D. Appleton and Company, 1858.

Acts of the Called Session of the General Assembly of Alabama, Held in the City of Montgomery, Commencing on the Second Monday in January, 1861. Montgomery, AL: Shorter and Reid, 1861.

Acts of the Second Called Session, 1861 and of the First Regular Annual Session of the General Assembly of Alabama, Held in the City of Montgomery, Commencing on the 28th Day of October and Second Monday in November, 1861. Montgomery, AL: Montgomery Advertiser and Job Office, 1862.

Acts of the Seventh Biennial Session, of the General Assembly of Alabama, Held in the City of Montgomery, Commencing on the Second Monday in November, 1859. Montgomery, AL: Shorter and Reid, 1860.

Acts Passed at the Annual Session of the General Assembly of the State of Alabama, Begun and Held in the City of Tuscaloosa, on the Third Monday in November, One Thousand Eight Hundred and Thirty-Four. Tuscaloosa, AL: David Ferguson, 1835.

Acts Passed at the Eighth Annual Session of the General Assembly of the State of Alabama, Begun and Held in the Town of Tuscaloosa, on the Third Monday in November, 1826. Tuscaloosa, AL: Grantland and Robinson, 1827.

Acts Passed at the Extra and Annual Sessions of the General Assembly of the State of Alabama, Begun and Held in the Town of Tuscaloosa, on the First Monday in November, One Thousand Eight Hundred and Thirty-Two. Tuscaloosa, AL: E. Walker, 1833.

Acts Passed at the First Biennial Session of the General Assembly of the State of Alabama, Begun and Held in the City of Montgomery on the First Monday in December, 1847. Montgomery, AL: McCormick and Walshe, 1848.

Acts Passed at the First Session of the First General Assembly of the Alabama Territory. St. Stephens, AL: Thomas East, 1818.

Acts Passed at the Fourth Annual Session of the General Assembly of the State of Alabama, Begun and Held at the Town of Cahawba, on the Third Monday of November, One Thousand Eight Hundred and Twenty Two. Cahawba, AL: William B. Allen, 1823.

Acts Passed at the Sixth Annual Session of the General Assembly of the State of Alabama; Begun and Held in the Town of Cahawba on the Third Monday in November, One Thousand Eight Hundred and Twenty Four. Cahawba, AL: William B. Allen, 1825.

Acts Passed at the Thirteenth Annual Session of the General Assembly of the State of Alabama, Begun and Held in the Town of Tuscaloosa, on the Third Monday in November, One Thousand Eight Hundred and Thirty-One. Tuscaloosa, AL: E. Walker, 1832.

Allen, A. B., ed. *American Agriculturist. 7 vols.* New York: Saxton and Miles, 1844.

Annual Report of the Chief of Engineers to the Secretary of War for the Year 1872, Washington, DC: Government Printing Office, 1872.

Annual Reports of the War Department. Washington D.C.: Government Printing Office, 1880.

Baldwin, Thomas, and Joseph Thomas. *A New and Complete Gazetteer of the United States: Giving a Full and Comprehensive Review of the Present Condition, Industry, and Resources of the American Confederacy*. New York: Lippincott, Grambo, and Company, 1854.

Battle, Cullen Andrews. *Third Alabama!: The Civil War Memoir of Brigadier General Cullen Andrews Battle, CSA*. Tuscaloosa: University of Alabama Press, 2000.

Benton, Jeffrey C. *The Very Worst Road: Travellers' Accounts of Crossing Alabama's Old Creek Indian Territory, 1820–1847*. Eufaula, AL: Historic Chattahoochee Commission of Alabama and Georgia, 1998.

Campbell, William S. *Report on the Alabama, Florida and Georgia Railroad*. E. G. Dorsey, 1838.

Carter, Clarence Edwin, ed. *The Territorial Papers of the United States: The Territory of Alabama, 1817–1819*. Vol. 18. Washington, DC: Government Printing Office, 1952.

Chappell, Frank Anderson, ed. *Dear Sister: Civil War Letters to a Sister in Alabama*. Huntsville, AL: Branch Springs Publishing, 2002.

Cloud, N. B. ed. *The American Cotton Planter*. 5 vols. Underwood & Cloud, 1860.

Colton, Calvin, and Henry Clay. *The Life, Correspondence, and Speeches of Henry Clay*. Vol. 4. New York: A.S. Barnes and Company, 1857.

Congressional Globe: 29th Congress, 1st Session. Washington, DC: Blair and Rives, 1846.

Constitution of the State of Alabama. Washington, DC: Gales and Seaton, 1819.

Cutrer, Thomas W., ed. *Oh, What a Loansome Time I Had: The Civil War Letters of Major William Morel Moxley, Eighteenth Alabama Infantry, and Emily Beck Moxley*. Tuscaloosa: University of Alabama Press, 2002.

De Bow, J. D. B. *The Seventh Census of the United States, 1850: Embracing a Statistical View of Each of the States and Territories*. Washington, DC: Robert Armstrong, 1853.

Garrison, William Lloyd. *The Letters of William Lloyd Garrison: A House Dividing Against Itself, 1836–1840*. Cambridge, MA: Harvard University Press, 1971.

Graham, James D. "Report, Pensacola, Florida, February 6, 1836." *American Railroad Journal and Advocate of Internal Improvements* 5 (1836): 452–55.

Grant, Ulysses Simpson. *Personal Memoirs of U. S. Grant*. New York: Charles L. Webster, 1894.

Hahn, Marilyn Davis. *Old Sparta and Elba Land Office Records and Military Warrants, 1822–1860*. Easley, SC: Southern Historical Press, 1983.

Hallock, Judith Lee, ed. *The Civil War Letters of Joshua K. Callaway*. Athens: University of Georgia Press, 1997.

Hilliard, Henry W. "Charles Carroll, of Carrollton. An Oration Delivered in the Representatives' Hall, Before the Legislature of Alabama and the Citizens of Tuscaloosa, December 7th, 1832." *Speeches and Addresses.* New York: Harper and Brothers Publishers, 1855.

———. *Politics and Pen Pictures at Home and Abroad.* New York: G.P. Putnam's Sons, 1892.

———. *Speeches and Addresses.* New York: Harper and Brothers Publishers, 1855.

Hodgson, Joseph, ed. *The Alabama Manual and Statistical Register for 1869 Showing the Geographical Position, Commercial Advantages, Agricultural and Manfactural Resources, and National Importance of the State of Alabama—A Statistical Guide for the Immigrant and Hand Book for the Citizen.* Montgomery, AL: Mail Building, 1869.

———. *The Cradle of the Confederacy: Or, the Times of Troup, Quitman, and Yancey. A Sketch of Southwestern Political History from the Formation of the Federal Government to A.D. 1861.* Mobile, AL Register Publishing Office, 1876.

Holcomb, Brent. *Marriage and Death Notices from the Southern Christian Advocate.* Vol. 1. Easley, SC: Southern Historical Press, 1979.

Hubbs, G. Ward. *Voices from Company D: Diaries by the Greensboro Guards, Fifth Alabama Infantry Regiment, Army of Northern Virginia.* Athens: University of Georgia Press, 2003.

Index to Miscellaneous Documents of the House of Representatives for the Second Session of the Fortieth Congress. Washington, DC: Government Printing Office, 1868.

Journal of the Called Session, 1862, and the Second Regular Annual Session of the House of Representatives of the State of Alabama, Held in the City of Montgomery, Commencing on the 27th October, and the Second Monday in November, 1862. Montgomery, AL: Montgomery Advertiser Book and Job Printing Office, 1863.

Journal of the Called Session, 1862, and the Second Regular Session of the Senate of the State of Alabama Held in the City of Montgomery, Commencing on the 27th October, and the Second Monday in November, 1862. Montgomery, AL: Montgomery Advertiser Book and Job Printing Office, 1863.

Journal of the Called Session of the House of Representatives of the State of Alabama, Held in the City of Montgomery, Commencing January 14, 1861. Montgomery, AL: Shorter and Reid, 1861.

Journal of the Congress of the Confederate States of America, 1861–1865. Vol. 5. Washington, DC: Government Printing Office, 1905.

Journal of the House of Representatives of the General Assembly of the State of Alabama, Begun and Held in the City of Tuscaloosa, on the First Monday in December 1842. Tuscaloosa, AL: Phelan, 1843.

Journal of the House of Representatives of the General Assembly of the State of Alabama, Begun and Held in the City of Tuscaloosa, on the First Monday in December 1844. Tuscaloosa, AL: Phelan, 1845.

Journal of the House of Representatives of the State of Alabama, Begun and Held at the Town of Cahawba, on the Third Monday in November 1822, Being the

Fourth Session of the General Assembly of Said State. Cahawba, AL: William B. Allen, 1823.

Journal of the House of Representatives of the State of Alabama, Begun and Held at the Town of Cahawba, on the Third Monday in November 1823. Being the Fifth Annual Session of the General Assembly of Said State. Cahawba, AL: William B. Allen, 1824.

Journal of the House of Representatives of the State of Alabama, Begun and Held at the Town of Cahawba, on the Third Monday in November, 1824, Being the Sixth Annual Session of the General Assembly of Said State. Cahawba, AL: William B. Allen, 1825.

Journal of the House of Representatives of the State of Alabama, Begun and Held at the Town of Tuscaloosa, on the First Monday in November, 1832, Being a Called Session of the General Assembly of Said State. Tuscaloosa, AL: E. Walker, 1832.

Journal of the House of Representatives of the State of Alabama, Begun and Held at the Town of Tuscaloosa, on the Third Monday in November, 1832, Being the Fourteenth Annual Session of the General Assembly of Said State. Tuscaloosa, AL: E. Walker, 1833.

Journal of the House of Representatives of the State of Alabama, Begun and Held At the Town of Tuscaloosa, on the Third Monday in November, 1826, Being the Eighth Annual Session of the General Assembly of Said State. Tuscaloosa, AL: Grantland and Robinson, 1827.

Journal of the House of Representatives, at the Annual Session of the General Assembly of the State of Alabama; Begun and Held in the City of Tuscaloosa, on the First Monday in November, 1840. Tuscaloosa, AL: Hale and Phelan, 1841.

Journal of the House of Representatives, of the State of Alabama, Begun and Held at the Town of Cahawba, on the Third Monday in November, 1825, Being the Seventh Annual Session of the General Assembly of Said State. Cahaba, AL: William B. Allen, 1826.

Journal of the House of Representatives, of the State of Alabama, Begun and Held at the Town of Tuscaloosa, on the Third Monday in November, 1833, Being the Fifteenth Annual Session of the General Assembly of Said State. Tuscaloosa, AL: May and Ferguson, 1833.

Journal of the Seventh Biennial Session of the House of Representatives of the State of Alabama, Session of 1859–1860, Held in the City of Montgomery. Montgomery, AL: Shorter and Reid, 1858.

Journal of the Sixth Biennial Session of the House of Representatives of the State of Alabama, Session of 1857–1858, Held in the City of Montgomery. Montgomery, AL: N.B. Cloud, 1858.

Journal of the Third Biennial Session of the House of Representatives of the State of Alabama, Session 1851–1852, Held in the City of Montgomery. Montgomery, AL: Brittan and De Wolf, 1852.

Journal of the Third Biennial Session of the Senate of Alabama, Session 1851–1852, Held in the City of Montgomery. Montgomery, AL: Brittan and De Wolfe, 1852.

Kennedy, Joseph Camp Griffith. *Agriculture of the United States in 1860; Com-*

piled From the Original Returns of the Eighth Census, Under the Direction of the Secretary of the Interior. Washington, DC: Government Printing Office, 1864.

———. *Population of the United States in 1860: Compiled from the Original Returns of the Eighth Census*. Washington, DC: Government Printing Office, 1864.

Mathis, Ray, and Mary Mathis. *Introduction and Index to the John Horry Dent Farm Journals and Account Books, 1840–1892*. Tuscaloosa: University of Alabama Press, 1977.

Matthews, James, ed. *Statutes at Large of the Confederate States of America*. Richmond, VA: R. M. Smith, 1862.

Olmsted, Frederick Law. *Journeys and Explorations in the Cotton Kingdom. A Traveller's Observations on Cotton and Slavery in the American Slave States. Based upon Three Former Volumes of Journeys and Investigations*. New York: S. Low and Son, 1861.

———. *A Journey in the Seaboard Slave States*. New York: Dix and Edwards, 1856.

Ordinances and Constitution of the State of Alabama, With the Constitution of the Provisional Government and of the Confederate States of America. Montgomery, AL: Montgomery Advertiser Book and Job Printing Office, 1861.

Owen, Marie Bankhead, and Emmett Kilpatrick, eds. "Alabama Census Returns 1820 and an Abstract of Federal Census of Alabama 1830." *Alabama Historical Quarterly* 6 (Fall 1944): 331–515

Owen, Thomas. *Alabama Official and Statistical Register*. Montgomery, AL: Brown Printing Company, 1915.

Public Laws of the Confederate States of America: Passed at the Fourth Session of the First Congress, 1863–1864. Richmond, VA: R.M. Smith, 1864.

Russell, Robert. *North America, Its Agriculture and Climate: Containing Observations on the Agriculture and Climate of Canada, the United States, and the Island of Cuba*. Edinburgh: A. and C. Black, 1857.

Shephard, John. *Reports of Cases Argued and Determined in the Supreme Court of Alabama*. Vol. 32. Montgomery, AL: Barrett & Wimbish, 1859.

Sherwood, Isaac R. *Memories of the War*. New York: H. J. Chittenden, 1923.

Smith, Eugene Allen. *Report on the Cotton Production of the State of Alabama*. s.n., 1884.

Smith, Scott R., trans. "Memoirs of the War, 1861–1865, Company B, 33rd Alabama: As Written by a Former Member of This Company from Dale County, W. E. Preston." *Pea River Trails* 36 (Spring 2011): 12–34.

Smith, William Russell. *The History and Debates of the Convention of the People of Alabama: Begun and Held in the City of Montgomery, on the Seventh Day of January, 1861: In Which Is Preserved the Speeches of the Secret Sessions, and Many Valuable State Papers*. Montgomery, AL: White and Pfister, 1861.

Starrett, Paul. *Appraisal Report: Lands in Southern Georgia and Southeastern Alabama Ceded by the Creek Nation, Before the Indian Claims Commission, Docket No. 21, Valued as of August 9, 1814*. s.n., 1957.

Sterkx, H. E. "Autobiography and Civil War Letters of Joel Murphree of Troy, Alabama." *Alabama Historical Quarterly* 19 (July 1957): 170–208.

Tribune Almanac and Political Register for 1856. New York: Greeley and McElrath, 1856. *War of the Rebellion: A Compilation of the Official Records of the Union and Confederate Armies, 128 Vols*. Washington, DC: Government Printing Office, 1880.

Watkins, Sam R. *Co. Aytch: A Confederate Memoir of the Civil War*. New York: Simon and Schuster, 2008.

Welles, Gideon, and Edgar Thaddeus Welles. *Diary of Gideon Welles in Three Volumes*. Vol. 2. New York: Houghton Mifflin, 1911.

Whig Almanac and Politicians Register for 1838. New York: George Dearborn and Company, 1838.

Williams, Clanton W. "Notes and Documents: Presidential Election Returns and Related Data for Antebellum Alabama." *Alabama Review* 1 (October 1948): 279–93.

———. "Notes and Documents: Presidential Election Returns and Related Data for Antebellum Alabama." *Alabama Review* 2, no. 1 (January 1949): 63–73.

Secondary Sources

Alexander, Thomas B. "Persistent Whiggery in Alabama and the Lower Class, 1860–1867." *Alabama Review* 12 (January 1959): 35–52.

Alexander, Thomas B., Kit C. Carter, Jack R. Lister, Jerry C. Oldshue, and Winfred G. Sandlin. "Who Were the Alabama Whigs?" *Alabama Review* 16 (January 1963): 5–19.

Alexander, Thomas B., and Peggy J. Duckworth. "Alabama Black Belt Whigs During Secession: A New Viewpoint." *Alabama Review* 17 (July 1964): 181–97.

Anbinder, Tyler G. *Nativism and Slavery: The Northern Know Nothings and the Politics of the 1850s*. New York: Oxford University Press, 1992.

Andrews, W. L. "Early History of Southeast Alabama." *Alabama Historical Quarterly* 10 (1948): 99–132.

Ballard, Michael B. *Vicksburg: The Campaign That Opened the Mississippi*. Chapel Hill: University of North Carolina Press, 2004.

Bardaglio, Peter. *Reconstructing the Household: Families, Sex, and the Law in the Nineteenth-Century South*. Chapel Hill: University of North Carolina Press, 1995.

Battles, Jason J. "Labor, Law, and the Freedmen's Bureau in Alabama, 1865–1867." In *The Yellowhammer War: The Civil War and Reconstruction in Alabama*. Edited by Kenneth W. Noe, 240–57. Tuscaloosa: University of Alabama Press, 2013.

Benners, Augustus. *Disunion, War, Defeat, and Recovery in Alabama: The Journal of Augustus Benners, 1850–1885*. Macon, GA: Mercer University Press, 2007.

Beringer, Richard E., Herman Hattaway, Archer Jones, and William Still. *Why the South Lost the Civil War*. Athens: University of Georgia Press, 1986.

Blair, William. *Virginia's Private War*. New York: Oxford University Press, 1998.

Bolton, Charles C. *Poor Whites of the Antebellum South: Tenants and Laborers in Central North Carolina and Northeast Mississippi*. Durham, NC: Duke University Press, 1994.

Bond, Bradley. "Herders, Farmers, and Markets on the Inner Frontier: The Mississippi Piney Woods, 1850–1860." In *Plain Folk of the South Revisited*, edited by Samuel C. Hyde Jr., 73–99. Baton Rouge: Louisiana State University Press, 1997.

Boyd, Gregory A. *Family Maps of Pike County, Alabama: With Homesteads, Roads, Waterways, Towns, Cemeteries, Railroads, and More*. Norman, OK: Arphax Publishing Company, 2007.

Brannen, Ralph. "John Gill Shorter: War Governor of Alabama, 1861–1863." PhD diss., Alabama Polytechnic Institute, 1956.

Braund, Kathryn E. Holland. *Deerskins and Duffels: The Creek Indian Trade with Anglo-America, 1685–1815*. Lincoln: University of Nebraska Press, 1993.

Brewer, Willis. *Alabama, Her History, Resources, War Record, and Public Men: From 1540 to 1872*. Montgomery, AL: Barrett and Brown, 1872.

Brinsfield, John Wesley. *The Spirit Divided: Memoirs of Civil War Chaplains: The Confederacy*. Macon, GA: Mercer University Press, 2006.

Bunn, Mike. *Battle for the Southern Frontier: The Creek War and the War of 1812*. Charleston, SC: History Press, 2008.

———. "Eufaula Regency." *Encyclopedia of Alabama*, 2010. http://www.encyclopediaofalabama.org/face/Article.jsp?id=h-2913.

Burton, Brian K. *Extraordinary Circumstances: The Seven Days Battles*. Bloomington: Indiana University Press, 2001.

Byrd, William. "Wiregrass: The Transformation of Southeast Alabama, 1880–1930." PhD diss., Auburn University, 2009.

Campbell, Jacqueline Glass. *When Sherman Marched North from the Sea: Resistance on the Confederate Home Front*. Chapel Hill: University of North Carolina Press, 2005.

Carey, Anthony Gene. *Parties, Slavery, and the Union in Antebellum Georgia*. Athens, GA: University of Georgia Press, 1997.

———. *Sold Down the River: Slavery in the Lower Chattahoochee Valley of Alabama and Georgia*. Tuscaloosa: University of Alabama Press, 2011.

Cashin, Joan E. *A Family Venture: Men and Women on the Southern Frontier*. New York: Oxford University Press, 1991.

Castel, Albert. *Decision in the West: The Atlanta Campaign of 1864*. Lawrence: University Press of Kansas, 1995.

Cecil-Fronsman, Bill. *Common Whites: Class and Culture in Antebellum North Carolina*. Lexington: University Press of Kentucky, 1992.

Clinton, Catherine. *The Devil's Lane: Sex and Race in the Early South*. New York: Oxford University Press, 1997.

Cole, Donald B. *Vindicating Andrew Jackson: The 1828 Election and the Rise of the Two-Party System*. Lawrence: University Press of Kansas, 2009.

Cooper, Edward S. *Louis Trezevant Wigfall: The Disintegration of the Union and Collapse of the Confederacy*. Madison, NJ: Fairleigh Dickinson University Press, 2012.

Cooper, William J. *Liberty and Slavery: Southern Politics to 1860*. New York: Alfred A. Knopf, 1983.

Cooper, William J., and Thomas E. Terrill. *The American South: A History*. Vol. 1. Lanham, MD: Rowman and Littlefield Publishers, 2009.

Cozzens, Peter. *This Terrible Sound: The Battle of Chickamauga*. Urbana: University of Illinois Press, 1992.

Crawford, Martin. *Ashe County's Civil War: Community and Society in the Appalachian South*. Charlottesville: University Press of Virginia, 2001.

Current, Richard Nelson, and T. Harry Williams. *Why the North Won the Civil War*. Baton Rouge: Louisiana State University Press, 1960.

Curtis, Michael Kent. *Free Speech, "The People's Darling Privilege": Struggles for Freedom of Expression in American History*. Durham, NC: Duke University Press, 2000.

Daniel, Larry J. *Shiloh: The Battle That Changed the Civil War*. New York: Simon and Schuster, 2008.

———. *Soldiering in the Army of Tennessee: A Portrait of Life in a Confederate Army*. Chapel Hill: University of North Carolina Press, 1991.

Davis, William C. *Look Away!: A History of the Confederate States of America*. New York: Simon and Schuster, 2003.

DeLombard, Jeannine Marie. *Slavery on Trial: Law, Abolitionism, and Print Culture*. Chapel Hill: University of North Carolina Press, 2007.

Denman, Clarence Phillips. *The Secession Movement in Alabama*. Montgomery: Alabama State Department of Archives and History, 1933.

Detzer, David. *Donnybrook: The Battle of Bull Run, 1861*. New York: Harcourt, 2005.

Dollar, Kent T. *Soldiers of the Cross: Confederate Soldier-Christians and the Impact of War on Their Faith*. Macon, GA: Mercer University Press, 2005.

Dorman, Lewy. *History of Barbour County, Alabama*. Eufaula, AL: Barbour County Genealogy and Local History Society, 2006.

———. *Party Politics in Alabama from 1850 through 1860*. Tuscaloosa: University of Alabama Press, 1935.

Durham, David I. *A Southern Moderate in Radical Times: Henry Washington Hilliard, 1808–1892*. Baton Rouge: Louisiana State University Press, 2008.

Durrill, Wayne K. *War of Another Kind: A Southern Community in the Great Rebellion*. New York: Oxford University Press, 1990.

Dyer, Thomas G. *Secret Yankees: The Union Circle in Confederate Atlanta*. Baltimore, MD: Johns Hopkins University Press, 2001.

Eaton, Clement. *History of the Old South*. New York: Macmillan Company, 1966.

Ellis, Richard E. *The Union at Risk: Jacksonian Democracy, States' Rights, and the Nullification Crisis*. New York: Oxford University Press, 1989.

Ellisor, John T. *The Second Creek War: Interethnic Conflict and Collusion on a Collapsing Frontier*. Lincoln: University of Nebraska Press, 2010.

Escott, Paul D. *After Secession: Jefferson Davis and the Failure of Confederate Nationalism*. Baton Rouge: Louisiana State University Press, 1992.

———. *Many Excellent People: Power and Privilege in North Carolina, 1850–1900*. Chapel Hill: University of North Carolina Press, 1988.

Ethridge, Robbie F. *Creek Country: The Creek Indians and Their World*. Chapel Hill: University of North Carolina Press, 2003.

Fallin, Wilson. *Uplifting the People: Three Centuries of Black Baptists in Alabama*. Tuscaloosa: University of Alabama Press, 2007.

Farmer, Margaret Pace. *One Hundred Fifty Years in Pike County, Alabama, 1821–1971*. Anniston, AL: Higginbotham, 1973.

Faust, Drew Gilpin. *The Creation of Confederate Nationalism: Ideology and Identity in the Civil War South*. Baton Rouge: Louisiana State University Press, 1989.

Fellman, Michael. *Inside War: The Guerrilla Conflict in Missouri During the American Civil War*. New York: Oxford University Press, 1989.

Fisher, Noel C. *War at Every Door: Partisan Politics and Guerrilla Violence in East Tennessee, 1860–1869*. Chapel Hill: University of North Carolina Press, 2001.

Fitzgerald, Michael W. *The Union League Movement in the Deep South: Politics and Agricultural Change During Reconstruction*. Baton Rouge: Louisiana State University Press, 2000.

Fleming, Mary Love Edwards. "Dale County and Its People During the Civil War: Reminiscences of Mary Love (Edwards) Fleming." *Alabama Historical Quarterly* 19 (Spring 1957): 61–110.

Fleming, Walter L. "The Buford Expedition to Kansas, 1899–1903." *Transactions of the Alabama Historical Society* 4 (1904): 178–79.

———. *Civil War and Reconstruction in Alabama*. New York: Columbia University Press, 1905.

Flewellen, Robert H. *Along Broad Street: A History of Eufaula, Alabama, 1823–1984*. Eufaula, AL: City of Eufaula, 1991.

Flynt, Wayne. *Alabama Baptists: Southern Baptists in the Heart of Dixie*. Tuscaloosa: University of Alabama Press, 1998.

———. *Dixie's Forgotten People: The South's Poor Whites*. Bloomington: Indiana University Press, 1979.

Foner, Eric. *Free Soil, Free Labor, Free Men: The Ideology of the Republican Party Before the Civil War*. New York: Oxford University Press, 1995.

Forbes, Robert Pierce. *The Missouri Compromise and Its Aftermath: Slavery and the Meaning of America*. Chapel Hill: University of North Carolina Press, 2007.

Ford, Lacy K. *Origins of Southern Radicalism: The South Carolina Upcountry, 1800–1860*. New York: Oxford University Press, 1988.

Frank, Andrew K. "Creek War." *Encyclopedia of American Indian History*. Edited by Barry M. Pritzker and Bruce E. Johansen, 220–21. Santa Barbara, CA: ABC-CLIO, 2007.

Frank, Joseph Allan, and George A. Reaves. *"Seeing the Elephant:" Raw Recruits at the Battle of Shiloh*. New York: Greenwood Press, 1989.

Freehling, William W. *The Road to Disunion: Secessionists at Bay, 1776–1854*. New York: Oxford University Press, 1990.

———. *The Road to Disunion: Secessionists Triumphant, 1854–1861*. New York: Oxford University Press, 2007.

Gallagher, Gary W. *The Confederate War*. Cambridge, MA: Harvard University Press, 1997.

———. "Disaffection, Persistence, and Nation: Some Directions in Recent Scholarship on the Confederacy." *Civil War History* 55 (2009): 329–53.

Gallman, James Matthew. *The North Fights the Civil War: The Home Front*. New York: Ivan R. Dee, 1994.

Garrett, William. *Reminiscences of Public Men in Alabama: For Thirty Years*. Atlanta, GA: Plantation Publishing Company, 1872.

Giddings, Paula. *When and Where I Enter: The Impact of Black Women on Race and Sex in America*. New York: W. Morrow, 1984.

Gienapp, William E. *The Origins of the Republican Party: 1852–1856*. New York: Oxford University Press, 1987.

Glatthaar, Joseph T. *Soldiering in the Army of Northern Virginia: A Statistical Portrait of the Troops Who Served Under Robert E. Lee*. Chapel Hill: University of North Carolina Press, 2011.

Gross, Ariela Julie. *Double Character: Slavery and Mastery in the Antebellum Southern Courtroom*. Princeton, NJ: Princeton University Press, 2000.

Hahn, Steven. *The Roots of Southern Populism: Yeomen Farmers and the Transformation of the Georgia Upcountry, 1850–1890*. New York: Oxford University Press, 1983.

Hall, Basil. *Travels in North America in the Years 1827 and 1828. 3 vols.* London: Simpkin and Marshall, 1829.

Harris, J. William. *Plain Folk and Gentry in a Slave Society: White Liberty and Black Slavery in Augusta's Hinterlands*. Middletown, CT: Wesleyan University Press, 1985.

Harrold, Stanley. *Border War: Fighting Over Slavery Before the Civil War*. Chapel Hill: University of North Carolina Press, 2010.

Harsh, Joseph L. *Taken at the Flood: Robert E. Lee and Confederate Strategy in the Maryland Campaign of 1862*. Kent, OH: Kent State University Press, 1999.

Hennessy, John J. *Return to Bull Run: The Campaign and Battle of Second Manassas*. New York: Simon and Schuster, 1994.

Hess, Earl J. *The Civil War in the West: Victory and Defeat from the Appalachians to the Mississippi*. The Littlefield History of the Civil War Era. Chapel Hill: University of North Carolina Press, 2012.

———. *Kennesaw Mountain: Sherman, Johnston, and the Atlanta Campaign*. Chapel Hill: University of North Carolina Press, 2013.

———. *Pickett's Charge: The Last Attack at Gettysburg*. Chapel Hill: University of North Carolina Press, 2001.

Hickman, Nollie W. *Mississippi Harvest: Lumbering in the Longleaf Pine Belt, 1840–1915*. Jackson: University Press of Mississippi, 1962.

Holt, Michael. *The Rise and Fall of the American Whig Party*. New York: Oxford University Press, 1999.

Howe, Daniel Walker. *What Hath God Wrought: The Transformation of America, 1815–1848*. New York: Oxford University Press, 2007.

Hume, Richard L. "The Freedman's Bureau and the Freedman's Vote in the Reconstruction of Southern Alabama: An Account by Agent Samuel S. Gardner." *Alabama Review* 37 (Fall 1975): 217–24.

Hundley, Daniel Robinson. *Social Relations in Our Southern States*. New York: Henry B. Price, 1860.

Hyde, Samuel C., Jr. "Plain Folk Reconsidered: Historiographical Ambiguity in Search of Definition." *Journal of Southern History* 71, no. 4 (November 1, 2005): 803–30.

Inscoe, John C. *Mountain Masters: Slavery Sectional Crisis Western North Carolina*. Knoxville: University of Tennessee Press, 1996.

Inscoe, John C., and Robert C. Kenzer, eds. *Enemies of the Country: New Perspectives on Unionists in the Civil War South*. Athens: University of Georgia Press, 2004.

Inscoe, John C., and Gordon B. McKinney. *The Heart of Confederate Appalachia: Western North Carolina in the Civil War*. Chapel Hill: University of North Carolina Press, 2000.

Jack, Theodore H. "Alabama and the Federal Government." *Mississippi Valley Historical Review* 3 (December 1916): 301–17.

———. *Sectionalism and Party Politics in Alabama*. Menasha, WI: George Banta, 1919.

Jackson, Carlton. "The White Basis System and the Decline of Alabama Whiggery." *Alabama Historical Quarterly* (Fall/Winter 1963): 246–53.

Jones, Allen W. "A Federal Raid into Southeast Alabama." *Alabama Review* (October 1961): 259–68.

———. "Unionism and Disaffection in South Alabama: The Case of Alfred Holley." *Alabama Review* 24 (April 1971): 114–42.

Jordan, Winthrop D. *White over Black: American Attitudes Toward the Negro, 1550–1812*. Chapel Hill: University of North Carolina Press, 1968.

Kenzer, Robert C. *Kinship and Neighborhood in a Southern Community: Orange County, North Carolina, 1849–1881*. Knoxville: University of Tennessee Press, 1987.

Kvach, John. *De Bow's Review: The Antebellum Vision of a New South*. Lexington: University Press of Kentucky, 2013.

LaFantasie, Glenn W. *Gettysburg Requiem: The Life and Lost Causes of Confederate Colonel William C. Oates*. New York: Oxford University Press, 2006.

———. *Twilight at Little Round Top: July 2, 1863—The Tide Turns at Gettysburg.* New York: Random House, 2007.

Laskin, Elisabeth Lauterbach. "Good Old Rebels: Soldiering in the Army of Northern Virginia, 1862–1865." PhD diss., Harvard University, 2003.

LeGrand, Phyllis LaRue. "Destitution and Relief of the Indigent Soldiers' Families of Alabama During the Civil War." PhD diss., Auburn University, 1964.

Little, John Buckner. *The History of Butler County, Alabama, 1815 to 1885: With Sketches of Some of Her Most Distinguished Citizens and Glances at Her Rich and Varied Resources.* Cincinnati, OH: Elm St. Printing Company, 1885.

Lonn, Ella. *Salt as a Factor in the Confederacy.* Tuscaloosa: University Alabama Press, 1965.

Martin, Bessie. *Desertion of Alabama Troops from the Confederate Army: A Study in Sectionalism.* New York: Columbia University Press, 1932.

———. *A Rich Man's War, a Poor Man's Fight: Desertion of Alabama Troops from the Confederate Army.* Tuscaloosa: University of Alabama Press, 2003.

Mathis, Ray. *John Horry Dent, South Carolina Aristocrat on the Alabama Frontier.* Tuscaloosa: University of Alabama Press, 1979.

McCaslin, Richard B. *Tainted Breeze: The Great Hanging at Gainesville, Texas, 1862.* Baton Rouge: Louisiana State University Press, 1997.

McCurry, Stephanie. *Confederate Reckoning: Power and Politics in the Civil War South.* Cambridge: Harvard University Press, 2010.

———. *Masters of Small Worlds: Yeoman Households, Gender Relations, and the Political Culture of the Antebellum South Carolina Low Country.* New York: Oxford University Press, 1997.

McDonough, James L., and Thomas L Connelly. *Five Tragic Hours: The Battle of Franklin.* Knoxville: University of Tennessee Press, 1983.

McIlwain, Christopher Lyle. *Civil War Alabama.* Tuscaloosa: University of Alabama Press, 2016.

McMillan, Malcolm Cook. *Constitutional Development in Alabama, 1798–1901: A Study in Politics, the Negro, and Sectionalism.* Chapel Hill: University of North Carolina Press, 1955.

———. *The Disintegration of a Confederate State: Three Governors and Alabama's Wartime Home Front, 1861–1865.* Macon, GA: Mercer University Press, 1986.

McPherson, James M. "American Victory, American Defeat." In *Why the Confederacy Lost.* Edited by Gabor S. Borritt, 15–42. New York: Oxford University Press, 1992.

———. *Battle Cry of Freedom: The Civil War Era.* New York: Oxford University Press, 1988.

McWhiney, Grady. "The Revolution in Nineteenth-Century Alabama Agriculture." In *From Civil War to Civil Rights, Alabama, 1860–1960: An Anthology From the Alabama Review.* Edited by Sarah Woolfolk Wiggins, 109–32. Tuscaloosa: University of Alabama Press, 1987.

———. "Were the Whigs a Class Party in Alabama?" *Journal of Southern History* 23 (November 1957): 510–22.

Mielnik, Tara Mitchell. "The Emancipator." *Tennessee Encyclopedia of History and Culture*. http://tennesseeencyclopedia.net/entry.php?rec=432.

Miller, James David. *South by Southwest: Planter Emigration and Identity in the Slave South*. Charlottesville: University of Virginia Press, 2002.

Miller, Robert J. *Both Prayed to the Same God: Religion and Faith in the American Civil War*. Lanham, MD: Lexington Books, 2007.

Mitchell, Reid. *Civil War Soldiers*. New York: Viking Press, 1988.

Moore, Albert B. *Conscription and Conflict in the Confederacy*. New York: Macmillan, 1924.

———. *History of Alabama*. Nashville, Tennessee: Benson, 1934.

———. *History of Alabama and Her People*. Chicago: American Historical Society, 1927.

Moore, Glover. *The Missouri Controversy, 1819–1821*. Lexington: University of Kentucky Press, 1953.

Morris, Thomas D. *Southern Slavery and the Law, 1619–1860*. Chapel Hill: University of North Carolina Press, 1996.

Murray, Paul. *The Whig Party in Georgia, 1825–1853*. Chapel Hill: University of North Carolina Press, 1948.

Myers, John B. "The Alabama Freedmen and the Economic Adjustments During Presidential Reconstruction, 1865–1867." *Alabama Review* 26 (October 1973): 252–66.

Noe, Kenneth W. "'Battle against the Traitors': Unionist Middle Tennesseans in the Ninth Kentucky Infantry and What They Fought For." In *Sister States Enemy States: The Civil War in Kentucky and Tennessee*. Edited by Kent T. Dollar, Larry H. Whiteaker, and W. Calvin, 123–39. Lexington: University of Kentucky Press, 2009.

———. "Exterminating Savages: The Union Army and Mountain Guerrillas in Southern West Virginia, 1861–1862." In *The Civil War in Appalachia: Collected Essays*. Edited by Kenneth W. Noe and Shannon H. Wilson, 104–30. Knoxville: University of Tennessee Press, 1997.

———. "'The Fighting Chaplain of Shiloh': Isaac Tichenor's Civil War and the Roles of Confederate Ministers." In *Politics and Culture of the Civil War Era: Essays in Honor of Robert W. Johannsen*. Edited by Daniel McDonough and Kenneth W. Noe, 204–64. Selinsgrove, PA: Susquehanna University Press, 2006.

———. *Perryville: This Grand Havoc of Battle*. Lexington: University Press of Kentucky, 2001.

———. *Reluctant Rebels: The Confederates Who Joined the Army after 1861*. Chapel Hill: University of North Carolina Press, 2010.

———. *Southwest Virginia's Railroad: Modernization and the Sectional Crisis*. Urbana: University of Illinois Press, 1994.

Oakes, James. *The Ruling Race: A History of American Slaveholders*. New York: Vintage Books, 1983.

Oates, William Calvin. *The War Between the Union and the Confederacy, and Its Lost Opportunities*. New York: Neale Publishing Company, 1905.

Owen, Thomas M. *History of Alabama and Dictionary of Alabama Biography*. 4 vols. Chicago: S. J. Clarke Publishing Company, 1921.

Owen, Thomas McAdory, and Marie Bankhead Owen. *History of Alabama and Dictionary of Alabama Biography*. 4 vols. Chicago, IL: S. J. Clarke Publishing Company, 1921.

Owens, Harry P. "The Eufaula Riot of 1874." *Alabama Review* 16 (July 1963): 224–37.

Owsley, Frank Lawrence. *Plain Folk of the Old South*. Baton Rouge: Louisiana State University Press, 1949.

Park, Robert E. "The Twelfth Alabama Infantry, Confederate States Army." *Southern Historical Society Papers* 33 (1905): 193–296.

Parsons, Lynn H. *The Birth of Modern Politics: Andrew Jackson, John Quincy Adams, and the Election of 1828*. New York: Oxford University Press, 2009.

Pfanz, Harry W. *Gettysburg: The Second Day*. Chapel Hill: University of North Carolina Press, 1987.

Phillips, Jason. *Diehard Rebels: The Confederate Culture of Invincibility*. Athens: University of Georgia Press, 2007.

Pruitt, Paul M. "William Calvin Oates (1894–96)." *Encyclopedia of Alabama*. http://www.encyclopediaofalabama.org/face/Article.jsp?id=h-1410.

Rable, George C. *Civil Wars: Women and the Crisis of Southern Nationalism*. Champaign: University of Illinois Press, 1991.

———. *God's Almost Chosen Peoples: A Religious History of the American Civil War*. Chapel Hill: University of North Carolina Press, 2010.

Remini, Robert Vincent. *Andrew Jackson and His Indian Wars*. New York: Viking, 2001.

———. *John Quincy Adams*. New York: Times Books, 2002.

Rhea, Gordon C. *The Battles for Spotsylvania Court House and the Road to Yellow Tavern, May 7–12, 1864*. Baton Rouge: Louisiana State University Press, 1997.

Riley, B. F, and Alabama Baptist Historical Society. *History of the Baptists of Alabama: From the Time of Their First Occupation of Alabama in 1808, Until 1894: Being a Detailed Record of Denominational Events in the State During Eighty-Six Years, and Furnishing Biographical Sketches of Those Who Have Been Conspicuous in the Annals of the Denomination, Besides Much Other Incidental Matter Relative to the Secular History of Alabama*. Birmingham, AL: Roberts and Son, 1895.

Roediger, David, and Elizabeth Esch, *The Production of Difference: Race and the Management of Labor in US History*. New York: Oxford University Press, 2012.

Rogers, William Warren, Robert David Ward, Leah Rawls Atkins, and Wayne

Flynt. *Alabama: The History of a Deep South State*. Tuscaloosa: University of Alabama Press, 1994.

Sarris, Jonathan D. "An Execution in Lumpkin County: Localized Loyalties in North Georgia's Civil War." In *The Civil War in Appalachia: Collected Essays*. Edited by Kenneth W. Noe and Shannon H. Wilson, 131–57. Knoxville: University of Tennessee Press, 1997.

Scott, Marvin. *History of Henry County, Alabama*. Pensacola, FL: Frank Parkhurst and Son, 1961.

Scribner, Robert Leslie. "A Short History of Brewton, Alabama." *Alabama Historical Quarterly* 11 (1949):1–131.

Sears, Stephen W. *Chancellorsville*. New York: Houghton Mifflin, 1998.

———. *Landscape Turned Red: The Battle of Antietam*. Boston: Houghton Mifflin Harcourt, 2003.

Sellers, Charles G., Jr. "Who Were the Southern Whigs?" *American Historical Review* (January 1954): 335–46.

Severance, Ben. "Confederate Alabama's Finest Hour: The Battle of Salem Church, May 3, 1863." In *The Yellowhammer War: The Civil War and Reconstruction in Alabama*. Edited by Kenneth W. Noe, 55–70. Tuscaloosa: University of Alabama Press, 2013.

———. *Portraits of Conflict: A Photographic History of Alabama During the Civil War*. Fayetteville: University of Arkansas Press, 2012.

Sheehan-Dean, Aaron Charles. *Why Confederates Fought: Family and Nation in Civil War Virginia*. Chapel Hill: University of North Carolina Press, 2009.

Smith, Timothy B. *The Untold Story of Shiloh: The Battle and the Battlefield*. Knoxville: University of Tennessee Press, 2008.

Southerland, Henry deLeon, and Jerry Elijah Brown. *The Federal Road through Georgia, the Creek Nation, and Alabama, 1806–1836*. Tuscaloosa: University of Alabama Press, 1989.

Sterkx, H. E. "Joel Dyer Murphree, Troy Merchant, 1843–1868." *Alabama Review* 11 (April 1958): 117–24.

———. *Partners in Rebellion: Alabama Women in the Civil War*. Plainsboro, NJ: Associated University Presses, 1970.

Stocker, Jeffrey D. ed., *From Huntsville to Appomattox: R.T. Coles History of 4th Regiment, Alabama Volunteer Infantry, C.S.A., Army of Northern Virginia*. Knoxville: University of Tennessee Press, 1996.

Storey, Margaret M. *Loyalty and Loss: Alabama's Unionists in the Civil War and Reconstruction*. Baton Rouge: Louisiana State University Press, 2004.

Sutherland, Daniel E. *A Savage Conflict: The Decisive Role of Guerrillas in the American Civil War*. Chapel Hill: University of North Carolina Press, 2009.

———. "Sideshow No Longer: A Historiographical Review of the Guerrilla War." *Civil War History* 46 (March 2000): 5–23.

Sword, Wiley. *Embrace an Angry Wind: The Confederacy's Last Hurrah—Spring Hill, Franklin, and Nashville*. New York: Harper Collins, 1992.

——. *Shiloh: Bloody April*. New York: Morrow, 1974.

Tatum, Georgia Lee. *Disloyalty in the Confederacy*. Chapel Hill: University of North Carolina Press, 1934.

Thompson, Illene D., and Wilbur E. Thompson. *The Seventeenth Alabama Infantry: A Regimental History and Roster*. Bowie, MD: Heritage Books, 2001.

Thornton, J. Mills. *Politics and Power in a Slave Society: Alabama, 1800–1860*. Baton Rouge: Louisiana State University Press, 1978.

Trudeau, Noah Andre. *The Last Citadel: Petersburg, Virginia, June 1864–April 1865*. Baton Rouge: Louisiana State University Press, 1993.

Turner, Maxine T. *Navy Gray: A Story of the Confederate Navy on the Chattahoochee and Apalachicola Rivers*. Tuscaloosa: University of Alabama Press, 1987.

Uchytil, Ronald. "Aristida Stricta." US Department of Agriculture, Forest Service, 1992. http://www.fs.fed.us/database/feis/plants/graminoid/aristr/all.html.

Vanovskis, Maris A. "Have Social Historians Lost the Civil War? Some Preliminary Demographic Speculations." *Journal of American History* 76, no.1 (June 1989): 34–58.

Venable, Austin. "Alabama's 'War of the Roses.'" *Alabama Review* 8 (October 1955): 243–59.

Walker, Juliet E. K. "Drivers, Slave." In *Dictionary of Afro-American Slavery*. Edited by Randall M. Miller and John David Smith, 296–98. Westport, CT: Praeger, 1997.

Walther, Eric H. *William Lowndes Yancey and the Coming of the Civil War*. Chapel Hill: University of North Carolina Press, 2006.

Ward, Wyley Donald. *Early History of Covington County, Alabama, 1821–1871*. Spartanburg, SC: Reprint Company, 1991.

Waselkov, Gregory A. *A Conquering Spirit: Fort Mims and the Redstick War of 1813–1814*. Tuscaloosa: University of Alabama Press, 2006.

Watson, Elbert. "James Pugh." *Encyclopedia of Alabama*, 2010. http://www.encyclopediaofalabama.org/face/Article.jsp?id=h-2972

Watson, Fred Shelton. *Coffee Grounds; a History of Coffee County, Alabama, 1841–1970*. Anniston, AL: Higginbotham, 1970.

Weitz, Mark A. *More Damning Than Slaughter: Desertion in the Confederate Army*. Lincoln: University of Nebraska Press, 2005.

West, Anson. *A History of Methodism in Alabama*. Nashville, TN: Barbee & Smith, 1893.

Wetherington, Mark V. *Plain Folk's Fight: The Civil War and Reconstruction in Piney Woods Georgia*. Chapel Hill: University of North Carolina Press, 2005.

Whites, LeeAnn. *The Civil War as A Crisis in Gender: Augusta, Georgia, 1860–1890*. Athens: University of Georgia Press, 1995.

Wilhelm, Blake. "Election Riots of 1874." *Encyclopedia of Alabama*. http://www.encyclopediaofalabama.org/face/Article.jsp?id=h-2484.

Williams, David. *Bitterly Divided: The South's Inner Civil War*. New York: New Press, 2013.

——. *Plain Folk in a Rich Man's War: Class and Dissent in Confederate Georgia.* Gainesville: University Press of Florida, 2002.

——. *Rich Man's War: Class, Caste, and Confederate Defeat in the Lower Chattahoochee Valley.* Athens: University of Georgia Press, 1998.

Williamson, Joel. *New People: Miscegenation and Mulattoes in the United States.* New York: Free Press, 1980.

Woodworth, Steven E. *While God Is Marching On: The Religious World of Civil War Soldiers.* Lawrence: University Press of Kansas, 2001.

Wright, Gavin. *Old South, New South: Revolutions in the Southern Economy Since the Civil War.* New York: Basic Books, 1986.

Yearns, W. Buck. *The Confederate Governors.* Athens: University of Georgia Press, 1985.

Index

Page numbers in italics refer to illustrations.